WORKSHOP TECHNOLOGY
for Mechanical Engineering Technicians

Book 1

SI Metric Edition

C. R. SHOTBOLT
C.ENG., M.I.MECH.E., F.I.PROD.E.,
M.I.Q.A., M.A.S.Q.C.
Senior Lecturer in Production Engineering,
Luton College of Technology

CASSELL · LONDON

CASSELL & CO. LTD—an imprint of
CASSELL & COLLIER MACMILLAN PUBLISHERS LTD
35 Red Lion Square, London WC1R 4SG
Sydney, Auckland
Toronto, Johannesburg
an affiliate of Macmillan Inc., New York

First published 1969
Second revised edition, September 1971
Second edition, third impression September 1974
Second edition, fourth impression 1976
Fourth edition, fifth impression March 1977

I.S.B.N. 0 304 93836 X

Printed in Great Britain by
The Camelot Press Ltd, Southampton

Preface to First Edition

This book is designed primarily to help students who are taking the Part I subject of Workshop Processes and Practice in the Mechanical Engineering Technicians' Course, no. 293, of the City and Guilds of London Institute. It will also be of use to students of the subject in a course for the Ordinary National Certificate in Engineering. It is hoped that Lecturers, too, will find the subject matter and its presentation of interest.

The author believes that for a student to do himself justice in this subject he must follow four types of study concurrently. In the classroom at College the principles are explained. At the same time these principles are demonstrated in the College laboratories and workshops, and put into practice at work under the guidance of skilled and experienced instructors. Furthermore, the student must study on his own to enlarge his understanding of the principles involved. Each type of study is essential to success, and if any one is omitted the student's progress and prospects will suffer. The book therefore sets out to explain principles rather than practice and to provide more background reading and amplification of topics than the time of the College course may allow. It makes no attempt to explain how to do a job except as an illustration of a principle. Thus in the Chapter on Workshop Measurements there are very few drawings of instruments; the student should become familiar with a vernier height gauge by handling it. There is, however, a detailed explanation of the principle of the vernier scale and of the different types of scale the student is likely to meet during his course of studies and subsequent career.

At the time of going to press the country is in the throes of 'going metric'. Students are going to be faced with the problem of using metric units in their studies although for many years, until machines and equipment are replaced, they will still be using inch units at their work. Accordingly the author has modified the original text to include metric units where appropriate. Generally where facts are stated they are in both inch and metric units, e.g. cutting speeds, gauge block sets, vernier and micrometer scales etc. Where a principle is illustrated by an example it may be in inch or metric units as the same principles follow whether inches, millimetres, or yards and metres are used in setting a machine. Thus the subject matter is predominantly in inch units with metric information where necessary. In subsequent editions the change will be phased in until the book is predominantly metric as the country changes.

Students may be surprised to learn that there is more time lost in industry through so-called accidents than through strikes. Various definitions of accidents are, 'Events which cannot be foreseen' and, 'Events due to chance causes'. The author believes that in industry there are no accidents—just Acts of God and carelessness, and Acts of God are rare indeed. The carelessness may not be the victim's but this is small consolation to a one-eyed toolmaker. Safety has been emphasised throughout the book by outlining hazards under the heading of Safety Notes in the text. These notes are in italics, either at the end of the chapter or at an appropriate point in the text.

The author gratefully acknowledges the assistance given to him so freely by various organisations: individual acknowledgements are made in the text and Appendices. Thanks are due also to colleagues at Luton College of Technology for their advice and assistance, particularly Mr W. Vann, C.Eng., M.I.Mech.E., M.I.Prod.E., M.I.Q.A., who so kindly read the proofs. Finally they are due to the ladies who so painstakingly translated the author's manuscript and prepared from it a readable typescript. Without the help of Mrs E. L. Duffield, Miss C. Duffield, Mrs J. Stimson, Miss P. Stimson, and Mrs B. Humphrey, this work would not have been possible.
Luton 1967.   C. R. Shotbolt

Preface to Second Edition

Since this work was first published there has been considerable progress in Great Britain towards using the metric system, and in particular SI units in engineering. Indeed the first-year student using this book will be working towards a wholly metric examination. At the same time industry is changing and new machinery and equipment will be metric, but for many years the young men in industry will be faced with a dual system of units. In this edition, therefore, the emphasis is on SI units but, particularly in chapter 5 dealing with Workshop Measurements, examples are also given in inch units.

During the change to the metric system it may well be the students, by virtue of their training, education and flexibility of mind, who will come to be considered the experts to whom older people, who are less amenable to change, will go for advice. If this work helps the student to develope that expertise in the applications of S.I. units, then its purpose will have been served.

Luton April 1971   C. R. Shotbolt

Contents

1
The Manufacture of Iron and Steel

Man is most fortunate in that he has had available an abundance of materials suitable for use in the technological form of society he has developed. Many of these are based on *iron* (Fe) which, when alloyed with *carbon* (C), gives a range of steels from the soft, ductile mild steel through the tough medium-carbon steels to the high-carbon steels. The latter can be made extremely hard and are used for cutting tools operating at low speeds; for higher speeds they have been superseded by more complex alloys. Different proportions of iron and carbon give another range of materials, the cast irons. These have different properties from the steels although produced from and containing the same materials, iron and carbon.

Fig. 1.1 is a simple flow chart of the production of steels and cast iron, on which the blocks represent the types of furnace used, while the materials entering the furnace and those obtained from it are shown by the arrows.

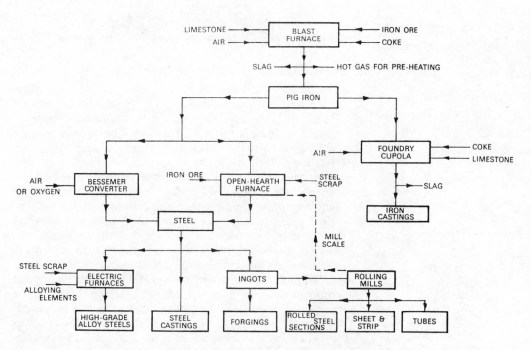

Fig. 1.1. Flow chart of the production of steel and cast iron

1

Fig. 1.2. The blast furnace (Reproduced by permission of the British Iron and Steel Federation)

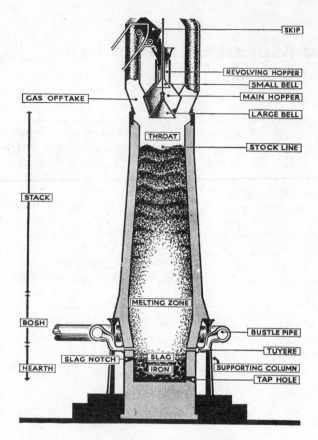

SKIP

REVOLVING HOPPER

SMALL BELL

GAS OFFTAKE

MAIN HOPPER

LARGE BELL

THROAT

STOCK LINE

STACK

MELTING ZONE

BOSH

BUSTLE PIPE

TUYERE

SLAG NOTCH

SLAG

IRON

SUPPORTING COLUMN

HEARTH

TAP HOLE

THE BLAST FURNACE (Fig. 1.2)

The source of all ferrous materials is *iron ore*, a chemical compound of iron and oxygen. The separation of the iron from its oxide, known chemically as a *reducing process*, is carried out in a *blast furnace*. The oxide is heated and brought into contact with the gas carbon monoxide, which combines with the oxygen in the ore to form carbon dioxide, leaving the molten iron to sink to the furnace hearth. The heat for the reaction is obtained by burning *coke*, an air blast being required to give the necessary temperature, and the resulting carbon monoxide reduces the iron ore. *Limestone* is included in the charge to combine with some of the unwanted impurities in the form of a slag, which floats on top of the molten iron and is tapped off separately.

The molten metal from the blast furnace is either tapped into ladles and used for immediate conversion into steel, or cast into conveniently sized slabs known as *pigs* for future conversion into cast iron or steel. In either case the iron contains too many impurities to be suitable for immediate use without further refining.

2

THE MANUFACTURE OF STEEL The main difference between steel and cast iron is in the amount of carbon they contain. Steel is an alloy of iron and carbon containing up to 1·8% of carbon, and the greatest proportion by far of all steel produced is mild steel, which contains only 0·1% to 0·2% carbon. Thus the pig iron, which contains nearly 4% carbon, must have its carbon content drastically reduced to be converted into steel. There are two major steelmaking processes in use today, as shown in fig. 1.1, and although they differ widely in method of operation they are identical in principle. In both cases, the excess carbon and other unwanted impurities are oxidised out.

THE BESSEMER PROCESS

This method of steelmaking was invented by Sir Henry Bessemer and does not use a furnace, in the accepted sense, but a *converter* of the type shown in fig. 1.3. It does not use any source of heat other than that obtained from the oxidising process used to remove the carbon.

The converter is filled with molten pig iron, the blast turned on and the whole converter is tilted to the upright position. The air blast, in passing through the molten steel, oxidises away the carbon and other impurities, leaving almost pure iron. It now remains to deoxidise the metal and add the precise amount of carbon necessary to produce the steel required.

For many years Bessemer steel was considered inferior to other types of steel for two reasons:
  (1) the rapidity of the process was such that the only control available was the furnace master's judgement of the flame:
  (2) the use of air for the blast caused metallic compounds of nitrogen to be formed, which reduced the quality of the steel.

Rapid methods of automatic analysis have largely overcome the first problem, while modern Bessemer converters are blown with a mixture of oxygen and steam to prevent the formation of harmful nitrides.

The great advantages of the process are its speed and flexibility. The converter can pour about 4000 kg of steel each hour and although it must be preheated it does not have to be fired in the accepted sense.

THE OPEN-HEARTH PROCESS

In this process the carbon is again oxidised out of the pig iron but the oxidising agent is iron oxide in the form of iron ore and of mill scale, the surface scale which flakes off the ingots in steel rolling mills.

The charge consists of pig iron, iron ore and mill scale,

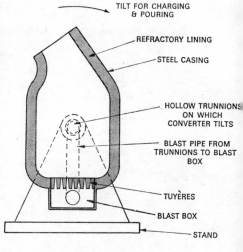

Fig. 1.3. The Bessemer converter

TILT FOR CHARGING & POURING

REFRACTORY LINING

STEEL CASING

HOLLOW TRUNNIONS ON WHICH CONVERTER TILTS

BLAST PIPE FROM TRUNNIONS TO BLAST BOX

TUYÈRES

BLAST BOX

STAND

3

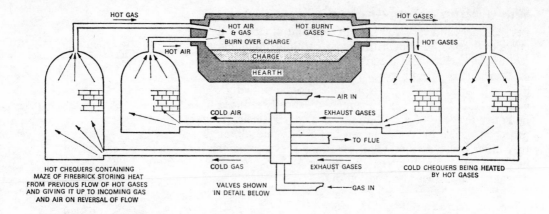

Fig. 1.4. Diagram of open-hearth furnace

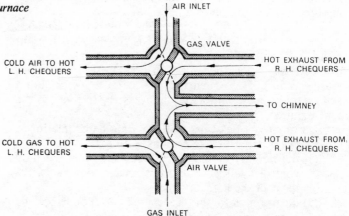

VALVES FOR REVERSING THE FLOW OF GASES THROUGH THE
THE OPEN-HEARTH FURNACE. THE DOTTED LINES INDICATE
THE VALVE POSITIONS WHEN THE FLOW IS REVERSED.

the heat necessary for the process being obtained in the conventional way by burning fuel. The furnaces are commonly gas-fired though many oil-fired furnaces are now in operation. Normally a gas/air combustion process will not generate enough heat to melt the iron and to overcome this difficulty the furnace is made *regenerative*. As the hot gases leave the furnace they pass through large chambers which contain chequered stacks of firebrick. The firebrick becomes hot and the flow of gas is then reversed, the new unburnt gases entering through the hot chambers and thus becoming preheated.

4

The furnace valves shown in fig. 1.4 are controlled to give optimum conditions and the gases enter the furnace at up to 1200°C. The energy of combustion, added to the internal energy which the gas and air already possess through preheating, is ample to melt the iron.

As the charge is melted, the carbon and other impurities are oxidised out by reacting with the iron ore and mill scale.

There are four major differences between this process and the Bessemer process:

(1) *Size:* furnace capacities of up to 200 tons are not uncommon;

(2) *Speed:* the process may take anything up to fourteen hours, which allows time for analysis and control during the process:

(3) *Method of oxidisation of impurities:* see above:

(4) *Source of heat:* see above.

In many steelworks there are large batteries of open-earth furnaces, backed up by Bessemer converters which may be brought into action at short notice to increase the manufacturing capacity.

THE 'BASIC' STEELMAKING PROCESS Phosphorus is the steelmaker's enemy, for a content of more than 0.02% of it has disastrous effects upon the mechanical properties of the steel. The processes already described do not remove the phosphorus, and for many years large sources of iron ore could not be exploited because of their high phosphorus content. The *basic process*, which overcame this defect, was developed specifically to use these hitherto untapped sources of ore. In both the Bessemer and open-hearth *basic* processes, a special furnace lining is used and, before the de-oxidation of the steel, large amounts of limestone are added to the charge, combining with the phosphorus to form a basic slag, which is later used as an agricultural fertiliser.

THE MANUFACTURE OF CAST IRON

THE FOUNDRY CUPOLA Cast iron is pig iron which has been refined by remelting in a foundry cupola and cast in a mould to the approximate shape and size required for the finished article.

The cupola is simply a miniature blast furnace, as shown in fig. 1.5, with certain modifications:

(1) The charge consists of pig iron
                    coke
                    limestone
                    scrap cast iron
accompanied by the air blast:

(2) The process is not continuous, and only sufficient iron is produced to meet the immediate need:

5

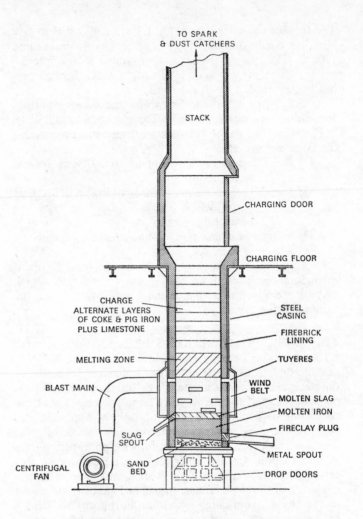

TO SPARK
& DUST CATCHERS

STACK

CHARGING DOOR

CHARGING FLOOR

CHARGE
ALTERNATE LAYERS
OF COKE & PIG IRON
PLUS LIMESTONE

STEEL
CASING

FIREBRICK
LINING

MELTING ZONE

TUYERES

BLAST MAIN

WIND
BELT

MOLTEN SLAG

MOLTEN IRON

FIRECLAY PLUG

SLAG
SPOUT

METAL SPOUT

CENTRIFUGAL
FAN

SAND
BED

DROP DOORS

Fig. 1.5. Diagram of foundry cupola

(3) To allow for complete emptying, the cupola is normally mounted on a stand and has a 'drop bottom'.

The cupola is first tapped to remove the slag and the cast iron is then tapped and stored in a ladle until poured into the mould. The process of moulding will be dealt with in Chapter 3.

HIGH QUALITY STEELS

High-grade steels and alloy steels are now usually made in electric furnaces, heated by either an electric-arc or an induction-heating process. The charge used is not pig iron, as in the other processes, but carefully selected scrap. This is further refined by the remelting and the addition of the required alloying elements. Both types of furnace are sealed and, burning no fuel, require no air. Thus there is no contamination of the charge through atmospheric attack.

Each of the furnaces has its own advantages; electric-arc furnaces can be made 'basic' and will then reduce the phosphorus content in the original charge. This is not the case in the high-frequency induction furnace, but the method of heating has the effect of stirring the charge, giving good mixing, which is beneficial for alloy steels.

From these steels are made the press tools, cutting tools and precise measuring equipment which are used in the manufacturing processes we shall discuss.

2
Heat Treatment of Steel

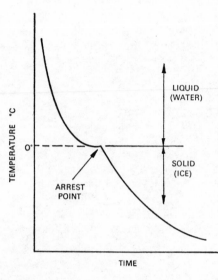

Fig. 2.1. Cooling curve for pure water

THE HEAT TREATMENT OF PLAIN CARBON STEELS

COOLING CURVES In order to understand the heat treatment of steel it is necessary first to understand the phenomena of cooling and the changes that take place in a material when it is cooled. If water is placed in the freezing compartment of a refrigerator it becomes solid and is then known as ice; a physical change has taken place. If a thermometer is placed in the water as it cools and the temperature is noted at regular intervals of time, a graph can be plotted of temperature against time. This graph might be expected to be a smooth curve but, in fact, is not. A pause occurs during the cooling, as shown in fig. 2.1. The drop in temperature is arrested for a short period and the pause is known as a *thermal arrest* or *arrest point*. It is at this temperature that the water changes from a liquid to a solid, i.e., a *physical change* takes place.

A physical change during cooling (or heating) is indicated by an arrest in the cooling (or heating) curve

THE COOLING OF LIQUID SOLUTIONS

It is well known that salt 'melts' ice. What actually happens is that the salt and water form a solution which has a lower melting point than that of water. If a cooling curve is plotted for a salt/water solution, as shown in fig. 2.2, two differences are apparent from the cooling curve for pure water:

(1) there are two arrest points;

(2) the temperature of the upper arrest point is lower than that of the single arrest point for pure water.

Observation during cooling shows that, at the upper arrest point, solid particles start to appear in the liquid solution and that these particles are solid water, or ice. As the temperature continues to drop, more and more pure water solidifies out until the lower arrest point is reached, when the remaining solution of salt and water freezes. The final solid therefore consists of:

(1) crystals of pure solid water (ice)

plus (2) crystals of a *solid solution** of salt and water.

If a second salt/water solution, containing a higher per-

*It is important to note that many materials can dissolve or remain dissolved in each other in the solid state to form what is known as a *solid solution*, in contrast to the liquid solutions which are more commonly encountered in everyday life.

8

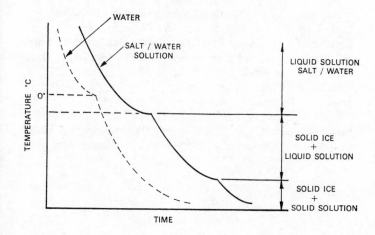

Fig. 2.2. *Cooling curves for pure water
and a weak salt/water solution*

centage of salt, is made up and the cooling curve is plotted,
the curve will again be found to have two arrest points, but
the temperature of the upper arrest will have dropped while
that of the lower arrest will be the same as before. As the
arrests are closer together, there is less time for the pure
water to freeze out between them and although the final
solid will again consist of a mixture of crystals of pure
water and crystals of a solid solution of salt and water, there
will be fewer crystals of water and more of the solid solution.

As more salt is added, the two arrests draw closer together,
with less pure water in the final structure, until eventually
the solution has only one arrest point. This particular solution is known as the *eutectic*, and has the following characteristics:

(1) it changes directly from a liquid to a solid, with no
    partially solid stage:
(2) the solid structure consists wholly of crystals of the
    solid solution:
(3) the solution has the lowest freezing point of all
    solutions of these two materials.

If the percentage of salt is increased beyond the eutectic
composition, the upper arrest point reappears. In this case
it is solid salt which freezes out between the arrests, and the
final structure consists of grains of pure salt and crystals of
the solid solution of salt and water.

During the cooling of a solution of *less* than eutectic composition (*hypo-eutectic*), the effect of freezing out pure water
is to *increase* the percentage of salt in the remaining solution.
This is readily apparent if one considers a bag containing
50 red balls and 50 green balls, i.e., 50% of each. If 25 red
balls are removed, the percentage of green balls left in the
bag will have increased to 67%.

9

Similarly, as a solution of *greater* than eutectic composition (*hyper-eutectic*) cools and the salt freezes out, the percentage of salt remaining in the solution decreases. In both cases, the change in the composition of the solution is such that, when the lower arrest point is reached, the remaining solution is of eutectic composition. Thus the solid materials produced by freezing any solution of salt and water will consist of *grains of solid eutectic plus crystals of one of the pure constituents*, depending on whether the original solution was of hypo-eutectic or hyper-eutectic composition.

Fig. 2.3. 'Family' of salt/water solution cooling curves

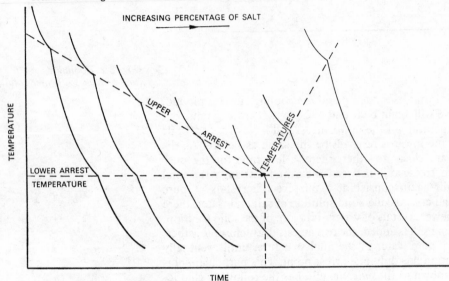

Fig. 2.4. Thermal equilibrium diagram for salt/water solutions

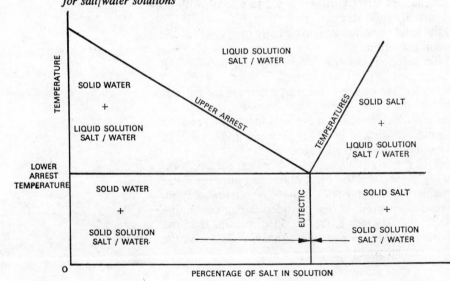

A family of cooling curves could therefore be produced, as in fig. 2.3, and the condition of the solution during each phase of cooling would be as shown. However, life is too short to draw a cooling curve for every possible solution of two materials, and by producing a few curves it is possible to draw a graph of arrest temperature against composition. Such a graph is called a *thermal equilibrium diagram*, that for salt and water being shown in fig. 2.4, with the condition of the solution in the various phases of the diagram also indicated.

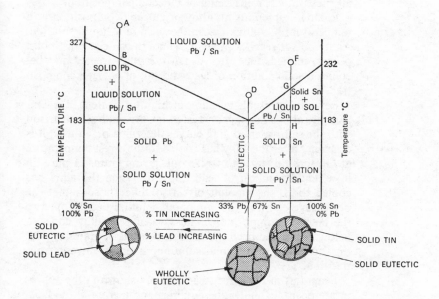

Fig. 2.5. *Thermal equilibrium diagram for lead/tin alloys (solders)*

THERMAL EQUILIBRIUM DIAGRAMS

Bearing in mind all that has been said about the cooling of salt and water solutions, consider now the cooling of an alloy more commonly encountered in the workshop, that of *lead* (Pb) and *tin* (Sn) an alloy more commonly known as *solder*.

The thermal equilibrium diagram for solder is shown in fig. 2.5. The melting point of pure lead is 327°C and that of tin is 232°C. The eutectic alloy, which contains 67% tin and 33% lead, melts at 183°C. This information provides the main points on the diagram, and the lines, which represent arrest temperatures, can be drawn in.

Now consider point A. This represents an alloy containing 80% lead and 20% tin at a temperature of 350°C. As it is above the upper arrest temperature, the alloy will be a *liquid solution of lead and tin* (Pb/Sn). As it cools, it reaches the upper arrest point at B, and pure lead starts to freeze out of

11

the solution. As the alloy cools further, more and more lead solidifies until the lower arrest point is reached at C. Thus between the two arrests the alloy consists of pure solid lead (Pb), and a liquid solution of lead and tin (Pb/Sn). By the time it has cooled to C, the amount of lead frozen out is such that the percentage of tin in the remaining solution has increased to the eutectic composition of 67%. Further cooling below this temperature causes the remaining liquid solution to freeze, so that the final solid alloy consists of grains of pure lead and grains of the solid solution of lead and tin, all these latter grains being of eutectic composition.

Point D represents an alloy of eutectic composition at a temperature of 200°C, i.e., in the form of a liquid solution. As it cools it reaches point E, where the single arrest point occurs, immediately after which the alloy freezes and becomes a solid solution of lead and tin, of eutectic composition.

Point F represents an alloy of high tin content at a temperature above the upper arrest point. Again, by comparison with the salt/water cooling curves described previously, it is clear that after the alloy has cooled to the arrest temperature at G, pure tin starts to freeze out, giving grains of pure tin in a liquid solution of lead and tin. When the alloy has cooled to H, the amount of tin solidified is such that the percentage of tin in the remaining solution has dropped to the eutectic composition. Thus, when this alloy cools to below 183°C and becomes solid, it consists of grains of pure tin and grains of the solid solution, again of eutectic composition.

Diagrams of the three structures are shown in the appropriate positions under the equilibrium diagram in fig. 2.5.

As stated earlier, an alloy of lead and tin is a solder, and it is of interest that there are two basic types of solder:

    (1) Tinman's solder, used for soldered assembly joints:
    (2) Plumber's solder, used for wiped joints in pipes and cables, and 'puddling', or covering and smoothing over welds in motor car bodies etc.

A solder used for assembly work, soldered connections in electronic equipment and the like must be one that sets, or solidifies, rapidly. For this reason, tinman's solder is of approximately eutectic composition. Above 183°C it is liquid, below this it is solid, and the joint sets almost immediately it is made, if not overheated.

On the other hand, a solder for smooth, wiped pipe-joints must be capable of being manipulated as it sets and must go through a stage when it is neither liquid nor solid, but pasty. A solder having a high lead content goes through just such a pasty stage as it cools between the upper and lower arrest temperatures, and plumber's solder is therefore of approximately 70% lead–30% tin composition.

12

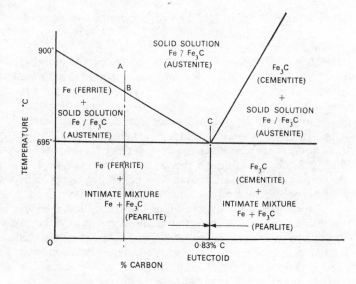

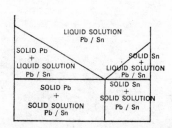

Fig. 2.6. *Iron/iron-carbide thermal equilibrium diagram (with lead/tin diagram for comparison)*

THE IRON/IRON-CARBIDE EQUILIBRIUM DIAGRAM

By now the reader will probably be wondering what salt water and solder have to do with the heat treatment of steel. There is a similar diagram for alloys of iron and carbon, called the *iron/carbon equilibrium diagram*, dealing with these alloys in the molten state at temperatures above 1100°C and with carbon contents up to 5% or more. We are, however, concerned only with the 'steel' part of this full diagram, that is, with alloys which have carbon contents up to 1·8% and *have already changed from the liquid to the solid state.* For this we use a second equilibrium diagram, called *the iron/iron-carbide diagram*, which shows what happens as plain carbon steels, in their solid state, cool from about 900°C. The diagram is very similar to that for lead/tin alloys and for convenience the two are shown side by side in fig. 2.6. There is one important difference, however, for the arrest points of the lead/tin diagram denote *changes from liquid to solid* whereas the arrest points of the iron/iron-carbide diagram denote *changes in the internal structure of the solid steel* as it cools.

The *crystals* or *crystal grains* of which iron and steel are composed are built up of exceedingly small cubes and the arrangement or spacing of the atoms of carbon and iron in these cubes, called the *space-lattice*, changes as the steel cools. Above the upper arrest point, the steel is a solid solution of iron and iron carbide, called *austenite*, and it is the relative proportions of iron and iron carbide which determine the temperatures of the upper arrest points, just as the

13

relative proportions of lead and tin determine the temperatures of the upper arrest points in solders. The arrest points are sometimes called *critical points* or *change points*.

With the lead/tin alloys, there was one alloy, the eutectic, which solidified completely without the formation of separate crystals of pure lead or pure tin. In the same way, there is one solid solution of iron and iron carbide which does not produce separate crystals of iron or iron carbide as it cools. This, since we are dealing with a solid solution, is called the *eutectoid*, where the percentage of carbon in the steel is 0·83%. Note that although the carbon in steel is always in the form of iron carbide, we classify the steel by the percentage of *carbon*, not iron carbide, which it contains.

In steels with a lower percentage of carbon than 0·83%, there is an 'excess' of iron and at the upper critical point crystals of pure iron, called *ferrite*, separate out within the austenite. In steels with a higher percentage of carbon than 0·83% there is an 'excess' of iron carbide and at the upper critical point crystals of iron carbide, called *cementite*, separate out.

The lower critical point, 695°C, is common for all steels and at this point the solid solution of austenite changes into an intimate mixture of iron and iron carbide called *pearlite*. The grains of pearlite consist of alternate and exceedingly thin layers, or laminates, of iron and iron carbide, and this laminated structure has a 'mother-of-pearl' or 'pearly' appearance under the microscope.

The eutectoid, 0·83% carbon, having no excess of ferrite or cementite, is pure pearlite. Steels with less than 0·83% carbon are a mixture of pearlite and ferrite; those with more than 0·83% carbon are a mixture of pearlite and cementite.

For reference purposes:

Austenite is the solid solution of iron and iron carbide, Fe/Fe_3C, above the critical range:

Ferrite is almost pure iron, Fe, and is very soft:

Cementite is iron carbide, Fe_3C, and is very hard:

Pearlite is an intimate mixture of fine alternate layers of iron and iron carbide, $Fe+Fe_3C$, and is the eutectoid of carbon steel, containing 0·83% carbon.

Bearing in mind the previous analysis of the cooling of salt/water solutions, and particularly of lead/tin alloys, consider point A on the iron/iron-carbide diagram (fig. 2.6). This represents a steel containing about 0·4% carbon and at a temperature of about 850°C. It is well above the upper critical temperature and will be in the form of a solid solution of iron and iron carbide (Fe/Fe_3C, austenite). As it cools, no changes occur until the temperature drops to the upper arrest point at B. Further cooling causes iron (Fe, ferrite) to come out of solution and the percentage of carbon left in the remaining solution is thus increased. By the time

14

the temperature has dropped to 695°C, the lower arrest temperature, the amount of ferrite precipitated is such that the carbon content of the *remaining solution* has risen to eutectoid composition of 0·83%C.

Further cooling causes this remaining solution to break down into the finely-divided layers of iron and iron carbide ($Fe + Fe_3C$) known as pearlite.

Thus, for a steel containing less than 0·83% carbon, the structures at the various phases of the diagram are:

(1) *Above the upper critical point:* solid solution of iron and iron carbide (austenite):

(2) *Between the arrest points:* mixture of iron and the solid solution (ferrite plus austenite):

(3) *Below the lower arrest point:* mixture of iron and the finely-divided layers of iron and iron carbide (ferrite plus pearlite).

This final structure is shown, as it would appear under a microscope, in fig. 2.7(a).

Fig. 2.7. Structures of slowly cooled steels of different carbon contents

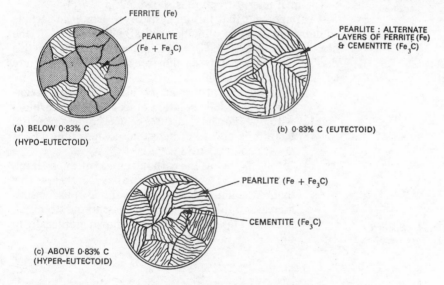

FERRITE (Fe)

PEARLITE
(Fe + Fe₃C)

PEARLITE : ALTERNATE
LAYERS OF FERRITE (Fe)
& CEMENTITE (Fe₃C)

(a) BELOW 0·83% C
(HYPO-EUTECTOID)

(b) 0·83% C (EUTECTOID)

PEARLITE (Fe + Fe₃C)

CEMENTITE (Fe₃C)

(c) ABOVE 0·83% C
(HYPER-EUTECTOID)

Consider now point C on the iron/iron-carbide diagram. This represents a steel containing 0·83% carbon at a temperature of 750°C. It is at a higher temperature than the single arrest point which occurs at this eutectoid composition and its structure will be that of a solid solution of iron and iron carbide (austenite). As it cools, no change occurs until it reaches the arrest temperature, at which point the solid solution breaks down into the mixture of the two constituents in finely-divided layers, which we know as pearlite. In this case there is no precipitation of either iron or iron carbide,

15

and the final structure is 100% pearlite, as shown in fig. 2.7(b).

When the carbon content is greater than 0.83%, iron carbide (Fe_3C, cementite) comes out of solution as the steel cools between the arrest points. As all the carbon in the steel is contained in the form of this constituent it follows that the percentage of carbon in the remaining solution is reduced until, by the time the temperature has fallen to the lower arrest point, the remaining solid solution is of eutectoid composition. Further cooling causes this solution to break down to finely-divided pearlite. Thus the structures occurring at the different temperature zones will be:

(1) *Above the upper arrest point:* solid solution of iron carbide (austenite):

(2) *Between the arrest points:* mixture of iron carbide and the solid solution (cementite plus austenite):

(3) *Below the lower critical point:* mixture of iron carbide and the finely-divided mixture of iron and iron carbide (cementite plus pearlite).

The final micro-structure is shown in fig. 2.7(c).

It is important that this analysis of the iron/iron-carbide equilibrium diagram should be clearly understood if the heat treatment of steel is to be appreciated, and for this reason the main points of the foregoing explanation are again emphasised as follows:

(1) All structures of steel are brought about by a breakdown of the solid solution of iron and iron carbide:

(2) All slowly cooled structures of steel contain pearlite:

(3) Pearlite is always of eutectoid composition, i.e., it always contains 0.83% carbon:

(4) It follows that as the carbon content of the steel approaches 0.83% from either above or below this figure, the amount of pearlite contained in the steel increases until, at this carbon content, the steel is all pearlite. This state of affairs is shown graphically in fig. 2.8.

Fig. 2.8. Graph of pearlite ($Fe + Fe_3C$) content against carbon

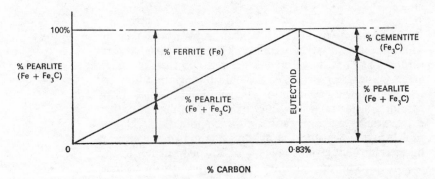

APPLICATION OF THE IRON/IRON-CARBIDE EQUILIBRIUM DIAGRAM TO THE HEAT TREATMENT OF STEEL

The 'steel' portion of the iron/carbon diagram, or the iron/iron-carbide diagram as we have called it, is the key to the heat treatment of plain carbon steels. Before it can be used, however, we must delve a little deeper into its implications and into the effects of the various combinations of the constituents involved. In order to understand these effects we must clearly appreciate the terms *mixture, solution* and *chemical compound*.

(1) *Mixture:*

To reduce the risk of accidents, icy roads are spread with a *mixture* of salt and sand. This is a typical mixture and has the characteristics of all mixtures. If a quantity of the two materials is shaken up in a test tube and examined, however intimately they are mixed it is found that:

(a) the separate grains of each can readily be identified:

(b) with a pair of tweezers and a magnifying glass we can separate the two by picking out the separate grains:

(c) when separated completely, the salt and sand are completely unaffected by having been mixed together.

(2) *Solution:*

A simpler way to separate the mixed salt and sand would be to add water. The salt will dissolve in the water which can then be poured off and filtered, leaving the sand. The water however, will have become salty and, of course, the salt solution will have taken the characteristics of a liquid. Furthermore, it takes very little salt to make water salty to the taste.

In a solution each material affects the other and the solution has some of the characteristics of both.

(3) *Chemical Compound:*

Salt is a typical chemical compound. It consists of the elements sodium (Na) and chlorine (Cl) combined chemically to produce sodium chloride (NaCl), common salt. Salt is an interesting material; we flavour our food with it, our health would suffer if we lacked it and, in submarines, factories and hot, humid climates, salt tablets are issued to combat heat fatigue. In short, we should find it hard to do without. However, if we took the sodium and the chlorine separately, the results would be very different.

If the metal sodium is dropped in water it fizzes about and gives off hydrogen. If swallowed its effect on the gastric juices could only be imagined! Chlorine is a dirty greenish-brown gas which is extremely poisonous and was, in fact, used as a poison gas in the 1914–18 war. Thus, here we have two materials which if taken internally, separately, would undoubtedly be fatal but, if taken in the correct chemically-combined form, the resulting compound, salt, is pleasant and beneficial.

Two materials combined chemically produce a 'new' material whose characteristics are different from those of its constituents.

In the iron/iron-carbide diagram all three of these combinations are encountered.

Iron carbide is a chemical compound of iron, which is soft, grey, ductile and malleable, and carbon, which is soft, black, and brittle (in its graphitic form, carbon is a very good lubricant). Iron carbide, the compound, is white, hard and brittle.

Steel is, of course, predominantly iron and contains a maximum of 1·8% carbon, so that even a high-carbon steel cannot contain much iron carbide. Thus, if the iron and iron carbide are in the form of a simple mixture, the physical properties of the material will be similar to those of iron, i.e., soft and malleable. As the amount of carbon increases, and hence the iron-carbide content increases, there is a change in hardness, strength and ductility as shown in fig. 2.9, but the change in hardness is small compared with that obtainable by heat treatment. Note that strength falls off when the carbon content exceeds 0·83%. The strength depends on the amount of pearlite in the steel, and the strongest plain carbon steel is wholly pearlitic with 0·83% carbon content.

In order to get the full effect of the hardness of the iron carbide it is necessary to ensure that all the iron is in solution with the hard constituent. This can be achieved by heating the steel to temperatures above those of the shaded zones of

Fig. 2.9. Effect of carbon content on strength, hardness and ductility of normalised plain carbon steel (compare with Fig. 2.8.)

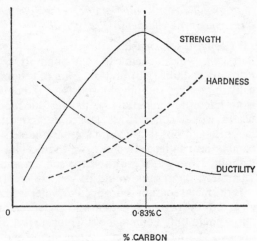

STRENGTH

HARDNESS

DUCTILITY

0·83% C

% .CARBON

18

the diagram shown in fig. 2.10(a). The steel must now be cooled so rapidly that the solution does not have time to break down into its former constituents. This, again fortunately, is easily done by a simple quench in water. We can draw a simplified diagram, fig. 2.10(b), showing the temperature zones to which the steel must be heated for the desired effects to take place. The main effects we shall consider are:

(1) *Hardening*

The steel is heated to the temperature zone shown in fig. 2.10(b) and quenched in water. This does not allow the solid solution, austenite, to break down into pearlite and a new, hard structure called *martensite* is formed.

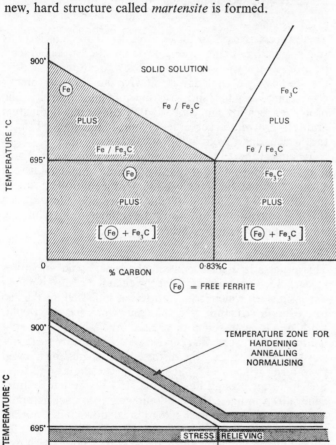

Fig. 2.10(a). Phases of iron/iron-carbide diagram which must be cleared to ensure that iron (Fe) is in solution with iron carbide

Fig. 2.10(b) Simplified iron/iron-carbide diagram showing temperatures to which plain carbon steel must be heated for various heat treatments

19

(2) Toughening

If steel is quenched rapidly it becomes hard. If it is cooled slowly it stays soft. It follows that there is a speed of cooling above which hardening occurs and below which it does not. This is called the *critical cooling speed*. If the steel is cooled just below the critical cooling speed, more slowly than in water, a partial but incomplete breakdown of the austenite takes place, giving a very fine-grained structure, much softer than martensite but very much tougher. This slightly slower cooling can be brought about by using an oil quench.

To toughen, heat the steel to the temperature zone shown in fig. 2.10(b) and quench it in oil.

(3) Annealing

This process is used to make a hardened piece of steel as soft as possible. If the steel is heated to the hardening temperature the martensite changes back to austenite and, if the steel is then cooled very slowly, the austenite breaks down completely to a soft structure containing pearlite. The prolonged heating and slow cooling cause the individual grains to grow into each other, giving a large-grained structure which, apart from being soft, is very weak.

To anneal, heat the steel to the temperature zone shown in fig. 2.10(b), 'soak' it at that temperature and cool it very slowly. This may be done by cooling at a controlled rate in the furnace, by switching off the furnace and allowing the furnace insulation to slow down the cooling, or by plunging the steel into dry sand or ashes.

(4) Normalising

This process is used to correct abnormal grain structures in steel. Such structures may be the enlarged grains of a fully annealed steel, which is too soft to machine well, or the distorted grain structure of a material which has been cold-worked, e.g., cold-rolled or pressed, and which might split if further cold work was carried out. To correct these unsatisfactory structures, the distorted grains must be allowed to re-form, which can be achieved by causing a solid solution to form through heating the steel to the temperature zone shown in fig. 2.10(b) and allowing it to cool naturally in air. This allows the austenite to break down into a normal pearlitic structure of the correct grain size, which is ideal for machining or will allow further cold work to be carried out.

To normalise, heat the steel to the temperature zone shown in fig. 2.10(b) and cool it in still air.

(5) Stress-Relieving, Sub-Critical Annealing or Process Annealing

These are all names given to a process which has certain advantages over normalising for low-carbon steels. The normalising process calls for cooling in air and, at the temperatures used, the oxygen in the atmosphere attacks the surface of the material, causing scaling. However, if the steel is heated to just below the *lower* critical point and cooled slowly, the grains of ferrite re-form, and since a low-carbon steel contains little other than ferrite, this process can be regarded as a normalising type of process for such a steel. Apart from its lower temperature, the process calls for slow cooling, which can be carried out in the furnace. If the furnace atmosphere is controlled and air is excluded, scaling will not occur and the parts will come out with nothing more than a slight tarnish. Subsequent operations can then be performed without the trouble of preiiminary de-scaling or cleaning, which is particularly valuable where stress-relieving is carried out between operations, e.g., in a press shop on large-scale production.

To stress relieve, heat the steel to just below the lower critical temperature and cool it slowly, as indicated in fig. 2.10(b).

(6) *Tempering*

If *hardened* plain carbon steel is reheated after hardening, the hard martensite starts to break down and the steel loses some of its hardness and gains in toughness. It is important to note that the loss of hardness and gain in toughness depend upon the temperature to which the steel is reheated. If a graph of hardness against tempering temperature is plotted it will be of the type shown in fig. 2.11 and will also show the two temperature zones used for different types of work:

    (a) low-temperature tempering
    (b) high-temperature tempering

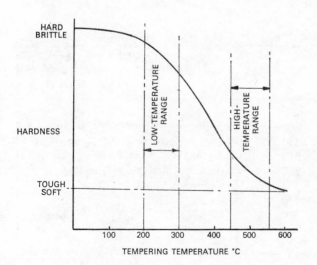

Fig. 2.11. Effect of tempering temperature on hardness

21

(a) *Low-temperature Tempering*

This is normally used for the range of work where the steel must be hard but must have enough brittleness removed to enable the tool to stand up to its task. Thus the temperature chosen must be related to the type of work the tool is required to do.

A scriber must retain its point without dulling for long periods but suffers little in the way of shock loads which might break it. It is therefore tempered at a low temperature of 200°C which, as the diagram shows, barely affects its hardness but just takes the edge off its brittleness.

A centrepunch has a slightly more arduous function, since it is struck lightly with a hammer and the point must not chip. It is thus tempered at a higher temperature of 260°C. Similarly, a cold chisel receives harder blows and is tempered at a still higher temperature.

SAFETY NOTE   *The head of any tool which is struck with a hammer must be soft. If the head is hard, a blow might cause it to chip and a splinter might enter the eye. The author knows a man to whom this happened, both of whose eyes became affected; as a result of the accident the man is permanently blind.*

Such tools can be tempered by heating the head of the tool with a gas blowlamp and allowing the heat to be conducted up the shank of the tool until the cutting edge attains the correct temperature. This is indicated by the changing colour of the film of iron oxide which forms on the polished surface of the tool during the heating and may be used as a guide to tempering temperature. The different colours, their associated temperatures and the type of work for which each is used are shown in the table below.

Table of Tempering Temperatures and Oxide Colours

Temperature deg. C	Tool	Colour
200	Scribers, gauges	Faint straw
230	Lathe tools	Pale straw
240	Drills	Dark straw
250	Taps	Brown
260	Centrepunches	Brown/purple
270	Press punches	Purple
280	Cold chisels	Dark purple
300	Springs	Blue

It is important to note that this method of tempering is not particularly reliable and should only be used for plain carbon steels, since the oxide colours differ with the composition of the steel. For accurate tempering, the steel should be heated in a suitable furnace where the temperature can be closely controlled. The furnace may be an oil-bath, salt-bath, lead-bath or hot-air furnace. If, after tempering, the tool head has to be softened, the head can be rapidly heated and then allowed to cool slowly while the cutting end is kept unchanged by immersion in a quenching medium.

SAFETY NOTE   *After prolonged use, the head of any tool which is struck with a hammer will 'mushroom' from the effect of the repeated hammer blows. The head has, in fact, been cold-worked and will therefore have become hard, brittle and liable to splinter. To avoid accidents, the head should be reground to its normal shape and re-annealed. Any punch or chisel with a mushroom head is a dangerous tool and its use can cause serious injury to the user, who ought to have more sense than to use it, and also to any innocent passer-by, since the splinters will fly in no predictable direction.*

(b) *High-temperature Tempering*

If *hardened* plain carbon steel is heated to a temperature of 450°C to 550°C, the breakdown of the hard martensite is more complete and a very fine-grained, tough structure is produced. Thus, to make a steel as tough as possible it should first be hardened, preferably using an oil quench, and then reheated to 550°C by immersion in a lead-bath or a salt-bath of neutral salt, for even heating, and allowed to cool. If the part is to be stabilised it can then be treated as described over without the toughened structure being affected.

Fig. 2.12. Constituents formed in plain carbon steel through different speeds of cooling.

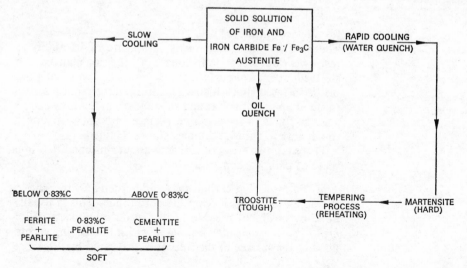

STRUCTURES FORMED DURING HEAT TREAT-MENT The above has covered the five basic processes used in heat treatment, viz., hardening, toughening, normalising, annealing and tempering. It will be noted that the structures produced are all formed by the breakdown of the solid solution of iron and iron carbide (Fe/Fe_3C) called austenite, and the type and properties of the structure depend upon the rate of cooling from the austenitic stage. These different structures are all given different names by the metallurgist, many of which have deliberately not been used in the text for the sake of simplicity. Fig. 2.12 shows in diagrammatic form the effects of the various treatments and also names the structures formed.

It now remains to discuss certain more specialised types of heat treatment but, as will be shown, these are really variants of the basic processes already mentioned.

(7) *Stabilising*

Heating followed by sudden cooling of the steel sets up internal stresses which, over a period of time, may cause the component to distort. If this happens to a gauge, the gauge may become inaccurate and start to reject good work, or worse still, accept work which should be rejected. Distortion must be prevented by relieving the internal stresses but the stress-relieving process described on page 20 cannot be used since it would soften the gauge, which must be hard to resist wear. Thus the temperature adopted must be that of a low-temperature tempering process. If the gauge is heated to 150°C for a period of five hours and cooled slowly it will still be of the required hardness but will also be extremely stable, and will retain its shape and size throughout its normal working life.

To stabilise, heat the steel to 150°C for five hours and cool it slowly.

(8) *Surface Hardening*

The hardness of a material is a measure of its ability to resist wear but it is an unfortunate fact that if a plain carbon steel is hardened enough to resist wear it is then usually too brittle to resist shock loads. Therefore, if we require a steel to stand up to both wear and shock loads in service we must arrange for it to have a hard surface to resist wear and a tough core to withstand blows and shock loads.

There are two ways of bringing about this condition in a piece of plain carbon steel:

(a) To use a high-carbon steel and harden only the skin to the depth required, leaving the core tough. This is usually done by means of a sophisticated electrical process called *high-frequency induction heating* in which the heating is confined to the surface of the steel and is so rapid that the core

24

does not have time to get hot enough to become hardened when the steel is quenched. The process is outside the scope of this book and is generally limited to large-production fully-automated heat-treatment shops with expensive electronic equipment, the complete treatment taking only a few seconds per component.

(b) To use a low-carbon steel and raise the carbon content of the case, or outer skin, to the required depth so that it can be hardened. This is the more common process, usually known as case-hardening, which we shall consider in some detail. The process requires three stages, which are usually separate:

  (i) carburising, to raise the carbon content of the case:
  (ii) core-refining, to toughen the core:
  (iii) case-hardening, to harden the case.

If a low-carbon steel of, say, 0·1% carbon content is heated to above the upper critical temperature in intimate contact with a carbon-rich material such as charcoal, a chemical reaction takes place and iron carbide is formed in the surface of the steel, producing a skin of high-carbon steel. During the period of high temperature, some of this iron carbide may spread into the core, raising its carbon content slightly so that the component may now have a skin containing 1·1% carbon and a core containing 0·3%. In most cases, the steel will have been held at above the upper critical temperature for a considerable time and its condition will be similar to that of fully annealed steel, viz., soft, weak and with an enlarged grain structure. It must now be treated to produce the tough core and hard case required, the temperatures for these treatments being shown on the heat-treatment diagram which is reproduced for convenience in fig. 2.13.

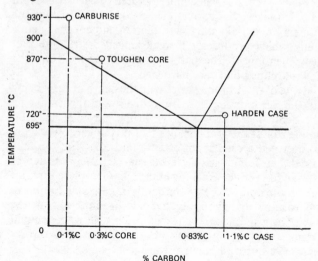

Fig. 2.13. Application of iron/iron-carbide diagram to case-hardening

Thus, the temperatures and quenches used in the process are:

      (i) Carburising: 950°C
      (ii) Core-refining: 850°C with an oil quench
      (iii) Case-hardening: 750°C with a water quench

Finally, a low-temperature tempering at 200°C may be used with prolonged heating and slow cooling, for the purposes of stress-relieving and stabilising.

The student should now be able to decide for himself the nature of the structures of the case and core, the case being a high-carbon steel, water-quenched from above the lower critical temperature, and the core a medium-carbon steel, oil-quenched from above the upper critical temperature and reheated to below this critical temperature when the case was hardened.

Various methods of surface hardening low-carbon steel are used, the stages described above being common to all of them. The main difference in the processes is the method of carburising, which can affect the subsequent treatment, but in all methods the general idea is the same, to raise the carbon content of the case and then harden it.

Methods of carburising differ in the material used to provide the carbon, which can be solid, liquid or gaseous.

(a) *Pack carburising* (*solid media*)

The workpieces are packed in charcoal, to which barium carbonate has been added to act as a catalyst, in a cast iron box which is sealed with fireclay, through which test pieces are left protruding. The box is then placed in the furnace at the required temperature of 950°C and left until the required case-depth is estimated to have been achieved, when a test piece is removed, quenched and fractured to check the depth of case. If the depth is correct the box is allowed to cool, the carburising material acting as insulation and enforcing slow cooling, which produces the weak annealed structure previously mentioned. The parts are now removed from the box, core-refined and case-hardened.

The rate of penetration varies with the depth of case, being about 0·3 per hour up to 0·5 mm depth and then reducing as the depth increases, as shown in the graph of fig. 2.14. Examination of the graph shows that it is not really practicable to exceed a case depth of 1·5 mm because of the time required. Nor in fact is it desirable, since greater case depths are prone to produce cracking and peeling, the case separating from the core. A common depth of case is 0·75 mm to 1 mm, to allow up to about 0·75 mm to be removed from the diameter by grinding after hardening. This allowance should be ample to cover any distortion and allow the workpiece to be cleaned up and brought to size.

26

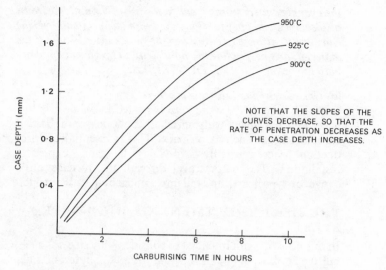

NOTE THAT THE SLOPES OF THE CURVES DECREASE, SO THAT THE RATE OF PENETRATION DECREASES AS THE CASE DEPTH INCREASES.

The pack-carburising process is most commonly found in toolrooms and small heat-treatment shops since, although it is a lengthy process, it can be carried out in standard furnaces, the only extra equipment needed being a cast iron box, a supply of carburising charcoal and some fireclay.

(b) *Cyanide Carburising* (*liquid media*)

Sodium cyanide is a salt extremely rich in carbon which melts at about 500°C, thus providing an extremely active carburising agent. It is heated to 950°C, the normal temperature for carburising, and the workpiece is suspended on a piece of wire and immersed in the bath. The liquid provides very even heating and gives minimum distortion with rapid penetration, ten minutes' immersion producing 0·25 mm depth of case. These values are for small parts, large components taking longer since they cool the salt on immersion and an initial heating period is then necessary to bring the bath up to the temperature required.

The speed of the process does not allow the usual grain growth to take place and in many cases the core-refining treatment can be omitted. This reduces still further the time required and also reduces the cost of case hardening where the type and quantity of work are suitable.

The cyanide process is widely used where large numbers of small parts are to be treated but requires specialised equipment of a comparatively expensive nature and is thus normally found only where the quantity of work warrants its installation.

SAFETY NOTE *Sodium cyanide is a deadly poison. An antidote must be kept in a readily accessible position in the shop where it is used, and instructions in the safe handling of the cyanide and its storage, and in the use of the antidote, must be displayed and obeyed. Common sense and personal hygiene can save a lot of grief; washing the hands after handling the material, and never allowing familiarity to breed contempt are both important. DON'T TAKE RISKS.*

(c) *Gas carburising (gaseous process)*

In this process the workpiece is heated in an electric furnace which is filled with enriched town gas or a bottled carbon-rich gas such as propane. This is essentially a production process, usually involving a large and expensive installation. The parts travel through the furnace on a conveyor-type hearth and fall into a quenching bath outside.

THE HEAT TREATMENT OF HIGH-SPEED STEEL

In this book it is not intended to consider alloy steels as such, but the book would be incomplete without mention of high-speed steel, which is so widely used for cutting tools that a young engineer becomes acquainted with it as soon as he enters a machine shop.

In our consideration of plain carbon steels we noted that a hardened plain carbon steel loses some of its hardness if it is reheated to a relatively low temperature, a process we know as tempering. This is a disadvantage if the steel is to be used as a cutting tool in machining, because the heat generated during cutting will produce the same effect and soften the tool, unless the cutting speed is kept so low that the small amount of heat produced can be easily dissipated.

If a steel is to be used for cutting at higher speeds it must be capable of retaining its hardness at higher temperatures, the reasoning that led to the development of high-speed steel by F. W. Taylor and his colleagues.

The commonest form of high-speed steel is known as 18–4–1 steel, the figures referring to the percentages of tungsten (W), chromium (Cr) and vanadium (V) in the steel. Each of these elements has its purposes but the combination produces a steel which retains its hardness when hot. The heat treatment for hardening the steel is more complex than that for plain carbon steel and is carried out in three stages:
  (1) heating slowly and carefully up to 850°C:
  (2) heating rapidly up to 1280°C:
  (3) quenching in oil.
Even then the steel is not fully hardened but may be hardened further by reheating to 600°C, a process known as *secondary hardening*. If this secondary hardening is not deliberately carried out it will probably occur to some extent early on in the life of the tool through the high temperature attained at its normal cutting speed, which is roughly three times that possible for a similar job with a high-carbon steel tool.

28

HEAT-TREATMENT EQUIPMENT

Steel can be hardened, tempered, annealed and normalised with no more equipment than a blow-torch and a bucket of water, but the variety of work would be limited and the results inconsistent. To carry out properly the full range of work for more than the simplest of tools it is necessary to use up-to-date equipment, consisting of:

(1) *Furnaces*, for correct heating of the work:

(2) *Temperature-Measuring Equipment*, to ensure that correct temperatures are employed:

(3) *Quenching Equipment*, to enable the hot steel to be quenched in the correct way under the best conditions:

(4) *Equipment for Testing Hardness and Toughness*, to check that the required results have been achieved.

(1) HEAT-TREATMENT FURNACES   Three basic types of furnace are required in a general heat-treatment shop: muffle furnaces for general work, salt-bath furnaces for more specialised work, and tempering furnaces. A wide range of work can be carried out by only a muffle furnace, but the range is still limited for present day requirements and it is better if all three types of furnace are available.

Fig. 2.15(a). Natural-draught gas-fired muffle furnace

Fig. 2.15(b). Electric muffle furnace with provision for atmospheric control (by courtesy of Wild-Barfield Ltd.)

Fig. 2.15(c). Natural-draught gas-fired semi-muffle furnace

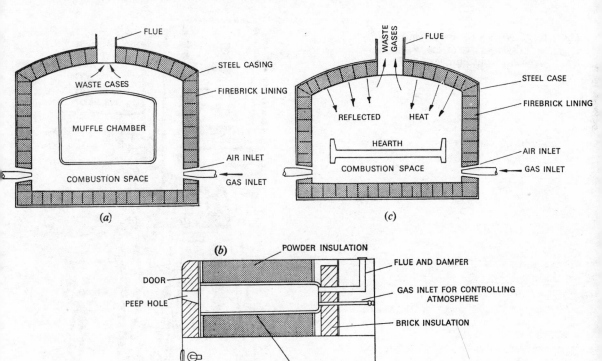

Muffle Furnaces

A muffle furnace is one in which the source of heat does not directly contact the work but circulates around the outside of the chamber, or muffle, in which the work is placed. This is true for either gas or electric furnaces as shown in figs. 2.15(a) and 2.15(b). Semi-muffle furnaces of gas-fired type are available, in which combustion takes place beneath the furnace hearth and the products of combustion pass through the work chamber, as shown in fig. 2.15(c). In this type of furnace the atmosphere is controlled by varying the proportions of gas and air which are burned together to produce the required temperature. Excess air, above that required for complete combustion of the gas, produces an oxidising atmosphere, while excess gas gives a reducing atmosphere. A neutral atmosphere, which is neither oxidising nor reducing, is obtained by using the correct mixture of air and gas for complete combustion. Thus, control of the combustion process gives some degree of atmospheric control. In the 'straight' muffle furnace the atmosphere is always oxidising unless the air is excluded by introducing an inert gas at a pressure slightly higher than atmospheric to keep out air.

Fig. 2.15(d). High-speed steels hardening furnace (by courtesy of the Wellman Incandescent Furnace Co. Ltd.)

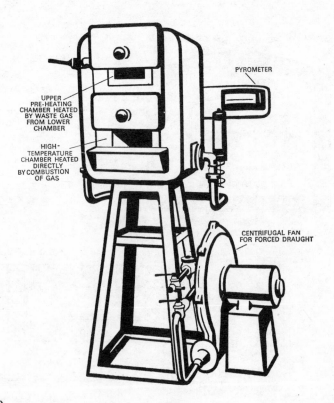

PYROMETER

UPPER
PRE-HEATING
CHAMBER HEATED
BY WASTE GAS
FROM LOWER
CHAMBER

HIGH-
TEMPERATURE
CHAMBER HEATED
DIRECTLY
BY COMBUSTION
OF GAS

CENTRIFUGAL FAN
FOR FORCED DRAUGHT

The High-Speed Steel Muffle Furnace

As stated on p. 28, high-speed steel must be heated slowly up to 850°C and then rapidly up to 1280°C. This is usually done by using a special type of muffle furnace, illustrated in fig. 2.15(d), which consists of two chambers, one above the other, but with a single source of heat. The lower, high-temperature chamber is heated directly but the upper chamber is heated by the waste gases from the high-temperature chamber and is therefore at a lower temperature. The work is usually placed on the sill of the lower-temperature, or pre-heating, chamber to warm up gradually and is then edged into the chamber. When the work has attained the required temperature both doors are opened simultaneously and it is transferred quickly to the hot chamber, for rapid heating to hardening temperature.

The Salt Bath Furnace (Fig. 2.16)

This type of furnace consists basically of a pot to contain the molten salt, a means of heating and an extraction system to remove the dangerous fumes. The furnace may be heated

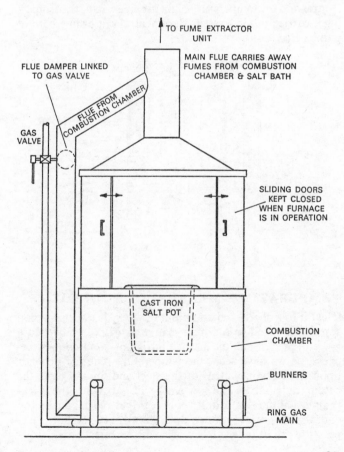

Fig. 2.16. Natural-draught salt-bath furnace

TO FUME EXTRACTOR UNIT

MAIN FLUE CARRIES AWAY FUMES FROM COMBUSTION CHAMBER & SALT BATH

FLUE DAMPER LINKED TO GAS VALVE

FLUE FROM COMBUSTION CHAMBER

GAS VALVE

SLIDING DOORS KEPT CLOSED WHEN FURNACE IS IN OPERATION

CAST IRON SALT POT

COMBUSTION CHAMBER

BURNERS

RING GAS MAIN

by gas, when combustion takes place beneath and around the pot in an enclosed combustion chamber, or by electricity. The electric type usually has a non-metallic pot into which a pair of electrodes project. The current passes between the electrodes through the salt and the resistance of the salt produces the required heating effect. In its solid state, the salt is non-conductive and the furnace is started by wedging a carbon rod between the electrodes. The rod is heated by the passage of the current and a pool of molten salt forms around it between the electrodes, in which the carbon rod dissolves. This conductive pool continues the heating process until the whole bath is molten.

The Tempering Furnace (Fig. 2.17)
This furnace runs at a lower temperature than either a muffle or a salt-bath furnace. It usually has a chamber in which the air is heated either electrically or by gas, and a built-in fan to give good circulation of air and even heating.

In some cases, as in the secondary hardening of high-speed steel, where it is important that the atmosphere should be neutral and the temperature higher than normal, the tempering is carried out in a salt-bath of neutral salt or in a bath of molten lead.

Fig. 2.17. Tempering furnace with forced-air circulation

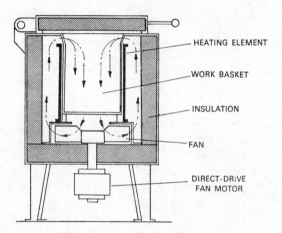

HEATING ELEMENT

WORK BASKET

INSULATION

FAN

DIRECT-DRIVE FAN MOTOR

TEMPERATURE-MEASURING EQUIPMENT

'Heat it to a cherry red and dip it in water' is the instruction sometimes given to a young man who wishes to harden a piece of steel. Such an instruction is not good enough because, as we have seen, the temperature required depends upon the carbon content of the steel and, in any case, the colour radiated by the hot steel will vary with the background lighting. In a dull room a bright red might be too cool and in a bright room a dull red might be too hot. Temperature can be judged by colour, with experience and knowledge of the conditions, but gaining the experience can be an expensive process. It is far better to start properly with accurate equipment for the measurement of temperature.

There are many forms of equipment available for temperature measurement and indeed for low-temperature work such as tempering there is much to be said for the use of the ordinary mercury thermometer, except for the high breakage rate which could be expected. The two commonest instruments in use today are:

(1) *the thermocouple pyrometer*
and (2) *the optical pyrometer.*

(1) THERMOCOUPLE PYROMETERS   These are based on a phenomenon known as the '*Seebeck Effect*'. If two dissimilar metal wires are joined at their ends to form a closed loop and the temperature of one joint, or junction, is raised above that of the other, an electric current will flow round the loop. The magnitude of the current will depend upon the *difference in temperature* between the hot and cold junctions. If an electrical measuring instrument is inserted into the loop so that its terminals form the cold junction, it can be calibrated to read in units of temperature, thereby producing a thermocouple pyrometer.

In practice it is not quite so simple, because the reading

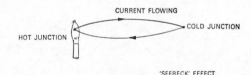

Fig. 2.18. Thermocouple pyrometer

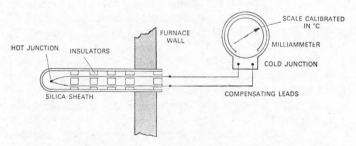

depends on the temperature *difference* between the junctions, and if the temperature of the cold junction varies, the reading correspondingly varies. It is also usually necessary to place the measuring instrument some distance away from the thermocouple to obtain a more convenient position for reading. This enables a simple means of cold-junction correction to be used, by making the leads from the thermocouple to the instrument also of dissimilar metals so that

33

they form, in effect, a second thermocouple to compensate for changes in temperature at the cold junction. These leads are thus called *compensating leads*.

The wires of the thermocouple must be insulated from each other by small ceramic insulators, or quills, and in the furnace the thermocouple is protected from damage by a silica sheath; the installation is shown in diagrammatic form in fig. 2.18.

Thermocouple Materials

The materials used for the wires of a thermocouple must be chosen so that:

(a) the current produced varies uniformly with the temperature throughout the working range:

(b) the melting points of the materials are above the working range:

(c) the materials have good corrosion resistance at high temperatures.

Materials in common use and their working temperature ranges are:

(i) iron/constantan: up to 700°C
(ii) chromel/alumel: up to 1100°C
(iii) platinum/platinum-rhodium: up to 1200°C

Constantan is an alloy containing 45% Ni and 55% Cu.
Chromel ,, ,, ,, ,, 90% Ni and 10% Cr.
Alumel ,, ,, ,, ,, 98% Ni and 2% Al.
Platinum/ ,, ,, ,, ,, 90% Pt and 10% Rh.
rhodium

Calibration of Thermocouples

It must be remembered that a thermocouple is a measuring instrument, that is to say, it compares an unknown standard with a known one. Over a period of time the accuracy of the instrument may fall off and it must therefore be checked at intervals. If a standard thermocouple of known accuracy is available, the thermocouple in question can be checked throughout its range by immersing the two side by side in a bath of molten metal and comparing the two readings as the metal cools.

If a standard thermocouple is not available, another method is to immerse the thermocouple in a bath of molten material of known freezing point, for example, pure sodium chloride, which freezes at 801°C. If a cooling curve for the salt is plotted, the difference between this temperature and that of the arrest point recorded by the thermocouple will be the error in the instrument *at this temperature*. The check can be repeated, using other materials, at other suitable fixed points over the range of the thermocouple.

A word of warning on the use of thermocouples is needed

34

at this point. The instrument does not necessarily give the temperature of the metal in the furnace, but that of the end of the thermocouple in its protective sheath. This temperature depends upon the position of the thermocouple in the furnace and upon whether the furnace temperature is uniform over the furnace volume. It will also depend upon how rapidly the furnace has been heated or cooled, since there will always be some lag between actual temperature and instrument reading unless the furnace has been held at constant temperature for a period. Thus, the skill and experience of the heat-treatment technician are important; even when he has good measuring equipment he must still be familiar with the performance of his furnaces to get the best results.

(2) OPTICAL PYROMETERS   If a material is heated to 500°C it starts to glow with a dull red colour, and as the temperature is increased the colour changes through bright red and orange to white, at which stage the material is at about 1200°C. These colours depend solely on the temperature of the material and not on its composition, although to the human eye the colours will appear to change as the background lighting changes, e.g., a hot object which appears black in a brightly lit room may appear to glow if the lights are switched off.

   If temperature is to be judged accurately by the colour of a heated substance, it must be compared with a known standard of colour and temperature. This is provided in the *optical pyrometer* by a standard bulb, lit from a battery through a variable resistance. The bulb is placed in the focal

Fig. 2.19(a). Arrangement of optical pyrometer of disappearing filament type

Fig. 2.19(b). Optical pyrometer

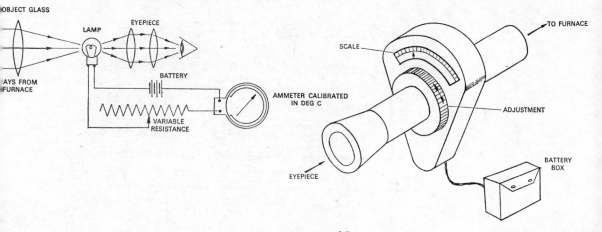

OBJECT GLASS

LAMP

EYEPIECE

RAYS FROM FURNACE

BATTERY

VARIABLE RESISTANCE

AMMETER CALIBRATED IN DEG C

SCALE

TO FURNACE

ADJUSTMENT

EYEPIECE

BATTERY BOX

plane of the objective lens of a telescope and the object in the furnace is viewed through the telescope so that the bulb filament is seen against the background of the hot substance. If the bulb is hotter than the substance it appears bright against the background, and if cooler it appears dark against a brighter background. When the filament is at the same temperature as the work it cannot be detected. The filament temperature depends upon the current passing through it, so an ammeter is built into the instrument, calibrated to read in degrees centigrade. The operator focuses the instrument on the work in the furnace, adjusts the variable resistance until the filament disappears into the background radiation and reads the temperature from the scale. The optical pyrometer is shown in figs. 2.19(a) and 2.19(b).

This type of pyrometer is, of course, limited to the radiant temperature range and at high temperatures a red filter is necessary to reduce glare, but it is portable, being battery-operated, and gives the actual temperature of the work rather than the temperature of one zone of the furnace containing the work, which may not be the same thing.

QUENCHING EQUIPMENT

As shown previously, different conditions are produced in a piece of steel by different methods of cooling, and these involve different cooling media. The cooling media are commonly:

    (1) an air blast, usually from the compressed-air line of the workshop:

    (2) a water quench:

    (3) an oil quench.

The latter two involve quenching tanks which should be designed so that the oil and water stay as nearly as possible at a constant temperature. This can be achieved by containing the oil tanks within the water tanks as shown in fig. 2.20 and having an overflow pipe, or sill, so that a steady flow of

Fig. 2.20. Water-cooled oil quenching tank

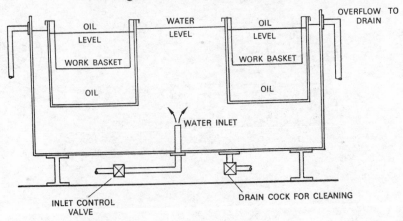

36

water carries the heat away. If another medium is required for a more drastic quench, brine may be used in one of the tanks.

SAFETY NOTE *The oil tanks should be provided with metal covers which can be used to snuff out rapidly any flare-up which may occur.*

EQUIPMENT FOR TESTING HARDNESS AND TOUGHNESS

HARDNESS TESTING   The easiest way to check whether a piece of steel is hard is to try to file it. Unfortunately this does not tell us how hard it is, and methods of measuring hardness based on numerical values are required so that comparisons can be made. Hardness is defined as the ability to resist indentation or scratching, and most machines designed to measure hardness do so by measuring the ability of a material to resist indentation by either a diamond or a hard steel ball under a standard load. Another method is based on a common phenomenon observed by anybody who has played a ball game, that a ball bounces higher from a hard surface than from a soft one. Yet another method, used at the National Physical Laboratory, is based on the fact that a different 'feel' is observed when a standard stylus is drawn over materials of different hardness.

Indentation Methods

(a) *The Brinell Test*
The Brinell hardness tester uses a hard steel ball as an indenter, which is impressed under a standard mass into the material to be tested. The hardness number is given by dividing the *applied mass* by the *surface area* of the indentation produced,

$$\text{i.e., Brinell hardness} = \frac{W}{1 \cdot 571 D(D - \sqrt{D^2 - d^2})}$$

where D =dia of ball, mm
d =dia of impression, mm
W =applied mass, kg

Normally, a mass of 3000 kg is used with a 10 mm ball but different balls and loads are used for soft materials and thin sheets. The test is not really suitable for very hard materials since the deformation of the ball affects the results, but a tungsten-carbide ball is sometimes used for such work.

(b) *The Vickers Pyramid Hardness Test*
A diamond indenter is used, in the form of a pyramid with a square base and an included angle of 136°. The hardness

number is again given by the surface area of the indentation divided into the load

i.e., Vickers pyramid no. (V.P.N.)$=\dfrac{2W\,\mathrm{Sin}\,\theta/2}{d^2}$

where $W=$applied mass, kg

$\theta\;=$included angle of pyramid, degrees

$d\;=$width of indentation *across the diagonals*, mm

The testing machine is fitted with a measuring microscope which is automatically aligned with the indentation, the operator's view through the eyepiece being as shown in fig. 2.21. The two knife edges are adjusted in the micrometer until they span the diagonal of the impression, and the micrometer reading is noted and converted into a hardness number, either by the use of the above formula or by reference to tables.

Fig. 2.21. Measuring microscope on Vickers hardness-testing machine

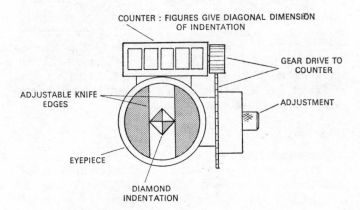

COUNTER : FIGURES GIVE DIAGONAL DIMENSION OF INDENTATION

GEAR DRIVE TO COUNTER

ADJUSTABLE KNIFE EDGES

ADJUSTMENT

EYEPIECE

DIAMOND INDENTATION

(c) *The Rockwell Hardness Test*

Both the Brinell and the Vickers tests give a hardness number which is based on the load per unit surface area of indentation, and a calculation or reference to a table of values is required after the test has been made. The Rockwell machine is different in that it is direct-reading, one reason for its popularity in industry, although in laboratories the Vickers or Brinell machines are usually preferred.

The Rockwell tester uses a conical diamond penetrator, with a 120° included angle and a 150 kg mass for harder materials on scale 'C', or a steel ball of 1·6 mm diameter with a 100 kg mass on scale 'B'. An initial mass of 10 kg is applied, to reduce the effects of slackness in the machine and any surface defects. The appropriate main mass is then applied and the *depth of penetration of the indenter* is measured. This measurement is shown on a dial gauge, built

38

into the machine and calibrated in the 'B' and 'C' scales for the appropriate penetrator and load.

(2) 'Bounce' Tests

The *Shore Scleroscope* consists of a glass tube graduated into 140 equal parts, down which a diamond-tipped hammer of mass 7·09 g is allowed to fall freely from a height of 250 mm on to the work. The height of the first rebound as shown on the scale is used as the Shore hardness number. If the material is hard, little energy will be expended in causing deformation and the hammer will bounce back to almost its original height. On the other hand, the deformation produced in a soft material will absorb a greater amount of the energy of the moving hammer and the hammer will not bounce back as far.

(3) Scratch Tests

The standard test for the hardness of minerals is the *Moh scratch test*, in which the mineral under test is scratched with stylii of graduated hardness, and the number allocated is one less than that of the stylus which just scratches the mineral. The scratch leaves a mark on the surface and the test is often regarded as not suitable for engineering purposes. However, a test which leaves no surface defect is described by the National Physical Laboratory.* A piece of silver steel is hardened and ground at one end to a smooth radius of about 0·50 mm, and mounted in a handle. The 'scriber' is drawn across the work surface and then across the surface of a number of graduated hardness standards of similar surface finish, the resulting marks being compared. This is particularly useful for testing the working surface of a gauge, for although a mark is produced no surface damage results.

TOUGHNESS TESTING Toughness is the ability of a material to withstand shock loads or impact. The easiest way to compare the toughness of different pieces of metal is to put them in a vice and hit them with a hammer. Those that fracture or bend most for a blow of given strength are the least tough, and those on which the hammer has least effect are the most tough. The hammer blows must be kept as consistent as possible and this, for an accurate test, is the difficulty. It is, however, quite simple to arrange for the blow always to have the same force by fixing the hammer to a pendulum and allowing it to swing from the same height for each test. The problem then is to judge the effect of the blow on the specimen. It is easier, in fact, to judge the effect on the hammer since, at the moment of impact, it contains

* N.P.L. Notes on Applied Science, No. 1—Gauge making and measuring.

energy equal to its effective mass multiplied by its original height. At impact some of this energy is used to break the specimen and therefore the hammer, as it continues its swing, will not reach its original height. The distance it swings short of its original height is a measure of the energy lost at impact.

Both the *Izod* and the *Hounsfield* impact testing machines operate on this principle, as shown in fig. 2.22. A slave poin-

Fig. 2.22. Principles of impact-testing machine

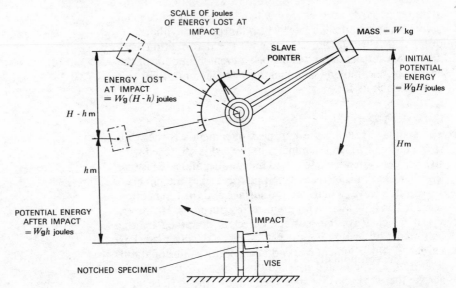

ter records the height to which the pendulum rises, reading against a scale of joules of energy lost in fracturing the specimen. The Izod machine is a large floor-mounted one with a single heavy pendulum delivering 160 joules of energy to a notched specimen which is held in a vice. The Hounsfield machine is smaller and has two pendulums, one swinging through the other, which carries the specimen. The energy lost at impact is again recorded by a slave pointer and is read off the scale in joule units.

SAFETY NOTE *These toughness tests are both dynamic tests and if the energy contained in the moving parts is expended on any part of the human anatomy the results are likely to be painful, if not disastrous, and may easily be fractures. The machines should be properly guarded and used with respect at all times.*

3
Primary Processes: Casting, Forging and Rolling

If the young engineer looks around he sees many components which are cast, forged, or rolled and then machined only where necessary. In most cases, further observation shows that had the part been machined from a solid piece or billet of metal, an enormous amount of swarf would have been produced, of comparatively small value as scrap, with a relatively small amount of metal remaining in the component. A good example of this is the cylinder barrel of an air-cooled motor cycle engine. From a solid billet the bore would have to be machined out and the cooling fins then machined, producing a small volume of metal around a large volume of air and an enormous heap of swarf.

In such cases, manufacture of the component proceeds in two stages:

(1) primary process: casting, forging, or rolling to the approximate size and shape required;
(2) secondary process: machining important sizes and working surfaces to the accuracy and surface finish specified, and required for efficient functioning of the component.

THE MANUFACTURE OF CASTINGS

One of several methods may be used to make a casting, depending upon the metal to be cast, the type and size of job, the number of parts required, and the speed at which they are to be produced. All the methods used, however, are common in that a cavity or *mould* is made, approximately of the size and shape of the required part, and is filled with molten metal which is then allowed to solidify. The mould is then opened and the casting removed. Methods of casting commonly used are:

(1) *Sand Casting* (including plate moulding)
(2) *Shell Moulding*
(3) *Investment Casting*
(4) *Die Casting*
(5) *Centrifugal Casting*.

For each of these processes we shall consider the stages involved in the manufacture of a typical part to be cast by that process.

Before manufacture starts, the designer of the casting must bear in mind certain points of importance in the

41

production of a good sound casting, and incorporate them in his design. Amongst these are:

(1) *Ease of manufacture*
In most cases, the pattern for the casting must be made so that it can be removed from the mould *without damaging the mould*. As shown in fig. 3.1, the designer can assist by:

    (a) avoiding undercuts

    (b) providing adequate 'draft' angles to allow the pattern or casting to free itself readily from the mould or die, in the same way that a pudding frees itself from a basin. The shape of a pudding basin is quite deliberate, to provide 'draft'.

Fig. 3.1. Casting modifications to ease withdrawal of pattern from mould

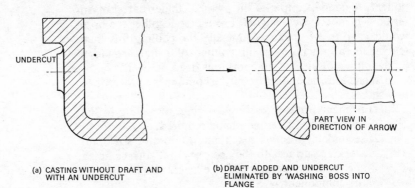

UNDERCUT

PART VIEW IN DIRECTION OF ARROW

(a) CASTING WITHOUT DRAFT AND WITH AN UNDERCUT

(b) DRAFT ADDED AND UNDERCUT ELIMINATED BY 'WASHING BOSS INTO FLANGE

Fig. 3.2. Modifications in casting to reduce likelihood of cracks

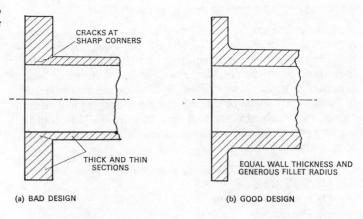

CRACKS AT SHARP CORNERS

THICK AND THIN SECTIONS

EQUAL WALL THICKNESS AND GENEROUS FILLET RADIUS

(a) BAD DESIGN

(b) GOOD DESIGN

(2) *Designing to avoid cracks*
Cracks in castings usually start at sharp corners, due to stress concentrations on cooling, or at changes in thickness, due to the uneven cooling rates of thick and thin sections. The part shown in fig. 3.2(a) is badly designed and its faults are corrected in fig. 3.2(b).

42

SAND CASTING

A sand casting is made by producing a cavity in moulding sand by ramming damp sand around a pattern of the shape required. The pattern is removed and the cavity filled with molten metal. Any holes in the casting are made by inserting *cores* in the mould, and provision must be made for feeding the metal into the mould and allowing the air in it to escape. The stages in manufacturing a simple flanged pipe, as shown in fig. 3.3, by sand casting are as follows.

(1) PATTERN MAKING The pattern is made of soft wood, usually yellow pine, and to allow removal from the mould must normally be split, the choice of split line being important as it usually determines the method of moulding. With cylindrical objects, the split is usually axial along a diameter, and the two halves of the pattern are dowelled so that they locate accurately together.

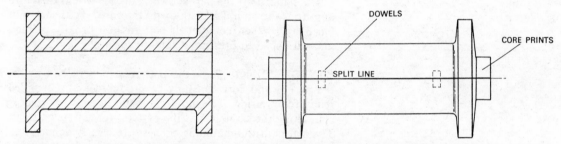

Fig. 3.3. *Simple flanged pipe casting*   Fig. 3.4(a). *Pattern for flanged pipe*

The patternmaker must also provide the draft and fillet radii, and add to the pattern any necessary *core prints*. These make cavities in the mould to locate and fix the *cores* which produce the holes required in the casting. Cores are made separately by ramming a special sand in a *core box*, which is usually in two halves and has a cavity the shape of the core required. On removal, the core is baked in an oven and becomes a stiff rod of sand, ready for insertion in the mould. When making the pattern for the casting, the patternmaker also makes any necessary core boxes.

As the casting cools it contracts, and the pattern must be

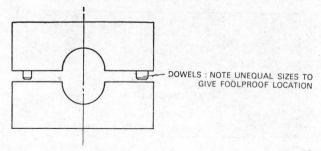

DOWELS : NOTE UNEQUAL SIZES TO GIVE FOOLPROOF LOCATION

Fig. 3.4(b). *End view of simple core box for flanged pipe casting. The halves are shown separated*

43

made oversize to allow for the contraction. To save calculations the patternmaker uses a *contraction rule* which has four scales, each nominally of 300 mm but whose length and graduations are increased by an amount depending on the contraction allowance for the metal being cast. These allowances are:

Cast iron, 10·67 mm/m.
Brass, 16 mm/m.
Aluminium, 21·3 mm/m.
Steel 16 mm/m.

Thus a 300 mm scale allowing a contraction of 21·3 mm/m for aluminium would actually be 306·39 mm long, divided into 30 equal parts for centimetres with the cm subdivided equally into millimetres. Each subdivision would therefore allow for the contraction of the casting during cooling.

The pattern for the part shown in fig. 3.3 would therefore appear as shown in fig. 3.4(a), with the core box as shown in fig. 3.4(b). When completed, patterns are usually painted and varnished to preserve a smooth surface.

(2) MOULDING With the pattern and core box made, the mould and core can now be produced and assembled ready for pouring. The mould is made in a two-part box, split along the same line as the pattern, for simple castings. The stages in the moulding process are clearly defined and the names of the materials and equipment used are given as the stages are described, below.

(a) LOWER HALF-MOULD Half of the pattern is placed face downwards on a *turnover board* and the lower half of the box, or *drag*, is placed around it. The pattern is packed around with *facing sand*, a fine sand to give a good finish, and the remainder of the cavity is rammed up with *green sand*. This is not green in colour but is so called because it is damp and contains clay to bond the grains together. At this stage the half-mould is as shown in fig. 3.5.

Fig. 3.5. First stage in making the mould

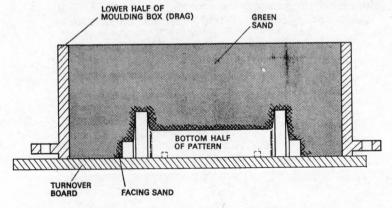

LOWER HALF OF
MOULDING BOX (DRAG)

GREEN
SAND

BOTTOM HALF
OF PATTERN

TURNOVER
BOARD

FACING SAND

(b) TOP HALF-MOULD The lower half-mould is inverted and the turnover board removed. The upper part of
the pattern is dowelled into place on its lower part and the
top half of the moulding box, or *cope*, is fitted to the drag.
The cope and drag are 'registered' by dowels, as shown in
fig. 3.6. The sand face is sprinkled with *parting sand* to prevent the two halves of the mould from sticking to each other.
Facing sand and green sand are again filled in and rammed
up, but this time provision must be made for pouring the
molten metal into the mould and allowing the hot air and
gases to come out. *A runner* must be made as an inlet and
risers formed wherever air will be entrapped, in this case on
top of the two flanges. The runner and risers are formed by
placing tapered wooden plugs in position and ramming the
sand around them. To provide an easy run-in, the metal
will be poured in the side of the mould cavity about halfway
along, so that it does not drop directly on to and break the
core yet spreads easily through the mould. Sections through
the mould at this stage are shown in fig. 3.6.

The core will have already been prepared in the core box
from a special bonded sand and baked hard to give it the
necessary strength.

(c) FINISHING THE MOULD The cope is gently lifted
off and turned over to reveal the pattern halves embedded
in the sand. A large wood screw or spike is driven into each
half of the pattern and tapped gently in all directions. This
rapping slightly enlarges the mould and allows the pattern
halves to be easily and cleanly removed. An *ingate* is cut at
the bottom of the runner in the lower half to provide a clean
run-in for the metal to the mould, and a *pouring cup* is
formed about the runner plug in the top half. Similar cups
known as *headers* are formed about the risers and the plugs
are removed. Wires are poked through the mould to provide
small vents so that gases generated by the action of the hot
metal on the damp sand can escape. The mould is then
finished off, loose sand is removed, any damage made good
and the cavity is painted or dusted with plumbago or black
lead to give a good finish to the casting. The core is placed
carefully in position and the two halves of the mould are
assembled, as shown in fig. 3.7, the cope and drag being
held together by cotters through the moulding-box dowels.
To prevent the top half of the mould 'floating' when the
molten metal is poured in, weights are usually placed on it
before pouring begins.

(d) POURING The molten metal is poured into the
runner as rapidly as possible, without overflowing the pouring cup, until it appears in the riser headers, indicating that

45

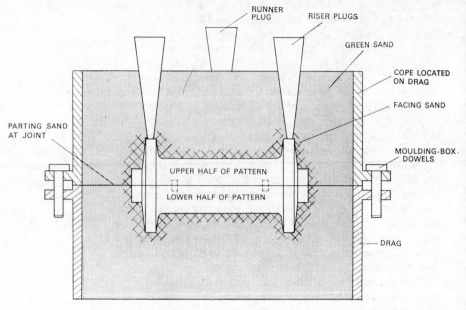

Fig. 3.6. Second stage in making the mould

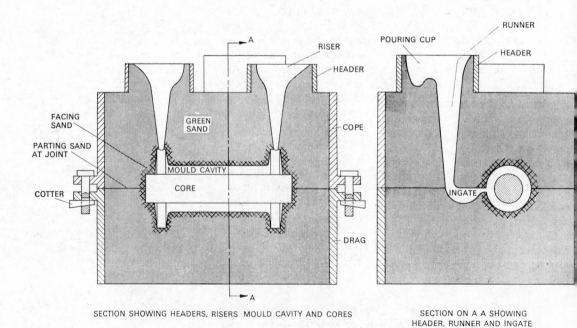

SECTION SHOWING HEADERS, RISERS MOULD CAVITY AND CORES

SECTION ON A A SHOWING HEADER, RUNNER AND INGATE

Fig. 3.7. Finished mould ready for pouring

46

the mould is full. Apart from this, the headers maintain a pressure, or head, of molten metal ensuring that the mould remains full. Since any bad metal, slag, bubbles of gas and displaced sand tend to float to the surface, they float into the risers, ensuring good metal in the mould and a sound casting.

(e) FINISHING THE CASTING When the casting has cooled, the boxes are vibrated to break up the sand and the rough casting is removed, looking rather different from the finished product. The *sprues* or sticks of metal formed by the runner and risers are broken off. The casting is pickled in a sulphuric acid solution to remove the scale, and then washed to remove the acid. Further dressing, or *fettling*, may be carried out by grinding, chipping and sand blasting until the casting is fully cleaned up. It is not yet ready for final machining, however, since it may warp and distort over a period of time as the internal stresses set up during cooling are dissipated. Castings are often stored in the open for this period and the treatment is known as *weathering*. When it is necessary for a casting to remain stable it is often first roughly machined and weathered in the open for a few months, to remove and release internal stresses, and is then finally machined to size. Weathering can be accelerated by heat treatment and by vibration, and small castings may be *tumbled* or *barrelled*, or shot blasted. In the barrelling process, the castings are placed in barrels or drums with small pieces of scrap, and the drums are rotated for about half an hour. The vibrations and light blows to which the castings are then subjected relieve the internal stresses and prevent subsequent distortion.

The above briefly outlines the process of sand casting. Points to note are:
- (i) the mould is used only once and if more than one part is required a new mould is necessary for each:
- (ii) sand casting is essentially a process for small numbers of parts but can be used for all sizes of castings:
- (iii) it can be used for all materials that readily cast:
- (iv) it does not give castings accurate to close limits, and even such functional details as hexagonal flats to fit spanners cannot be cast accurately enough to obviate machining.

PLATE MOULDING This is a modification of the sand-casting process used for the mass-production of small parts. The two halves of a metal pattern are set opposite each other on the two sides of a metal plate which is placed between the boxes while both are rammed together. Thus when the plate is removed its thickness, separating the pattern halves, is 'lost' and the two mould halves come together as shown in fig. 3.8

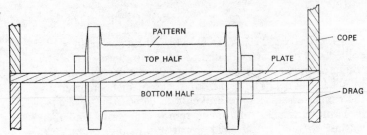

Fig. 3.8. Plate pattern for flanged pipe. When the plate pattern is removed and the cope and drag are brought together again, the thickness of the plate is 'lost'

It is not generally worthwhile making a plate pattern for a single casting and the plate usually carries patterns for a number of castings. These patterns are connected by raised sections which form channels to allow the molten metal to flow to all the moulds. Thus a simple plate pattern for moulding our flanged pipes four at a time would appear as in fig. 3.9. The plate-moulding process is therefore a sand-casting process about which the following points should be noted:

(i) the mould is used only once:

(ii) the process lends itself to mechanisation, i.e., to machine ramming, and is essentially a production process:

(iii) the pattern plates are more expensive than single patterns, but their cost is more than offset by the quantity production of castings.

Fig. 3.9. Plan view of plate pattern for four flanged pipes

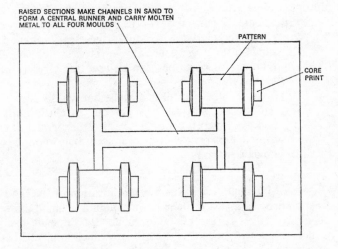

SHELL MOULDING

This is a fairly recent development in casting processes and provides a conveniently rapid method of moulding, on a production basis, castings accurate to within $\pm0{\cdot}13$ mm on dimensions up to about 100 mm.

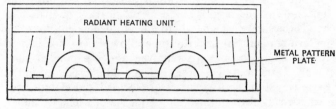

STAGE 1 : HEATING THE PATTERN PLATE

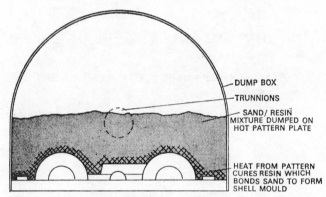

STAGE 2 : HOT PATTERN PLATE IS PLACED ON DUMP BOX
WHICH IS THEN INVERTED.

Fig. 3.10. Stages in the manufacture of a casting by the shell-moulding process

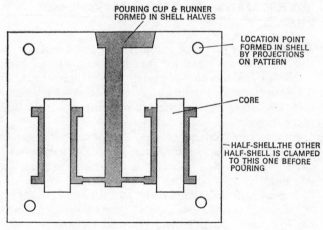

STAGE 3 : FINISHED MOULD WITH HALF-SHELL REMOVED.
THE SHADED ZONE IS THE CAVITY TO BE FILLED
BY METAL

49

A metal pattern plate is made, similar to that used for plate moulding but including location points so that the two mould halves will later locate accurately together. This is heated and placed on a *dump box* which contains a mixture of sand and uncured synthetic resin. The box is turned over and the sand and resin mixture is thus 'dumped' on to the hot pattern. The resin is cured by the heat of the plate and bonds the sand permanently to a depth dependent upon the pattern temperature and the time allowed. The box is then turned back, the pattern removed and the bonded sand 'shell' is lifted out. The other half-mould is produced in the same way and the two halves are located and clamped together ready for pouring. The sequence of events is shown diagrammatically applied to our flanged pipe in fig. 3.10.

Apart from the accuracy obtainable, which eliminates the need for machining non-critical working surfaces, e.g., hexagonal flats to fit spanners, other advantages are:

(1) Rapidity; a mould can be produced in from three to ten minutes:

(2) Small components can be moulded and cast in groups:

(3) *Complex* castings can be made accurately and require minimum fettling;

(4) No vents or risers are required. The runner provides a head, and air and gases escape easily through the shell since it is porous. This lends itself to complex shapes such as an air-cooled engine cylinder.

INVESTMENT CASTING (LOST-WAX PROCESS)

This method of precision casting is one of the oldest known and was certainly used for making the brass and bronze statues of Buddha and other religious images throughout the East. Because of the high degree of accuracy obtainable, it is used nowadays for precision casting of high melting-point alloys.

An accurate permanent metal mould for the required component is made, in which a replica of the component is cast in wax, complete with runner sections. This expendable wax model is now dipped in a slurry, or suspension in water, of a ceramic material which dries to form a coating adhering to the wax. Further coats are given until a sufficient body of ceramic is built up and dried. The whole is fired or baked to harden and strengthen the ceramic mould, during which the wax replica melts and burns out, so that it is 'lost'.

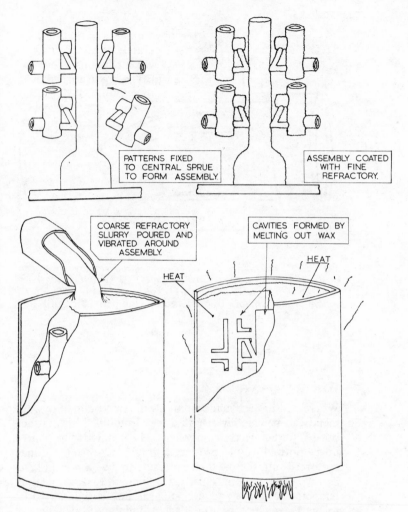

PATTERNS FIXED
TO CENTRAL SPRUE
TO FORM ASSEMBLY.

ASSEMBLY COATED
WITH FINE
REFRACTORY.

COARSE REFRACTORY
SLURRY POURED AND
VIBRATED AROUND
ASSEMBLY.

CAVITIES FORMED BY
MELTING OUT WAX

HEAT

HEAT

Fig. 3.11. Stages in making a mould for an investment casting by the lost-wax process (by courtesy of the British Investment Casters Technical Association)

By this means a very precise *mould* with good surface finish is made, in which it is possible to cast high melting-point alloys and produce a casting which requires a minimum of machining. As many of these alloys are extremely difficult to machine the expense of the casting process is more than justified. Fig. 3.11 shows the sequence of events involved in the manufacture of an investment casting and fig. 3.12, a typical part produced.

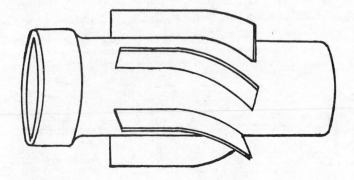

Fig. 3.12. Swirl vanes for air cleaner produced by Investment Casting in stainless steel. Casting limits ±0·13 mm. If machined from solid bar the finished part would weigh only 20% of the weight of the bar stock (reproduced by kind permission of B.S.A. Precision Castings Ltd.)

DIE CASTING

Where castings are made from low melting-point alloys, the metal can be cast directly in a metal mould, which is then opened to remove the component. The metal may be poured in the normal way to produce a *gravity die-casting*, or may be forced into the die under pressure to give a *pressure die-casting*. The materials used are limited to low melting-temperature alloys and a zinc-base alloy is generally used for parts which carry little load. Aluminium is also die-cast and, in isolated cases, brass, but its melting point is the limit of temperature at which the process is used.

It is important to note that the dies which form the mould must be designed so that the casting can be removed in one piece, without damaging the mould. The split line must be chosen with great care and in some cases multi-part dies with more than one split line are used. Ejector pins are provided to remove the solidified casting from the dies as they open. The dies are usually designed to produce more than one component per cycle of the die-casting machine, according to the component size, and up to twelve-impression dies may be used for small components.

After the component has been cast, the sprue is broken off and any flash is removed, usually by a clipping operation in a press.

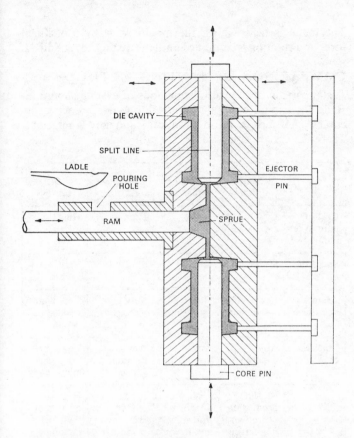

Fig. 3.13. Simple die-casting dies producing two flanged pipes per cycle. Note that the split line corresponds to that of casting methods and that draft in the pattern is still necessary.

Sequence of Operations

1. *Dies closed with ram withdrawn beyond pouring hole.*
2. *Core pins inserted.*
3. *Measured quantity of molten metal poured into pouring hole.*
4. *Ram moved forward, forcing metal into die cavity under pressure (position shown).*
5. *Core pins withdrawn.*
6. *Dies opened, ram staying in position shown. Casting ejected by ejector pins and ram.*

Arrows indicate motions of moving parts.

The accuracy available is such that machining of the component can be kept to a minimum, being carried out only where a particular fit is required. An indication of the quantity of work produced by die casting can be gained by listing some of the components in a modern motor car which are made by this process. It should be noted that all these components carry very little load. They include:

(1) Fuel pump body   (2) Speedometer body
(3) Carburettor body   (4) Petrol gauge 'sender' unit
(5) Door handles   (6) 'Hardware', including mascots, names, badges and decorative brightware.

Pressure die-castings can be produced as tiny parts such as small gears for instruments or as large as 35 kg in mass.

A die for our flanged pipe is shown in fig. 3.13, two pipes being produced per 'shot'.

CENTRIFUGAL CASTING

Where long pipes of uniform wall thickness are required, they can be produced by rotating the mould and pouring the metal into it through a runner which moves along the mould.

53

The metal is held against the mould walls by centrifugal force and rotation is continued until the casting has solidified.

COMPARISON OF CASTING METHODS

A comparison of the various methods of casting should include the capital cost of equipment, speed of process, accuracy and surface finish produced, and any limitations. These factors are compared in the table below.

	Sand Casting	Shell Moulding	Investment Casting	Die Casting
Cost of pattern or mould	Low	Low	High	High
Speed of process	Slow	Fast	Slow	Very fast
Accuracy and finish	Low ±0·40 mm	High ±0·12 mm	Very high ±0·003 m per m	Very high ±0·003 m per m
Materials cast	Any material	Any material	Any material	Low melting-point alloys only
Uses	Medium production of iron and non-ferrous castings	High production of iron and non-ferrous castings	Production of high-accuracy castings in high melting-point alloys	High production of low melting-point alloys

THE FORGING PROCESS

Forging and casting are complementary to each other as primary processes, but whereas castings are made by pouring molten metal into a mould, a forging is made by heating the metal until it is plastic and hammering, pressing, or bending it into shape.

Forgings may be made by hand by a blacksmith, often assisted by his mate, or by various types of power-operated machinery. Quantity production of small and medium-sized forgings is usually performed by *drop hammers* or *forging machines,* in both of which the hot metal is hammered or squeezed between metal dies in which impressions have been cut to produce the shape of forging required. Larger forgings are generally shaped by *power hammers* or *hydraulic presses,* some of which can handle forgings of very large size e.g., big gun barrels and ships' mainshafts. Smaller power hammers fitted with dies are sometimes used in place of drop hammers. A recent development is that of high-energy-rate forming, where the tup, or hammer, strikes a billet in the die at very high speed, and the energy thus generated is used to produce a good quality forging in one stroke.

HAND FORGING

Some people think that a blacksmith heats a piece of metal and hammers it into intricate shapes simply by using a hammer and his anvil. This is a misconception, for the blacksmith uses a variety of tools, each having its own particular purpose, as does any other skilled man. The most-used tools are undoubtedly the hammer and anvil, but frequently the anvil is used as a mount for pairs of tools between which the work is forged by hammer blows. Many forging operations require two men, the smith and his mate or *striker*. The smith is the skilled man, holding the work in tongs and positioning the upper tool on it. By a system of signals, and an understanding built up during years of working together, he instructs the striker where, when, and with what force the blows are to be struck.

The smith and the striker use a range of hammers, of different weights and shapes to suit the operation in hand. The smith's own hand hammer is usually about 4 kg in mass of head, while the striker generally uses heavier hammers, called *sledge* hammers, from 8 kg to 14 kg, or more, mass of head.

Before considering the various operations performed by the smith, let us examine the anvil and the use of its various parts (see fig. 3.14). The main body of the anvil is made of mild steel, with a hardened *top face* welded on. The *beak* is soft and, with an increasing diameter of cross-section, is useful for producing bends of different radii. The *ledge* between the beak and the anvil face is soft and can be used as

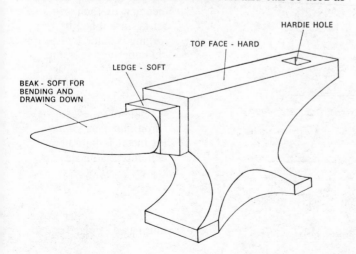

Fig. 3.14. A smith's anvil

HARDIE HOLE

TOP FACE - HARD

LEDGE - SOFT

BEAK - SOFT FOR BENDING AND DRAWING DOWN

a base for cutting operations with *hot chisels*, i.e., chisels shaped to cut hot metal. Cutting should not be done on the anvil face since this might spoil the face whose hardness might also damage the edge of the chisel. Near the end of the anvil face is a square hole, or *hardie hole*, used for holding the shank of the lower member of a pair of tools.

A large anvil may have a mass up to 250 kg and its face is positioned at a comfortable working height, usually about 0·7 m. This is achieved by mounting it on a large solid block of wood or a heavy metal stand whose shock-absorbent qualities help to spread the shock loads and reduce damage to the floor.

HAND FORGING OPERATIONS

Most of the forgings produced by a blacksmith are the result of a sequence of fairly standard operations. These and the tools used are considered in turn below.

(1) CUTTING   Cutting is normally done by chisels. These may be *hot chisels* for cutting hot metal or *cold chisels* for cutting cold metal. Both are normally fitted with a long handle, the chisel being held on the work and struck with a hammer.

The cold chisel is similar to a fitter's chisel, except that it is longer and has a handle. Its edge is hardened and tempered, and its point angle is 60°.

The hot chisel has a point angle of 30° and is soft. To harden and temper it would be pointless, since its contact with hot metal would soften it.

Fig. 3.15. Use of chisels in forging

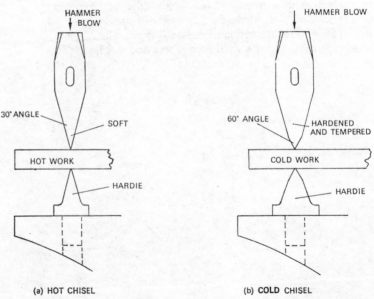

HAMMER BLOW

30° ANGLE

SOFT

HOT WORK

HARDIE

(a) HOT CHISEL

HAMMER BLOW

60° ANGLE

HARDENED AND TEMPERED

COLD WORK

HARDIE

(b) COLD CHISEL

56

Chisels are often used in pairs, the lower tool then being known as a *hardie*, which has a square shank to fit the hardie hole. The work is positioned between the hardie and the top chisel by the smith, as shown in fig. 3.15, and the top chisel is struck by the striker.

(2) UPSETTING   This process consists of increasing the cross-section of the material locally at the expense of its length. Only the part to be upset is heated to forging temperature, and the bar, or work, is then struck at the end, usually between the hammer and the anvil, as shown in fig. 3.16.

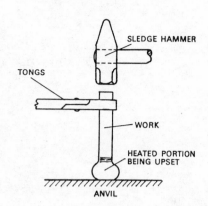

Fig. 3.16. Upsetting

(3) DRAWING-DOWN   This is the opposite of upsetting, i.e., the section of the bar is reduced locally, with an increase in length. The point where drawing-down is to start is usually first notched, or necked, by *fullers*, and drawing-down is continued from that point either between a pair of fullers or against the corner edge of the anvil. This leaves an undulating surface which is usually finished with a *flatter* or *set-hammer*, as shown in fig. 3.17.

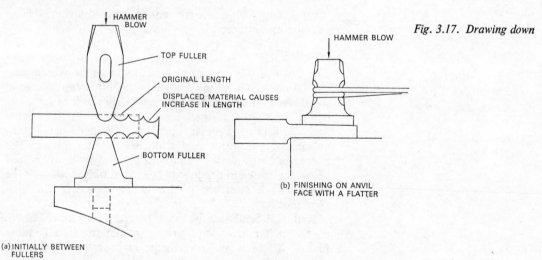

Fig. 3.17. Drawing down

(4) SWAGING   Swaging is the process of finishing a round or hexagonal section of bar between a pair of swages of the appropriate size. These may be separate tools, top and bottom, or held together by a long spring handle, as shown in fig. 3.18. In place of the bottom swage, the smith may use a *swage block*. This is a large square block of cast iron mounted on a heavy stand; around its four sides are semi-circular, half-hexagon and vee-shaped grooves, of increasing sizes, which correspond to bottom swages and other bottom tools. In the face of the swage block is a series of holes of

57

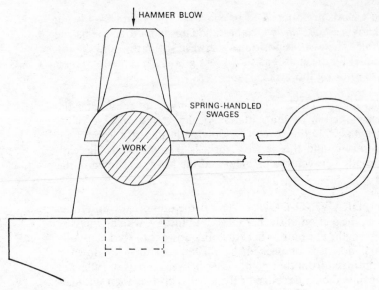

↓ HAMMER BLOW

SPRING-HANDLED
SWAGES

WORK

Fig. 3.18. Swaging

various shapes which are convenient for holding bars during bending operations.

(5) BENDING   Bends may be made to a sharp angle or to a radius. Sharp bends can be made in a vice, or by hammering the work over the anvil edge, but in either case the metal should be thickened by upsetting on the *outside* of the bend before the bend is started. This compensates for the distortion which takes place at the corner, the metal being compressed on the inside and stretched on the outside. The effect can be shown by bending a piece of indiarubber and observing the bend produced. The metal bulges wider at the inside and is stretched further at the outside, with local thinning.

Radiused bends can be made over the beak of the anvil, around a bar in a vice or round a mandrel in a bending fixture. There is again a change in cross-section but the tendency is less severe, and the change in width is corrected after bending.

(6) PIERCING   The smith often produces a hole in the work by piercing the metal with a *punch*, over the hardie hole or over a *die*, which is a block of metal with a hole through it corresponding in size to the punch. Use of a punch and die gives a more accurate hole than using the punch alone. Holes other than round can be produced by first making a round hole and then driving through a tool called a *drift*, which tapers from round at the point to the

58

size and shape required at the shank. Alternatively, a round hole can be filed or machined to a different shape when the workpiece has cooled.

MACHINE FORGING OPERATIONS

Hand forging processes are suitable for relatively small work but when larger pieces of metal have to be forged the energy available from a hand-operated sledge hammer is not enough. Consequently, power hammers are used, driven by water power, compressed air, steam or friction. In most of these the sledge hammer is replaced by a heavy power-operated upper anvil called the *tup*, which is lifted up and then falls, or is driven, down on to the lower anvil which is built into the base of the hammer. When the tup falls under its own weight, its potential energy at the top of the stroke is changed to kinetic energy as it gains speed. When impact occurs, this kinetic energy is released and the work done on the hot metal is equal to it.

Similar pairs of tools to those used in hand forging can be used and a similar range of operations carried out.

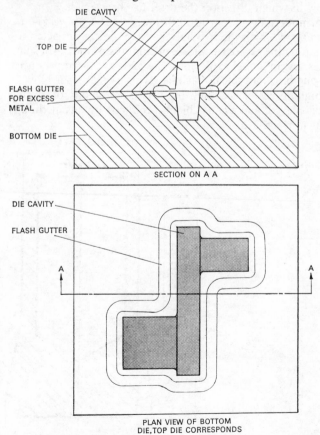

DIE CAVITY

TOP DIE

FLASH GUTTER
FOR EXCESS
METAL

BOTTOM DIE

SECTION ON A A

DIE CAVITY

FLASH GUTTER

A   A

PLAN VIEW OF BOTTOM
DIE. TOP DIE CORRESPONDS

Fig. 3.19. Dies for drop-forging a single-sided crank

DROP FORGING This is a machine forging process used to produce large numbers of similar parts. A pair of dies with appropriate impressions are fitted to the tup and anvil and accurately aligned by using a dummy component to set them in position. The hot blank to be forged is often pre-formed to a suitable size and shape before it is placed in the lower die. The top die, attached to the tup, then drops on to the blank and the energy of its fall squeezes the metal until it fills the impressions of the dies, any excess forming a flash, or fin, which is clipped off later. This process is used for a wide diversity of parts whose sizes vary from rocker arms for internal-combustion engines to wheels for railway trucks and carriages. The dies for a single-sided crank are shown in fig. 3.19.

It should be noted that in this process, as in casting, allowance must be made for shrinkage, and for extracting the forging from the dies. Draft and a suitable split line are necessary, since there must be no undercuts. Examination of a drop forging will usually reveal the split line of the dies, where the fin has been trimmed off, and the draft angle will show in which direction the draft has been made.

A modern development of this process is *high-energy-rate forming* in which the two halves of the die are impacted together by the explosive release of compressed air or, in some cases, by an actual explosion. The parts are often produced by one blow, a typical machine giving 17,000 J per blow. A high degree of accuracy and very good quality of forging are achieved, and a collet blank produced by this method is shown in fig. 3.20.

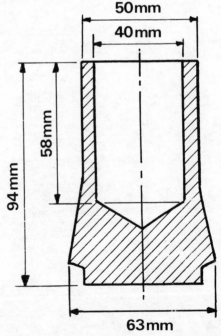

Fig. 3.20. Collet blank produced from 0·60% carbon steel in one blow by a high-energy process. Billet size: 49·3 mm dia. × 50·8 mm long. Concentricity held within 0·08 mm

THE ROLLING PROCESS

HOT ROLLING   Molten steel from the Bessemer or open-hearth process is normally cast into *ingots* of roughly square section and weighing up to 10 tonf, while most of the material required by the engineer, other than castings or forgings, is of much smaller section. The ingots are usually reduced to the size and section required by passing between pairs of cylindrical rolls under high pressure in a *rolling mill* to reduce the thickness and width, with increase in length. This process takes place in stages, the ingot first being heated to 1200°C in a soaking pit, and then reduced to *blooms* which are cut to length before reduction to the section finally required.

The rolling process may require up to twelve sets of rolls of different sizes and shapes, each set approaching nearer to the section wanted, and the billet is passed through each set in turn. If the rolling is not continuous the various reductions are made by different-sized grooves along the length of roll. The bar, or stock, moves forward on the first pass, back on the second, forward on the third and so on. The final rolls for a channel section are shown in fig. 3.21.

If steel plate or strip is required the process is similar, except that the blooms first pass through a *slabbing mill* to

Fig. 3.21. Hot rolling

(a) FINISHING ROLLS FOR
CHANNEL SECTION

TOP ROLL

BOTTOM ROLL

(b) OTHER HOT-ROLLED
SECTIONS

produce slabs, which are then reduced between successive parallel rolls to the thickness required. For steel strip, used by the motor industry in large quantities, a continuous-strip mill is often employed, the slab passing through a succession of rolls each of which produces a reduction in section and an *increase in length*. The speed of each set of rolls must be carefully controlled in relation to the one preceding it to maintain the correct tension in the strip. At the final stage the strip, moving at speeds of up to 100 km/h, is wound into coils ready for despatch to the user.

COLD ROLLING   This process is basically similar to the hot rolling process except that the material is rolled cold, i.e., at room temperature. As in hot rolling, the section of the material is reduced and the length correspondingly increased. The material is initially hot rolled near to size and pickled in acid to remove the scale. It is then cold rolled between rolls whose surface has a high finish, to produce a corresponding finish on the rolled metal. The pressures are, of course, very much higher since the cold metal cannot be 'moved' so easily, and the reduction per pass is less, but a much greater degree of control can be exercised and the thickness can be kept accurate to less than 0·03 mm.

COLD DRAWING OR WIRE DRAWING

Much of the bar and rod used in engineering is known as *bright-drawn mild steel*, or B.D.M.S. The metal is first hot rolled to produce *black* bar which is pickled to remove the scale, and then pulled cold through dies so that the section is reduced, and the length increased.

The die holes are conical in shape and must, of course, be very hard to maintain their size and finish against wear through the high pressures involved. Small dies for thin wires are made from diamond or tungsten carbide, larger sizes from hardened tool steel and the very large sizes from chilled cast iron.

With cold drawing, as with the rolling processes, all the materials produced have a 'grain', i.e., the grains of metal are elongated in the direction of drawing or rolling and tend to increase the strength of the metal in this direction. Thus if a piece of bright mild steel is bent across the grain it will normally withstand the bending stresses, but if the bend is along the bar, in the same direction as the grain, the bar may crack unless it has first been normalised.

THE EXTRUSION PROCESS

Just as toothpaste is squeezed from a tube and comes out with the same shape as the hole, metal may be forced through a die under pressure and will emerge with the same shape as

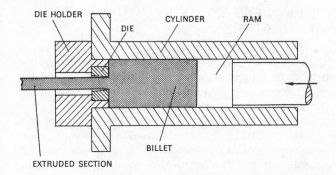

DIE HOLDER DIE CYLINDER RAM

EXTRUDED SECTION

BILLET

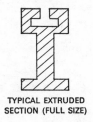

TYPICAL EXTRUDED
SECTION (FULL SIZE)

the die. A much higher pressure is required than for tooth-paste, of course, and the process is normally limited to brass, copper, and the aluminium alloys, all of which have a fairly low tensile strength. Extremely complex sections, solid or hollow, may be extruded, a typical section being shown with a diagram of the process in fig. 3.22. These sections can be extremely thin and of insufficient strength to withstand wire drawing, yet the same high degree of accuracy can be achieved.

IMPACT EXTRUSION   If a metal which is extremely plastic when cold is struck by a punch moving at very high speed, the material 'splashes' back up the punch and produces a tube. This process is called impact extrusion and is used for the manufacture of toothpaste tubes, electrical-consenser cans, ignition-coil cans for motor cars, cigar tubes etc. All of these are made from aluminium supplied in the form of slugs, the tube shown in fig. 3.23 being produced from the slug by a single blow.

Fig. 3.22. Simple forward extrusion and a typical extruded section

Fig. 3.23. Impact extrusion. A toothpaste tube is produced by a single blow on a slug of aluminium

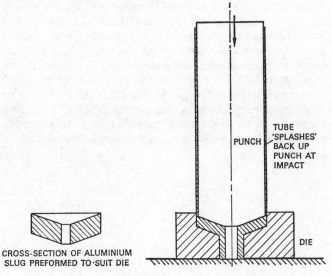

PUNCH

TUBE
'SPLASHES'
BACK UP
PUNCH AT
IMPACT

DIE

CROSS-SECTION OF ALUMINIUM
SLUG PREFORMED TO·SUIT DIE

63

THE PROPERTIES OF CASTINGS AND FORGINGS

At the end of the section on casting we made a comparison of the various casting processes. Now we can ask why are two types of process required, the casting process and the forging process. The reason is simply that the properties of materials and the properties of parts produced by the two processes are very different. Cast iron will not forge and, generally, the ferrous casting has low tensile strength and is brittle, easily broken by impact. The forging, on the other hand, has high tensile strength and the ability to withstand shock loads. Further, steel is not amenable to casting, having a higher melting temperature and not flowing so easily as cast iron. It is a much more difficult material in which to produce a sound casting.

The forging process can, however, readily be carried out on steel, and the 'grain' of the steel can be arranged to lie in the best direction to withstand the applied loads. Thus forgings are used where a high tensile strength and an ability to withstand shock loads are required.

There are cases where materials are required to withstand shock loads but the very shape of the part demands that it should be cast. In these cases it is possible to heat-treat the castings to make them more malleable. The heat treatment consists of packing the castings in either iron ore or rolling mill scale and heating them to 900°C for up to five days. The carbon is oxidised out of the thin sections, giving a structure similar to that of mild steel and reducing the risk of fracture due to a shock load. This process of removing the carbon is called the *whiteheart* process.

Another process, which does not remove the carbon, is called the *blackheart* process. Here the castings are packed in neutral material to exclude air and heated to 800°C. The brittle cementite breaks down to ferrite and carbon, which is dispersed in 'rosettes' throughout the casting and does not break up the structure, as do the flakes of graphite in grey iron castings. A later process has been evolved in which alloying elements added to the iron cause the carbon to be produced as spheroids in the casting process. This iron, known as S.G. (spheroidal graphite) iron, is becoming common where the casting must withstand shock loads.

64

4
Metal Joining Processes

Apart from casting and forging, another method used by the engineer to save machining and materials is fabrication, the building up of a larger part or structure from a number of smaller parts. These are joined together either by mechanical methods, using screws, rivets, shrinkage or press fits etc or by 'bonding' the parts together using another material such as solder, brazing metal or some of the more recent high-strength glues based on epoxy resins. Welding is considered a bonding process since it gives a permanent joint, although it does not generally employ a different material. When a metal welding rod is used in fusing the joint it is normally similar to the metal being joined.

MECHANICAL JOINTS

LOCATION Regardless of the method of joining, it is good practice to make the parts *self-locating* where possible. Consider two shaft flanges bolted together to join two shafts. There must be clearance between the bolts and their holes to allow the bolts to enter easily and take up any misalignment between the holes, and this clearance could allow the flanges and shafts to move out of line as shown in fig. 4.1.

Fig. 4.1. Use of spigot and recess to give self location of flanged couplings

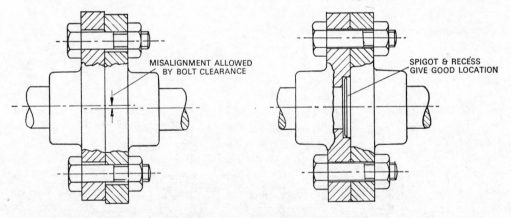

MISALIGNMENT ALLOWED BY BOLT CLEARANCE

SPIGOT & RECESS GIVE GOOD LOCATION

If a spigot is machined on one flange and a corresponding recess in the other so that the two register with each other, misalignment is limited to any clearance between spigot and recess, which would be much smaller than that between bolts and holes.

TAPER LOCATIONS If a spigot and recess are made correspondingly tapered and drawn into each other by a bolt, there should be no misalignment. This method is used widely on machine parts, the shank of a shell end-milling cutter being a good example. However, the taper alone gives only a friction drive and, to make the drive positive, tenons are incorporated as shown in fig. 4.2.

Fig. 4.2. Location and positive drive of shank for shell end-milling cutter (see also Fig. 6.26)

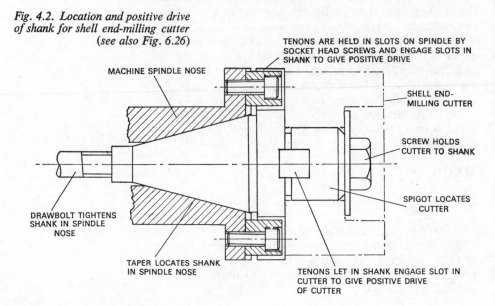

Fig. 4.3. Use of dowels, bushes and pillars to locate parts of press tool

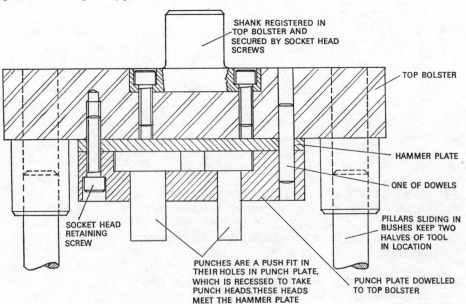

DOWEL PINS A third method of location is to use dowels, which pass through both parts and are a push fit in their holes to give precise location, with screws to hold the parts together. This method is frequently used where parallel or taper registers are not practicable and especially where flat surfaces have to be located on each other, as in press tools. Fig. 4.3 shows the top bolster and punches of a small press tool in which the following points should be noted.

(1) The two halves, or bolsters, of the tool are located by sliding pillars and bushes:
(2) The two punches are a press fit in the punch plate and are therefore self-locating:
(3) The punch plate and hammer plate are dowelled to the top bolster and held by screws (only one dowel and one screw are shown):
(4) The tool shank is registered into the top bolster and held by screws.

BOLTS AND NUTS Bolts and nuts are generally used to clamp two parts together, as shown in fig. 4.1, and are normally fitted only where a spanner can be applied to each part to tighten the nut and prevent the bolt from turning. If a thread is stripped by over-tightening, it requires the replacement of only the nut and bolt, but a stripped thread in the component itself can mean an expensive repair or replacement.

Many applications of nuts and bolts require a locking device to prevent them from coming loose through vibration. There are a number of locking devices in use of which the commonest are:

(1) spring lock washers:
(2) a second nut or locknut:
(3) proprietary 'Nylock' nuts. (There are also other proprietary locking nuts):
(4) castellated nuts and split pins.

The first two tend to strain the thread in the bolt and nut, and the third relies on the friction between a nylon insert in the nut and the bolt thread. The castellated nut and split pin is used to give a positive lock which in no way relies on friction.

SCREWS Screws are used where a spanner cannot be applied to both nut and bolt because of the inaccessibility of one or the other. This means that one of the components must be tapped to receive the screw, as in fig. 4.3, where all the screws shown are socket-head screws which can be screwed down very tightly with a hexagonal key. If the head need not be recessed, a hexagon headed screw may be used and if the joint need not be very tight, a cheese-head screw or a countersunk screw tightened with a screw-driver can be used, as in fig. 4.4.

SAFETY NOTE *Always use the correct size of spanner when tightening a screw or nut and only use an adjustable spanner as a last resort, for this slips all too easily.*

STUDS Studs are double-ended screws used to hold a cover on a casting with a gasket between to form a gas-tight joint. The stud end which screws into the casting often has a coarse thread while the other end, for the nut, has a fine thread. The reason for this is given on page 69 but the arrangement will usually allow the fine thread on the nut end to strip rather than the coarse thread in the casting, thus preventing damage to the casting. Studs are used on pump end cases, motor car cylinder heads etc. as shown in fig. 4.4.

Fig. 4.4. Use of studs for holding end plate to cast housing. Note the spigot location and the use of undercuts to give clearance at corners

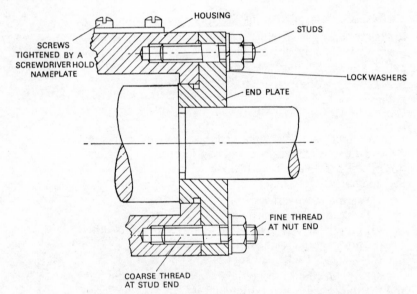

USES OF COARSE AND FINE THREADS The young engineer soon becomes aware that in several systems of screw threads there are *coarse thread series* and *fine thread series*. British Standard Whitworth and British Standard Fine threads, and Unified Coarse and Unified Fine threads, are examples. In each case the thread form is the same but the pitch of the thread is different for similar diameters of bolts and screws.

Let us consider a 12 mm diameter screw being tightened into a casting with spanner of effective length 150 mm, the thread being coarse in one case and fine in the other. In each case let the spanner make one revolution.

The distance moved by the spanner force will be $2\pi \times 150$ mm.

(1) 12 mm $\times$ 1·75 mm pitch.

For one revolution the screw moves 1·75 mm.

Assuming 100% efficiency:

Mechanical Advantage $=$ Velocity Ratio

$$= \frac{\text{Distance moved by effort}}{\text{Distanced moved by load}}$$

$$= \frac{2\pi \times 150}{1·75}$$

$$= 171\pi$$

(2) 12 mm $\times$ 1·25 mm pitch.

For one revolution the screw moves 1·25 mm.

$$\text{Mechanical Advantage} = \frac{2\pi \times 150}{1·25}$$

$$= 240\pi$$

Thus, the mechnical advantage for the fine thread is much the greater and the joint is pulled down much tighter by the same force on the spanner.

If a fine thread is used in a weak material such as cast iron or aluminium it will be much more likely to strip than a coarse one. It follows that fine threads should only be used in strong materials such as steel, and coarse threads in castings and weak materials.

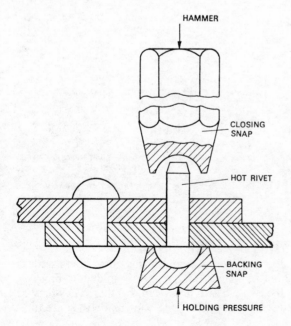

HAMMER

CLOSING SNAP

HOT RIVET

BACKING SNAP

HOLDING PRESSURE

Fig. 4.5. Riveting snaphead rivets

RIVETS The joints made by rivets may be classed as semi-permanent, since to break the joint the rivet head must be cut off or the rivet drilled out. Riveted joints are usually confined to plate or sheet material as used in ships and aircraft, and to rolled steel sections as used in bridges and steel-framed buildings.

For the latter type of work snap-head rivets are most common. The rivet, which has one head already formed, is heated to forging temperature and passed through the holes in the two plates. The head end of the rivet is held tightly against one plate by the riveter's mate, using a rivet snap, and the other end is forged to shape over the other plate by the riveter, using a similar snap and a hammer, or a pneumatic riveting tool. As the rivet cools it contracts and draws the plates more tightly together. Such a joint is shown in fig. 4.5.

'POP' RIVETS In the aircraft industry a need developed for a rivet which could be closed from the outside without support from the inside. Such rivets are often tubular aluminium rivets with a steel rod running through the centre which has a head at the unclosed end of the rivet, as shown in fig. 4.6. A tool is used to hold the head of the rivet in place and draw the rod into the rivet so that its end spreads the unclosed end of the rivet. The steel stem has a weak 'neck' so that when the rivet is closed the head breaks off and the stem is withdrawn.

Fig. 4.6. Hollow or 'pop' rivets

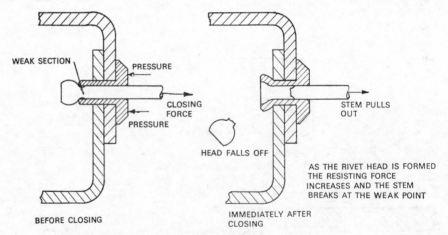

WEAK SECTION

PRESSURE

CLOSING
FORCE

PRESSURE

HEAD FALLS OFF

STEM PULLS
OUT

AS THE RIVET HEAD IS FORMED
THE RESISTING FORCE
INCREASES AND THE STEM
BREAKS AT THE WEAK POINT

BEFORE CLOSING

IMMEDIATELY AFTER
CLOSING

SOLDERING AND BRAZING

Joints made by soldering and brazing may be classed as bonded joints in that a foreign metal, solder or brass, is fused into the two parts to join them together. They may be classed as permanent joints since once made they are difficult to break, either by mechanical force or by heat, without causing damage to one or both parts. Basically there are three types of joint, depending upon the strength required:

(1) *soft soldered:* low temperature and low strength:
(2) *silver or hard soldered:* higher temperature and greater strength:
(3) *brazed:* high temperature and great strength.

As the temperature required increases, the strength of the joint obtained increases.

In all cases the fundamentals are the same. The parts must be thoroughly cleaned, either mechanically or chemically, a flux must be applied to them to maintain cleanliness and prevent atmospheric attack, and the parts must be heated until the solder or brass melts and fuses into them, thus creating the joint.

It is important to note that the *work* must be heated to a temperature at which the solder will flow. It is not enough to melt the solder and drop it or flow it on; this gives a 'dry' joint which is weak and easily broken.

SOFT SOLDERING For most mechanical assembly joints, tinman's solder is used, whose characteristics were given in Chapter 2. It melts at 183°C and is composed of two parts of tin and one of lead. It changes directly from a solid to a liquid state and vice-versa without an intermediate pasty stage.

Small joints can be made by using a *soldering iron*, which is ironically made of copper, while larger areas may be 'sweated' together. In either case the work must be heated to above the melting temperature of the solder either by the heat from the soldering iron or by a gas flame, or other source of heat.

USE OF THE SOLDERING IRON Soldering irons are made of copper because it is a good conductor of heat and readily transfers the heat from the body of the iron, through the tip, to the work. The bit is usually large and heavy so that it can contain a large quantity of heat to be given up to the work. Note: copper does not retain the heat—it gives it up.

The work must be clean, free from grease and clear of any oxide film, and the initial preparation of the work is most important. It should be cleaned by filing or rubbing with *dry* emery cloth until any oxide coating is removed, and the area of the joint should then be coated with flux. While this is being done the iron is heated to a temperature at which it readily melts solder. While hot, the iron is filed clean to remove any oxide film, dipped in flux to maintain chemical cleanliness and 'tinned' or coated with solder. If it is not properly tinned, fresh solder applied for the joint will not adhere to it nor flow freely from it.

The iron is now drawn along the joint slowly enough to heat the parts to a temperature above the melting point of solder, at which temperature the solder will flow from the iron to the job and 'make' the joint as it cools. Fresh solder is added as the joint is being 'run'. At the same time as it heats the work, the iron boils the flux and creates a gaseous shield which prevents atmospheric oxygen from attacking the joint.

In a properly soldered joint, the solder fuses into the parent metal at the point of contact so that the final joint should consist of the parent metal, a layer of solder and parent metal fused together, a layer of solder (the thinner the better), a second layer of solder and parent metal fused together, and the parent metal again, as shown in fig. 4.7.

It cannot be emphasised enough that soldering itself is a simple operation. It is the preparation and cleanliness which make the joint sound, and more soldered joints have been spoiled by bad preparation than by any other cause.

Fig. 4.7. Diagrammatic cross-section through soldered joint (highly magnified)

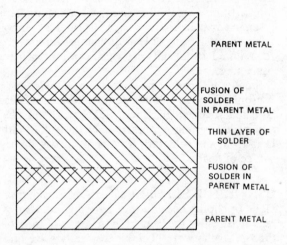

PARENT METAL

FUSION OF SOLDER IN PARENT METAL

THIN LAYER OF SOLDER

FUSION OF SOLDER IN PARENT METAL

PARENT METAL

SWEATED JOINTS When large solid parts have to be joined, the soldering iron will not raise the temperature of the work enough to cause the solder to flow; the heat is conducted away too quickly by the mass of metal. In such cases the areas to be joined are first 'tinned'. They must again be thoroughly cleaned and fluxed, and heated by being placed on a hot plate or by a blow torch until the solder will 'take'. When using a torch it is inadvisable to heat the surface to be tinned directly since the hot gas may cause contamination. Heat should be applied from outside the surface and conducted to it.

72

When both surfaces have been tinned they are refluxed, held together under pressure and again heated until the solder fuses to form the joint. An example is shown in fig. 4.8.

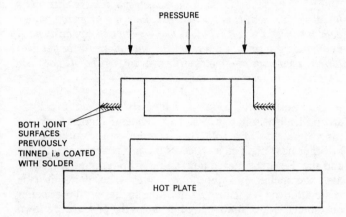

Fig. 4.8. A sweated joint. Note self-location

USE OF CAPILLARY ACTION   Where two cylindrical parts are to be soldered one into the other, such as the tube into the flanged end shown in fig. 4.9, they are first cleaned. The tube is then fluxed and fitted into the flanged end and a ring of solder is placed around the tube as shown. The assembly is heated by a blow torch until the solder melts, when it is drawn down into the joint by capillary action. On mass-production work the heating can be done by electrical induction methods, and then takes only about five seconds.

This method of soldering can give a very strong joint, but only when the clearance between the parts is not excessive. The maximum strength is obtained with about 0·13 mm

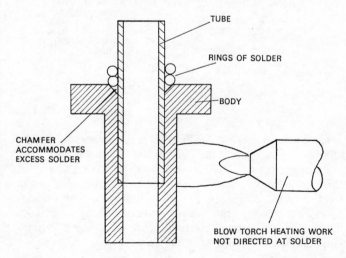

Fig. 4.9. Making a soldered joint by capillary action

clearance all round. If the clearance is much less the solder will not flow into the joint, and if it is much greater the solder itself will fail, in shear.

SAFETY NOTE *In soldering electrical joints, care must be taken that heat is not conducted along the wires to damage delicate parts or the insulation. This conduction can be avoided by clamping a pair of pliers on the wire close to the joint to form a heat sink and conduct heat away, so that it does not pass along the wire.*

HARD SOLDERING AND BRAZING   These processes are basically similar in that they demand higher temperatures than that of a soldering iron and both require flame or other heating. The essence of the job is again cleanliness and the use of a suitable flux, and it is not enough merely to melt the spelter and hope it will stick. The work must be heated above the melting point of the spelter until the spelter on it melts. Under similar circumstances the procedure shown in fig. 4.9 can be used. A common application of brazing is the joining of cemented-carbide tool tips to a carbon steel shank. Here the spelter takes the form of a strip of shim thickness which, after the work has been cleaned and fluxed, is placed in position at the joint, with the tip in place. Pressure is now applied and the shank heated until the spelter melts and forms the joint, as shown in fig. 4.10.

Fig. 4.10. Brazing a cemented-carbide tip to a steel tool shank

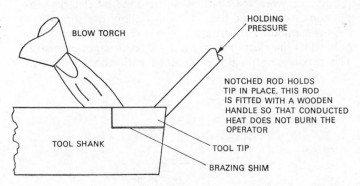

Copper brazing is a specialised form of brazing used generally for production work. The parts are made self-locating and copper plated. They are then put together and passed through a furnace so that the copper fuses and forms the joint. A small American motor car firm once built engines by copper brazing the water jacket around the cylinder liners, and the process is used to braze cooling fins on lengths of tube for heat transfer units.

74

FLUXES Fluxes are of two types:

(1) those which chemically clean and protect the surface:

(2) those which only protect an already clean surface.

Those which have a chemical action are usually corrosive and the work must be thoroughly washed after the joint has been made. If this is not possible, a non-active or passive flux must be used.

Active fluxes

These fluxes are most commonly used for soft soldering and the best-known is chloride of zinc or 'killed spirit'. Proprietary brands may be purchased, or the flux can be made by adding an excess of zinc to concentrated hydrochloric acid. When the liquid stops bubbling it is strained off and then ready for use. After its use the joint must be well cleaned to prevent corrosion.

Passive fluxes

There are many of these. Tallow is sometimes used but the commonest is resin, and for electrical joints a resin-cored solder is used in which the flux is contained within a hollow wire or rod of solder which is thus ready for immediate use. This type of flux does not clean the work in any way, and the work must be thoroughly cleaned of any oxide film or other impurity before soldering is commenced.

For hard soldering and brazing, borax is generally used as a flux. It may be applied directly as a powder, or more conveniently made into a paste with water and painted on.

WELDING

Welding differs from soldering in that generally no foreign metal is used to make the joint. The parts are heated locally to melting point until they fuse and flow together. Thus a welded joint should be continuous, and ideally, even microscopic examination should not reveal the joint. As the weld proceeds, a filler rod of similar metal supplies additional metal to fill the joint and make good any losses.

Heating must be very rapid to confine it to a local area, and an oxy-acetylene flame or an electric arc is used. The flame must be supplied by a correct balance of oxygen and acetylene so that it is neither oxydising nor carburising, since either of these flames would weaken the weld. In arc welding, the electrode is coated with a 'flux' which vaporises and provides a gaseous shield to prevent atmospheric attack.

Electrical-resistance welding is used to weld sheet metal in mass-production work, e.g., in the automobile industry. The parts are heated to the plastic state by the passage of an electric current and under pressure immediately weld together. Spot welding, stitch welding, seam welding and projection welding are all examples of this technique.

Finally let us consider factors influencing the choice of one of these types of joint.

(1) *Strength* If high strength is required a high temperature method must generally be used.

(2) *Temperature* The operating temperature of the joint must be below the melting point of the jointing material. It is no good using solder, which melts at 183°C, for a joint working at 300°C.

(3) *Cost* Generally, the lower the temperature required to make the joint, the lower the cost.

5
Workshop Measurements

As man's industrial techniques have progressed and the equipment we accept as part of everyday life has become more complex, there have been two parallel developments in engineering equipment. One has been in the machinery used to produce articles and components, and the other has been in the measuring equipment used to measure them. These are extremely closely related, since it is of little value to use a machine capable of working to ± 0.005 mm if our only measuring equipment is a rule and a pair of calipers. On the other hand, a wood turner making a chair leg is not likely to use a dial gauge or a micrometer. Thus it is important for the student to study measuring techniques and their applications as well as production processes.

MEASURING STANDARDS

How accurately must we be able to measure in modern engineering? Consider a part whose diameter is required to be 25 ± 0.05 mm. It is no good measuring it with a rule, for this will only be accurate to ± 0.15 mm in the hands of a skilled man. We need an instrument which can measure to ± 0.005 mm, i.e., one-tenth of the allowable variation in the part size.

In order to maintain this measuring instrument we need to check it against a standard of length whose accuracy is again within one-tenth of the instrument accuracy, i.e., ± 0.0005 mm, which, put in another way, is ± 0.5 *thousandths of a mm*. The first-year apprentice checking his micrometer with *gauge blocks*, or *slip gauges*, is therefore handling equipment whose order of accuracy is measured in fractions of a micrometre. To check these standards, still higher orders of accuracy are required and the highest standards, *grade* 00 blocks, are checked against the legal standard of length which is nowadays based on the wavelength of a particular colour of light.

These grade 00 gauge blocks are made to an accuracy of $\pm 5 \times 0.00001$ mm and are used only in a Standards Room, for checking inspection-grade blocks, which are then used for testing equipment and gauges.

SLIP GAUGES OR GAUGE BLOCKS These are hardened, ground and lapped rectangular blocks of high-carbon

steel (sometimes of cemented carbide) made so that:
(1) opposite faces are flat:
(2) ,, ,, ,, parallel:
(3) ,, ,, ,, accurately the stated distance apart:
(4) ,, ,, ,, of such a high degree of surface finish that when two blocks are pressed together with a slight twist by hand they will wring together, i.e., remain firmly attached to each other.

These properties of gauge blocks enable them to be built up, by wringing, into combinations which give sizes varying by steps of 0·01 mm and whose overall accuracy is of the order of 0·00025 mm, even with workshop-grade blocks. They are supplied in sets of 50, 78, or 105 pieces, and protective blocks are provided for use with inspection and workshop grades. These protective blocks should, where possible, be used as the end blocks of all combinations.

In the case of metric sizes B.S.S. 4311 recommends four sets of gauge blocks, two of which are set out below. The smallest increment possible with these sets is 0·0025 mm. Manufacturers do make sets which enable steps of 0·001 mm to be achieved.

Set no. M78

1·01 mm to 1·49 mm by 0·01 mm steps	— 49	blocks
0·50 mm to 9·50 mm by 0·50 mm steps	— 19	,,
10, 20, 30, 40, 50, 75, and 100 mm	— 7	,,
1·0025 mm	— 1	block
1·005 mm	— 1	,,
1·0075 mm	— 1	,,
	78	blocks

Set no. M50

1·01 mm to 1·09 mm by 0·01 mm steps	— 9	blocks
1·10 mm to 1·90 mm by 0·10 mm steps	— 9	,,
1 mm to 25 mm by 1 mm steps	— 25	,,
50, 75, and 100 mm	— 3	,,
1·0025, 1·0050, and 1·0075 mm	— 3	,,
0·050 mm	— 1	block
	50	blocks

Inch gauges are made in 41- or 81-piece sets, the 81-piece set being as follows:

0·1001 in to 0·1009 in by 0·0001 in steps	— 9	blocks
0·101 in to 0·149 in by 0·001 in steps	— 49	,,
0·050 in to 1·000 in by 0·050 in steps	— 20	,,
2 in, 3 in and 4 in blocks	— 3	,,
	81	,,

The 41-piece set is made up in a similar manner but not quite as many combinations can be achieved, the blocks provided being:

0·1001 in to 0·1009 in by 0·0001 in steps	—	9	blocks
0·101 in to 0·109 in by 0·001 in steps	—	9	,,
0·110 in to 0·190 in by 0·010 in steps	—	9	,,
0·100 in to 0·900 in by 0·100 in steps	—	9	,,
0·050 in, 1 in, 2 in, 3 in and 4 in blocks	—	5	,,
		41	,,

COMBINATIONS OF GAUGE BLOCKS In wringing combinations of gauge blocks the smallest possible number of blocks should be used. This can be achieved by working in a systematic manner by subtraction as follows.

Example:

Select suitable gauge blocks for making up a pile whose height is 81·83 mm.

(1) *Using a 78-piece set*

			Blocks used
	81·83		
2 protective slips	2·00	(subtract)	2 × 1·00 protectives
	78·83	remainder	
	79·83	remainder	
Select 2nd decimal	1·33	(subtract)	1·33
	78·50	remainder	
Select 1st decimal	3·50	(subtract)	3·50
	75·00	remainder	75·00
	Total	81·83 (check)	

(2) *Using a 50-piece set*

	81·83		
2 protective slips	2·00	(subtract)	2 × 1·00 protectives
	79·83	remainder	
Select 2nd decimal	1·03	(subtract)	1·03
	78·80	remainder	
Select 1st decimal	1·80	(subtract)	1·80
	77·00	remainder	
Select 1st unit	2·00	(subtract)	2·00
	75·00	remainder	75·00
	Total	81·83 (check)	

Note that six blocks are required with the 50-piece set and only five with the 78-piece set.

As examples the student should work out the combinations required to make up lengths of 3·4159 in and 5·281 in using the inch sets.

Fig. 5.1. Use of gauge block accessories

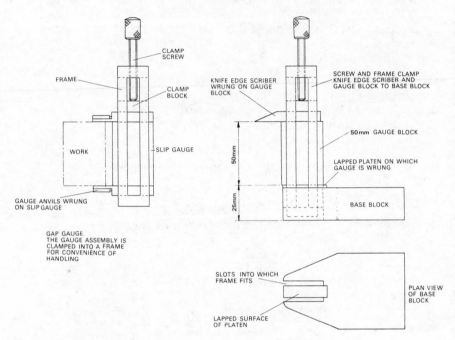

(b) HEIGHT GAUGE SET ACCURATELY AT **75mm**

APPLICATIONS OF GAUGE BLOCKS The simplest application of gauge blocks is their use as checking pieces for measuring instruments. They are also used as setting blocks for accurate measuring instruments such as comparators, and for setting sine bars to angular measurements. Their use is greatly increased if a set of gauge block accessories is available, since these can then be made into gap gauges and height gauges, as shown in fig. 5.1.

SAFETY NOTES *Gauge blocks must be handled carefully and protected from damage. The slightest burr will destroy their accuracy and wringing ability.*

(1) Always wring with a twisting movement, not a longitudinal rubbing movement.

(2) Always clean the blocks with chamois leather, or lintless cloth.

(3) Handle the blocks over a cloth so that if dropped they do not fall on a hard surface, which might raise a burr.

80

(4) *Do not put any blocks back into the box until all work with them is finished. All blocks that have been handled should then be cleaned and lightly greased as they are put away.*

THE MAGNIFICATION PRINCIPLES USED IN MEASURING

The eye cannot unaided detect from a scale a size difference smaller than about 0·1 mm and divisions of this size drawn on a scale would be so close together as to be difficult to distinguish. To see these small measurements clearly it is necessary to magnify the movement of the measuring face so that larger divisions can be used. Three common principles of magnification are used:

    (1) the micrometer principle:
    (2) the vernier principle:
    (3) the dial gauge principle.

THE MICROMETER   If we take a nut with a pitch of 1 mm, braze it into a 'U' shaped frame and pass a bolt through it whose head has 10 equally-spaced lines, in one revolution the bolt will advance 1 mm through the nut. The ten divisions on the head enable one revolution to be sub-divided into tenths of a revolution and each division there-fore represents $\frac{1}{10}$ mm of movement of the bolt. A section of perspex rule with 1 mm divisions, attached to the frame, would enable these fractions to be read off, and we have then made a rough micrometer to read to $\frac{1}{10}$ mm. By estimating between the divisions we can measure to less than this.

In practice the screw of a micrometer has a pitch of 0·50 mm, and the barrel has a scale sub-divided into 0·5 mm divisions. Thus one revolution of the thimble, or screw, moves the anvil 0·50 mm. The circumference of the thimble is graduated into 50 equal divisions, each equal to $\frac{1}{50}$ of a revolution, which represents $\frac{1}{50} \times 0·50 = 0·01$ mm, as shown in fig. 5.2(b).

Fig. 5.2(a). Simple micrometer to read to 0·10 mm

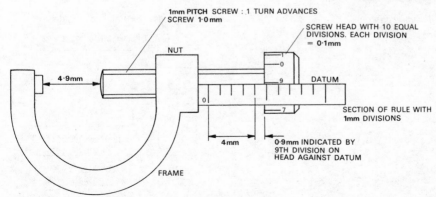

1mm PITCH SCREW : 1 TURN ADVANCES SCREW 1·0 mm

SCREW HEAD WITH 10 EQUAL DIVISIONS. EACH DIVISION = 0·1mm

NUT

4·9mm

DATUM

SECTION OF RULE WITH 1mm DIVISIONS

4mm

0·9mm INDICATED BY 9TH DIVISION ON HEAD AGAINST DATUM

FRAME

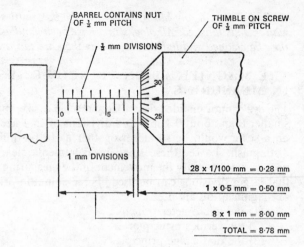

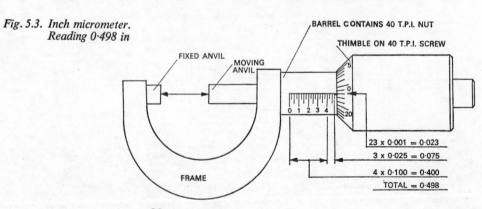

Fig. 5.2(b). Scales of metric micrometer.
Reading 8·78 mm

Other micrometers for more accurate work have larger thimbles and barrels so that each 0·01 mm unit on the thimble can be subdivided into 10 equal parts, each representing 0·001 mm.

Note that the micrometer principle is:

(1) to provide linear movement of the anvil through rotary movement of a screw thread:

(2) to divide the pitch of the screw into a convenient number of equal parts of the thimble, each of which represents the basic unit of measurement.

The same principle is applied to lead screws operating slides on machine tools. A screw may have a pitch of 5 mm, with the scale at the handwheel divided into 500 equal parts, each representing 0·01 mm movement of the slide.

THE INCH MICROMETER In the inch system the micrometer is designed to read to $\frac{1}{1000}$ in. The screw has a pitch of 0·025 in, and the thimble is graduated into 25 equal divisions each representing $\frac{1}{1000}$ in. Fig. 5.3 shows a reading of 0·498 in on the inch micrometer scale.

Fig. 5.3. Inch micrometer.
Reading 0·498 in

THE VERNIER PRINCIPLE The magnification on the vernier scale is given by two scales sliding over each other, the divisions on one being smaller than those on the other. The eye can detect which of these divisions are in line with each other, and it is this fact which enables us to read a vernier to 0·02 mm.

The basic principle is that *the smallest unit of size to which the vernier can be read is equal to the difference in length between the divisions on each scale.*

Thus, if we require a vernier to read to 0·02 mm, the divisions on the vernier scale must be 0·02 mm smaller than the divisions on the main scale. If the main scale divisions are 0·50 mm (a convenient size corresponding to the divisions on a micrometer barrel), each division on the vernier scale= 0·50 mm−0·02 mm=0·48 mm. Since we wish to measure the 0·50 mm division of the main scale in 0·02 mm units there must be 25 divisions on the vernier scale

∴ Length of vernier scale=25×0·48 mm=12 mm.

If we now consider the vernier to be reading zero, i.e., both zero marks are in line, and we move the vernier scale 0·02 mm, the first division on the vernier scale will be in line with the next division on the main scale. If we move the vernier 0·18 mm, the ninth division on the vernier scale will be in line with the next division on the main scale and so on.

Thus, to read the vernier setting shown in fig. 5.4(a):

(1) Read mm units on main scale   =43·00 mm
(2) Read ½ mm units on main scale

                                        = 0·50 mm

(3) Read the particular mark on the vernier scale which is exactly opposite a division on the main scale   = 0·18 mm

                            Total   =43·68 mm

The vernier scales used to illustrate this section are non-standard. They are meant to explain the vernier principle and show how it may be applied in different ways. For standard vernier scales see B.S. 887.

Fig. 5.4(a) Standard metric vernier scale. Reading 43·68 mm

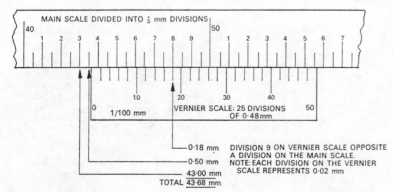

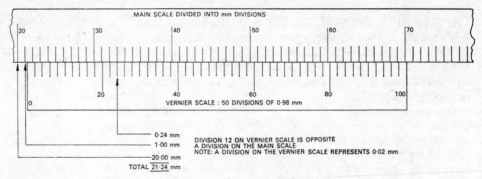

VERNIER SCALE : 50 DIVISIONS OF 0·98 mm

0·24 mm
1·00 mm
20·00 mm
TOTAL 21·24 mm

DIVISION 12 ON VERNIER SCALE IS OPPOSITE
A DIVISION ON THE MAIN SCALE
NOTE: A DIVISION ON THE VERNIER SCALE REPRESENTS 0·02 mm

*Fig. 5.4(b). Extended metric vernier
(1 mm divisions). Reading 21·24 mm*

Another scale, with more widely spaced divisions, also reads to 0·02 mm but the main scale divisions are 1 mm long.

∴ Division of vernier scale=1 mm−0·02 mm=0·98 mm

∴ Length of vernier scale =0·98 mm×50 =49 mm

Fig. 5.4(b) shows this scale reading 21·24 mm.

These represent two of the vernier scales available, others being shown in B.S. 887 and B.S. 1643. Similarly different scales are available in inch units, as shown below.

THE INCH VERNIER   The inch vernier normally reads to 0·001 in and the main scale divisions are 0·001 in

∴ Division of vernier scale=0·025 in−0·001 in=0·024 in

To sub-divide 0·025 in into 0·001 in units there must be 25 equal divisions on the vernier scale

∴ Length of vernier scale=0·024 in×25=0·600 in

Fig. 5.5(a) shows this scale reading 3·195 in.

*Fig. 5.5(a) Standard inch vernier scale.
Reading 3·195 in*

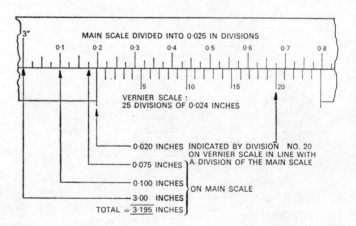

3″
MAIN SCALE DIVIDED INTO 0·025 IN DIVISIONS
0·1   0·2   0·3   0·4   0·5   0·6   0·7   0·8

5   10   15   20
VERNIER SCALE :
25 DIVISIONS OF 0·024 INCHES

0·020 INCHES INDICATED BY DIVISION NO. 20
ON VERNIER SCALE IN LINE WITH
A DIVISION OF THE MAIN SCALE
0·075 INCHES

0·100 INCHES   ON MAIN SCALE
3·00 INCHES
TOTAL = 3·195 INCHES

To separate the divisions more widely another *extended vernier scale*, with 0·050 divisions on the main scale, can be used.

Then:

Division of vernier scale $=0·050-0·001=0·049$ in
$\therefore$ Length of vernier scale $=0·049$ in $\times 50 =2·45$,,
This scale is shown reading 4·836 in in fig. 5.5(b).

Fig. 5.5(b) Extended inch vernier scale (0·050 in divisions). Reading 4·836 in

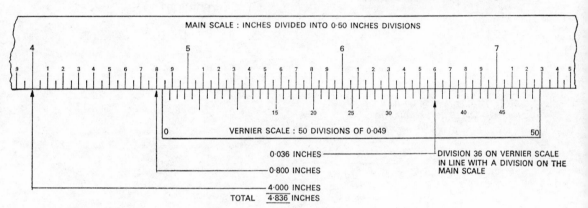

THE VERNIER PROTRACTOR   The vernier principle can equally well be applied to a protractor scale by having a vernier scale of suitable radius sliding over the protractor scale, as shown in figs. 5.6(a) and 5.6(b). Most vernier protractors read to units of five minutes of a degree. If the main scale is divided into degrees and the vernier scale is made relative to 2°, then:

Division of vernier scale $=120'-5' =115'$
Length of vernier scale $=115' \times \frac{60}{5} =1380'=23°$
The vernier scale shown in fig. 5.6(a) reads 39° 20.
A scale reading to $\frac{1}{20}°$ or 3' can also be obtained.
Division of main scale $=1°=60'$
$\therefore$ Division of vernier scale $=60'-3'=57'$
Arc length of vernier scale $=57' \times \frac{60}{3}=1140'=19°$

This type of scale is often used on rotary tables etc. of much larger radius than that of a vernier protractor, and where the degree units are more widely spaced. That shown in fig. 5.6(b) reads 20° 27′

Fig. 5.6(a). Vernier protractor scale reading to 5 minutes of arc, as used on the vernier bevel protractor

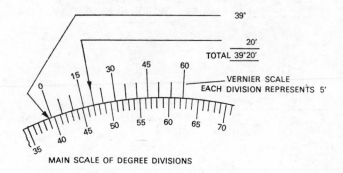

Fig. 5.6(b). Vernier protractor as used on large-radius scales, reading to 3 minutes of arc

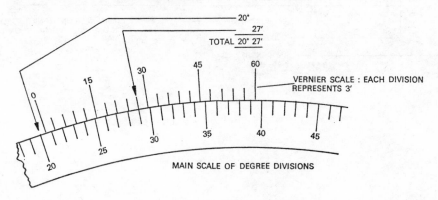

THE VERNIER MICROMETER. The vernier principle is applied to the inch micrometer to sub-divide the thimble divisions by 10; the micrometer can be read to 0·0001 in.

Division of the thimble $= 1$ unit

$\therefore$ Division of the vernier scale $= 1$ unit $- \frac{1}{10}$ unit

$$= \frac{9}{10} \text{ unit}$$

$\therefore$ Length of vernier scale $= \frac{9}{10} \times 10 = 9$ units of the thimble.

These 10 divisions of the vernier scale are engraved round the barrel of the micrometer over an arc length equal to 9 divisions of the 0·001 in units on the thimble, as indicated in fig. 5.7.

The micrometer shown in fig. 5.7 reads 0·5282 in.

86

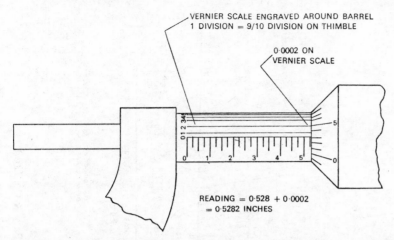

VERNIER SCALE ENGRAVED AROUND BARREL
1 DIVISION = 9/10 DIVISION ON THIMBLE

0·0002 ON
VERNIER SCALE

READING = 0·528 + 0·0002
= 0·5282 INCHES

Fig. 5.7. vernier principle applied to an inch micrometer. The 0·001 in micrometer scale is subdivided by the vernier scale to read to 0·0001 in

Very precise micrometers are made, with large barrels and thimbles on which the 0·002 mm units are shown directly. By applying the vernier principle to these instruments the 0·002 mm units can be sub-divided to read to 0·000 2 mm. These instruments are normally found in gauge testing rooms and metrology laboratories rather than in workshops, but they employ the same basic principles of the hand micrometer and the vernier combined.

THE DIAL TEST INDICATOR   The dial gauge employs yet another method of magnifying small movements so that they can be detected by the human eye. The linear movement of a plunger is changed into rotary movement of a pointer whose tip moves over a circular scale. The circle of the scale is divided into equal parts representing 0·01 mm or 0·001 mm, or inch units, depending upon the sensitivity required.

Internally, the plunger usually has a rack or straight gear which drives a small pinion. This is fixed to a larger gear which drives a second small pinion. This also is fixed to a second larger gear which in turn drives a third small pinion to which the pointer is attached. Thus a compound gear train is used to produce a magnified plunger movement at the pointer tip. A spring exerts a return force on the plunger to keep it in contact with the item being measured, while a hair spring assists the rotary motion and takes out backlash. A typical dial gauge mechanism is shown in fig. 5.8. This also shows a reverse compound train of third and fourth gears which drive a second pointer to show the number of turns of the main pointer.

An important feature of the dial gauge is that the scale can be rotated by a ring bezel, enabling it to be readily set to zero. The gauge can thus be used as a *comparator*, or instrument for comparative measurements, as well as for direct measurements. Many dial gauges read plus in a clockwise

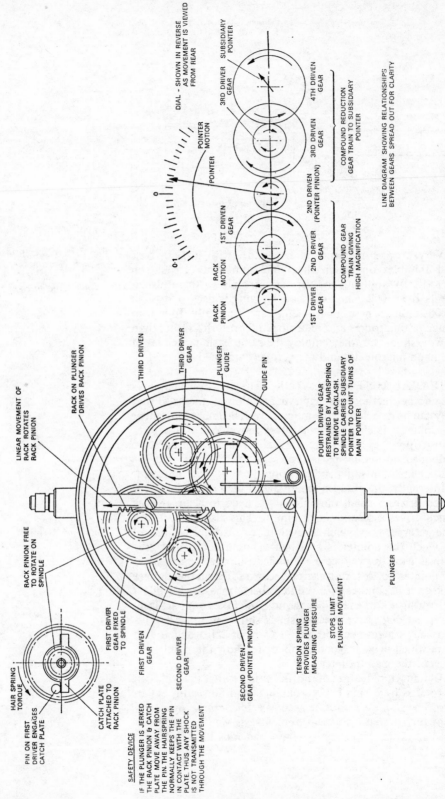

Fig. 5.8. Dial gauge movement (diagram produced with assistance of J. E. Baty & Co. Ltd.)

DIAL - SHOWN IN REVERSE AS MOVEMENT IS VIEWED FROM REAR

3RD DRIVER GEAR

SUBSIDIARY POINTER

4TH DRIVEN GEAR

3RD DRIVEN GEAR

Compound Reduction Gear Train to Subsidiary Pointer

POINTER MOTION

POINTER

2ND DRIVEN GEAR (POINTER PINION)

1ST DRIVEN GEAR

RACK MOTION

RACK PINION

2ND DRIVER GEAR

1ST DRIVER GEAR

Compound Gear Train Giving High Magnification

Line diagram showing relationships between gears spread out for clarity

THIRD DRIVEN

THIRD DRIVER GEAR

PLUNGER GUIDE

GUIDE PIN

LINEAR MOVEMENT OF RACK ROTATES RACK PINION

RACK ON PLUNGER DRIVES RACK PINION

FOURTH DRIVEN GEAR RESTRAINED BY HAIRSPRING TO REMOVE BACKLASH. SPINDLE CARRIES SUBSIDIARY POINTER TO COUNT TURNS OF MAIN POINTER

HAIR SPRING TORQUE

RACK PINION FREE TO ROTATE ON SPINDLE

FIRST DRIVER GEAR FIXED TO SPINDLE

FIRST DRIVEN GEAR

SECOND DRIVER GEAR

PIN ON FIRST DRIVER ENGAGES CATCH PLATE

CATCH PLATE ATTACHED TO RACK PINION

SECOND DRIVEN GEAR (POINTER PINION)

TENSION SPRING PROVIDES PLUNGER MEASURING PRESSURE

STOPS LIMIT PLUNGER MOVEMENT

PLUNGER

SAFETY DEVICE

IF THE PLUNGER IS JERKED THE RACK PINION & CATCH PLATE MOVE AWAY FROM THE PIN. THE HAIRSPRING NORMALLY KEEPS THE PIN IN CONTACT WITH THE PLATE. THUS ANY SHOCK IS NOT TRANSMITTED THROUGH THE MOVEMENT

direction from zero and minus in a counter-clockwise direction, thus giving plus and minus indications and measurements.

THE RULE The engineer's rule is made of steel, hardened and tempered, with scale divisions engraved upon it. A metric scale and two types of inch scale are provided, one divided into tenths of an inch with sub-divisions down to $\frac{1}{100}$ in, and the other divided into sub-divisions of $\frac{1}{2}$ in, $\frac{1}{4}$ in, $\frac{1}{8}$ in, $\frac{1}{16}$ in and, for parts of its length, $\frac{1}{32}$ in and $\frac{1}{64}$ in. The smallest division the eye can usefully distinguish is about 0·25 mm and even this is difficult without the use of a magnifying lens. The markings themselves are about 0·1 mm wide, so further sub-division than 0·5 mm serves no useful purpose. In measuring a width by a rule, the greatest accuracy is obtained by working between divisions and not from the end. The end is only used when measuring to a shoulder or when the rule is used as a scale to which a surface gauge or scribing block is set.

THE ACCURACY OF MEASUREMENT

How accurately can these measuring instruments be used? First we must decide what we mean by accuracy. Some measuring instruments can be *read* to a greater accuracy than others by estimating fractions of the divisions provided. A micrometer has divisions representing 0·01 mm units but these can be sub-divided by estimation to about 0·002 mm. A vernier, on the other hand, cannot practicably be read to a measurement finer than that provided by the divisions. Thus a 0·01 mm vernier can only be read to 0·01 mm. This is called *reading* accuracy.

If an instrument is to be *set* to a given dimension, how accurately can this be done? A micrometer scale can probably be set to 0·002 mm, but this does not take into account any errors in the zero setting or pitch errors in the screw. Thus the setting accuracy is about ±0·002 mm over the whole length, and rather less for a vernier.

Finally we have the *measuring* accuracy. This involves both reading and setting accuracies, and the human elements of feel, touch and experience. Some instruments are more cumbersome to use than others and with them delicacy of touch has less effect. Bearing all these factors in mind, the accuracies with which measurements may be carried out *consistently* are as follows, based on a length of 25 mm:

Steel rule used directly	±0·25 mm
Steel rule used to set a scribing block	±0·125 mm
Vernier calipers, external	±0·03 mm
Vernier calipers, internal	±0·05 mm

89

0—25 mm micrometer used directly	±0·007 mm
0—25 mm micrometer preset to gauge blocks	±0·005 mm
Dial gauge over its complete range	±0·003 mm to 0·02 mm
Dial gauge as comparator over a small range	±0·0001 mm to 0·003 mm

THE SURFACE PLATE AND STRAIGHT EDGE If a large workpiece with widely-separated dimensional features is to be checked, all such dimensions must generally be referred to a flat surface. A typical example of the effects of using as a reference plane a non-flat surface is shown in fig. 5.9, producing error in the marked-out positions of the hole centres.

Fig. 5.9. Effect of marking-out from non-flat surface. Note that the errors in the hole positions are equal to the flatness errors

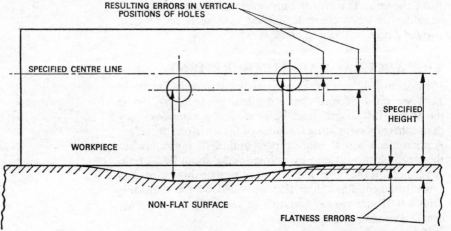

The reference planes used in engineering are the *surface table* and the *surface plate*, the former being free-standing and the latter mounted on a bench. These plates are usually of good-quality grey cast iron which has been stress-relieved to ensure that they do not distort over a period of time. The better grades are scraped and the cheaper ones are merely planed, the accuracy of a planed table depending upon the accuracy of the machine producing it. B.S.817* sets out standards of accuracy for surface plates; a grade 'A' plate of diagonal length 1 metre has to be flat within ±0·008 mm over its whole surface, and to within ±0·004 mm over any 300 mm.

Generally, grade 'C' planed plates are suitable for workshop use, grade 'B' scraped plates are used for inspection work and grade 'A' plates for high-precision and standards-room work.

* B.S. 817 has not been metricated at the time of writing. These figures are conversions from the inch standard.

90

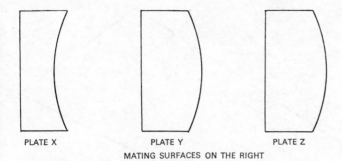

PLATE X   PLATE Y   PLATE Z
MATING SURFACES ON THE RIGHT

Fig. 5.10. The Whitworth principle: plate X will mate with plates Y and Z, but Y and Z will not mate. All three mate only when all three are flat

THE WHITWORTH PRINCIPLE How does one obtain a flat surface? It is easy to say it is scraped but how does one know where to take off the high points? Sir Joseph Whitworth pointed out that if three plates are compared with each other in alternate pairs, they will all only mate perfectly in all positions when they are absolutely flat. Thus, if we have three plates X, Y and Z and scrape X to Z and X to Y, X will mate with both Y and Z. However, if X is concave, Y and Z will both be convex, as shown in fig. 5.10, and will not mate together. When all three mate in all positions, all three are quite flat.

Fig. 5.11. Cast iron bow-shaped or 'camel-back' straight edge

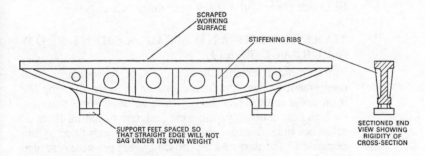

SCRAPED
WORKING
SURFACE

STIFFENING RIBS

SUPPORT FEET SPACED SO
THAT STRAIGHT EDGE WILL NOT
SAG UNDER ITS OWN WEIGHT

SECTIONED END
VIEW SHOWING
RIGIDITY OF
CROSS-SECTION

Once a flat surface has been obtained it can be used as a datum against which other surfaces are checked.

The same principles apply to straight edges, which are sometimes made of thin-section hardened tool steel and given a knife edge, in the small sizes used by toolmakers. The knife edge gives a reduced bearing area which allows very small clearances to be observed, particularly if viewed against a light box. Larger straight edges are made of cast iron to the shape shown in fig. 5.11. These can be used for checking flat surfaces by lightly smearing the face with engineer's blue and registering it on the surface under test, or vice versa.

When a surface is checked by a straight edge it must be tested in directions not only parallel to its edges but also

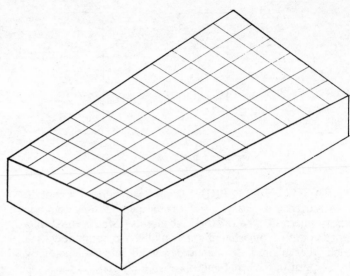

Fig. 5.12. This surface appears flat if checked parallel to the sides. Checking the diagonals reveals the error in flatness

across its diagonals. Fig. 5.12 shows a surface which appears flat along all the lines shown but is not flat across the diagonals. This is because such a surface consists of an infinite number of straight lines and all that a straight edge tests is straightness. For the surface to be flat, all these lines must lie in one plane and a check over diagonals tests this.

MARKING-OUT AND MEASUREMENT FROM A SURFACE PLATE

Marking-out is essentially a process of reproducing on a component or part the dimensions given in the drawing for it, in order to establish the positions of the various features, such as hole centres, surfaces etc., relative to datum faces or reference lines. The datum faces will have been fixed by the designer of the part and he should, where possible, arrange that the largest faces are chosen. This ensures that the part will stand firmly on the surface plate and give a rigid base from which to work.

A hole is usually positioned from two datum faces at right angles to each other and even if the relationship of the holes is an angular one it is normal to set out their positions by means of rectangular co-ordinates, as shown in figs. 5.13(a) and 5.13(b).

The instrument selected for marking-out will depend upon the accuracy required, but the principles are the same in all cases. For an accuracy of, say, 0·1 mm, a rule and scribing block may be used; for one of ±0·02 mm, a good vernier height gauge is required; for less than this, gauge blocks and accessories are needed. In all cases a scriber or knife is required to produce the line and must be sharp.

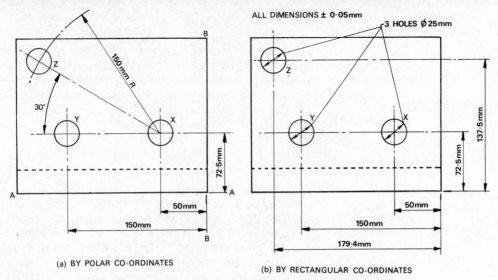

ALL DIMENSIONS ± 0·05mm

(a) BY POLAR CO-ORDINATES

(b) BY RECTANGULAR CO-ORDINATES

Fig. 5.13. Two methods of dimensioning hole centres

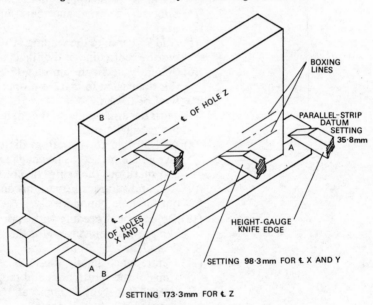

Fig. 5.14(a). Marking out of angle plate completed

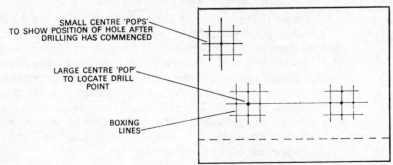

Fig. 5.14(b). Marking out hole-centres from face AA

Consider marking-out the holes in the angle plate shown in fig. 5.13. The dimensions given in (a) have already been converted into rectangular co-ordinates in (b) and we therefore work from faces AA and BB, these being the datum faces. The accuracy demanded calls for the use of a height gauge but the knife edge cannot then be dropped down to the surface plate, so the angle plate is mounted on parallel strips. The procedure is then as follows, illustrated by figs. 5.14(a) and 5.14(b).

(1) Register the height gauge on top of the parallel strips and note the reading, say 35·8 mm. This represents our datum reading and all others are related to it.

(2) Add 62·5 mm to the datum giving a reading of 98·3 mm and mark-out the horizontal centre line of the two holes X and Y.

(3) Add 12·5 mm to this dimension and mark-out 'boxing lines' at the approximate positions of the holes.

(4) Subtract 25·0 mm and mark-out the lower boxing lines.

(5) Add 75·0 mm to the reading of 108·3 mm and mark-out the centre line of the single hole Z.

(6) Similarly add and subtract 12·5 mm to and from this dimension to mark-out upper and lower boxing lines of the hole.

(7) Turn the angle plate so that datum face BB rests on the parallel strips.

(8) Add 50 mm to the datum dimension 35·8 mm to give 85·8 mm. Set the height gauge to this dimension and mark-out the centre line of hole X.

(9) Add and subtract 12·5 to this dimension and mark-out the hole boundaries.

(10) Repeat the procedure with appropriate additions to the previous dimension for the two remaining holes Y and Z.

(11) Centrepunch lightly the hole centres, the intersections of the centre lines and the 'boxed' holes, then deepen the centre 'pops' at the hole centres for location of the drill point.

The complete marked-out face is shown in fig. 5.14(b).

Note the procedure of boxing the holes. If, when drilling is started, the initial 'cone' wanders off-centre, the error can be observed and corrected (see Chapter 7). Sometimes the apprentice is told to centre punch the hole centre and use dividers to mark-out concentric circles to indicate the accuracy of drilling, but this can lead to error. If the centre 'pop' is not accurately positioned the scribed circles will also be off-centre and will tend to cause inaccurate work rather than assist its correction. The 'boxing' of a hole is independent of the centre mark.

Incidentally, a sharp centre punch can be 'felt' into the scribed lines and positioned accurately. The small centre 'pops' on the hole boundary lines are useful since they will not be scratched out by the swarf during drilling and will serve as witnesses to the accuracy of the drilling.

The calculations for marking-out work such as this should always be set out clearly on a clean sheet of paper, not old scrap paper, and kept until the job is checked. Neat orderly calculations make for accurate work and less likelihood of error. For these reasons, the calculations are set out below.

Parallel strips: 25 mm   *Datum on height gauge: 35·8 mm*
Datum face A A
Holes X and Y

Datum	35·8	boxing 108·3		108·3
height	62·5+	12·5+		12·5−
	108·3 mark C L	120·8 mark		95·8 mark

Hole Z

Datum	35·8	boxing 173·3		173·3
height	137·5+	12·5+		12·5−
	173·3 mark C L	185·8 mark		160·8 mark

Datum face B B
Hole X

Datum	35·8	boxing 85·8		85·8
height	50+	12·5+		12·5−
	85·8 mark C L	98·3 mark		73·3 mark

Hole Y

Datum	35·8	boxing 185·8		185·8
height	150+	12·5+		12·5−
	185·8 mark C L	198·3 mark		173·3 mark

Hole Z

Datum	35·8	boxing 215·2		215·2
height	179·4+	12·5+		12·5−
	215·2 mark C L	227·7 mark		202·7 mark

A similar method can be used for checking hole positions, by inserting fitting plugs in the holes and registering their top heights with a height gauge. A greater degree of accuracy

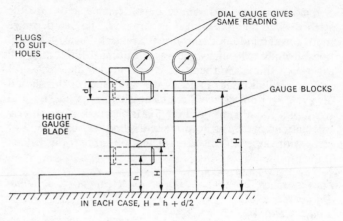

Fig. 5.15. Two methods of checking hole positions relative to base

DIAL GAUGE GIVES SAME READING

PLUGS TO SUIT HOLES

GAUGE BLOCKS

HEIGHT GAUGE BLADE

IN EACH CASE, H = h + d/2

Fig. 5.16(a). Checking axis of hole for parallelism with base

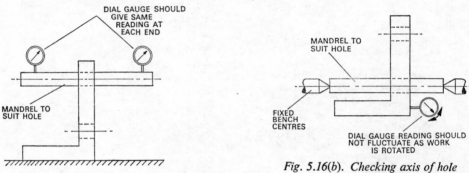

DIAL GAUGE SHOULD GIVE SAME READING AT EACH END

MANDREL TO SUIT HOLE

MANDREL TO SUIT HOLE

FIXED BENCH CENTRES

DIAL GAUGE READING SHOULD NOT FLUCTUATE AS WORK IS ROTATED

Fig. 5.16(b). Checking axis of hole for squareness with face

can be achieved if the heights to the tops of the plugs are calculated and gauge blocks made up to these heights, comparisons then being made directly by a dial gauge, as shown in fig. 5.15.

A check that the holes are parallel to the base can be achieved by replacing the plug with a longer, close-fitting, parallel mandrel and checking over the mandrel at each end, as shown in fig. 5.16(a). If the readings are the same, parallelism has been achieved but note that this does not check that the hole is square to the face of the plate. If the faces of the angle plate are square to each other and the drilling and its set-up have been correct, squareness should have been achieved, but a better check is to mount the mandrel between fixed centres and rotate the work with a dial gauge held against the face, as shown in fig. 5.16(b). Any movement shown on the dial gauge will indicate that the hole is not square to the face.

ANGULAR SETTING

A protractor fitted with a vernier scale as already described is most useful for marking off angles and checking angled faces. It is, however, a little cumbersome, can only be read

96

to 5 min of arc, and when it is used for measuring, as distinct from setting, the problem of 'feel' arises. The same applies to an even greater extent to the protractor of a combination set and if accurate checking or setting of angles is required a sine bar should be used.

The sine bar is a hardened and ground steel bar of rectangular section with a hardened steel precision roller at each end, the distance between the centres of the rollers being accurately set. If the sine bar is placed on a surface plate with gauge blocks of height h mm under one roller, as shown in fig. 5.17(a), the height h is opposite to angle θ and the centre distance l is the hypotenuse of triangle ABC. Therefore:

$$\sin \theta = \frac{h}{l}$$

or $\quad h \, \text{mm} = l \sin \theta$

Thus, to set up angle θ, multiply $\sin \theta$ by l and use a gauge block combination of this height to raise one end of the sine bar.

Metric sine bars are available with lengths of 100 mm, 200 mm and 250 mm. In this case $h = l \sin \theta$ where $l = $ sine bar length.

An error in height h obviously produces an error in angle θ. What is not so obvious is the fact that, as angle θ increases, the same error in h produces a *greater* error in θ. The sine bar should therefore not be used for angles greater than 45° if this can be avoided. The work can often be turned through 90° and the complement of the angle used.

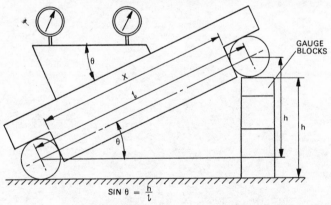

GAUGE BLOCKS

SIN $\theta = \dfrac{h}{l}$

Fig. 5.17(a). Simple sine bar for checking angles

With the aid of a sine bar, an angle can be accurately marked-out by a height gauge or checked by a dial gauge and stand, as indicated in fig. 5.17(a). The accuracy of this simple sine bar depends upon the distance X, since the rollers are pulled into the cutaways by socket-head screws. If this distance is inadvertently ground *undersize*, the sine bar can only be corrected by packing the cutaway at one

97

Fig. 5.17(b). Improved sine bar

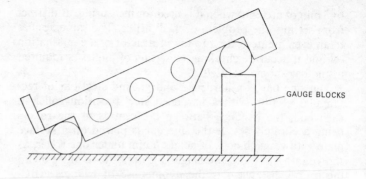

GAUGE BLOCKS

end with shim, which is not good practice. An improved type of sine bar is shown in fig. 5.17(b). In this, if the length is oversize it can be corrected by grinding off one cutaway face, and if undersize by grinding off the other.

SAFETY NOTE *A sine bar and slip gauge set-up tends to be unstable and can easily be knocked over. Always support it against an angle plate and lightly clamp it where necessary. This also helps when the work is aligned with the sine bar to avoid compound-angle errors.*

THE SINE TABLE The sine table is a more robust piece of equipment and is used for heavier work and in machining. It employs the sine-bar principle, as shown in fig. 5.18, and can be mounted on a grinding or other machine for angles to be ground or machined to a high degree of accuracy.

Fig. 5.18. Sine table used in grinding work to a precise angle

$$\text{Sin } \theta = \frac{h}{100}$$

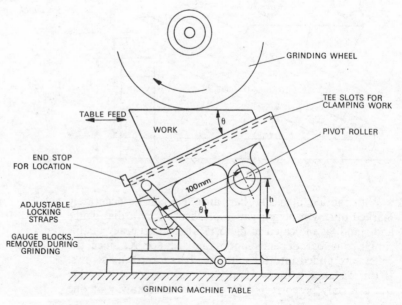

GRINDING WHEEL

TEE SLOTS FOR CLAMPING WORK

TABLE FEED

WORK

θ

PIVOT ROLLER

END STOP FOR LOCATION

100mm

ADJUSTABLE LOCKING STRAPS

θ

h

GAUGE BLOCKS, REMOVED DURING GRINDING

GRINDING MACHINE TABLE

For a high degree of accuracy, five-figure tables should be used. As an example, consider setting up the angle 23·5°, with a 100 mm sine bar using four-figure tables.

$$h = 100 \sin \theta$$
$$= 100 \text{ mm} \times 0\cdot3987$$
$$= 39\cdot87 \text{ mm}$$

The fourth figure in four-figure tables is not reliable, and when multiplied by 100 becomes the second decimal figure in our slip gauge pile. If we use five-figure tables we get

$$h = 100 \times 0\cdot39875$$
$$= 39\cdot875 \text{ mm}$$

This error of 0·005 mm in h can be avoided by using appropriate gauge blocks as follows:

	39·875	*Blocks used*
2 protective slips	2·000 subtract	$2 \times 1\cdot000$ protectives
	———	
	37·875	
	1·005 subtract	1·005
	———	
	36·87	
	1·47 subtract	1·47
	———	
	35·4	
	1·40 subtract	1·40
	———	
	34·00	
	4·00 subtract	4·00
	———	
	30·00	30·00
	———	———
	Total =	39·875 Check
		———

INTERCHANGEABLE MANUFACTURE

The ability to measure to a high degree of accuracy is the most important factor in modern production techniques. It is this ability that allows us to make large numbers of parts independently of each other and know that any pair of parts, selected at random, will fit together properly and function as an assembly. If this were not so, each pair of mating parts would have to be 'made to suit' until the desired fit was obtained

It must be noted, however, that we cannot achieve absolute accuracy. Nothing can be made to an exact size, and if by chance a size was exact we could not measure it accurately enough to prove this. The highest grade of gauge blocks is only accurate to within $\pm0\cdot00005$ mm of their stated size, up to 25 mm in length. As their size increases the permitted error also increases.

If we consider a shaft which is to be a running fit in a bush which itself is to be pressed into a housing as shown in fig. 5.19, ideally we should like to dimension it as shown, so that:

(1) the bush has precisely 0·05 mm interference with the housing

(2) the shaft has precisely 0·025 mm clearance in the hole.

Fig. 5.19. Housing, bush and shaft with 'ideal' dimensions which cannot be made exactly as dimensioned

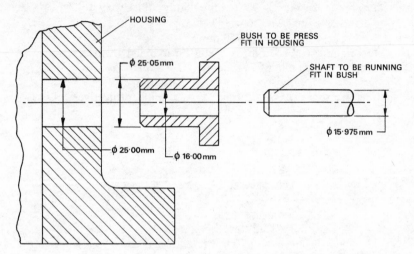

HOUSING

BUSH TO BE PRESS FIT IN HOUSING

SHAFT TO BE RUNNING FIT IN BUSH

φ 25·05 mm

φ 25·00mm

φ 16·00 mm

φ 15·975 mm

These ideal conditions are unobtainable since we cannot work to exact sizes, but we can say that if there is less than 0·05 mm interference the bush may slip, and if there is less than 0·025 mm clearance the shaft may seize in the bush. These then are minimum values which provide a starting point. If we now consider each part in turn and decide the amount of size variation we can *tolerate* for each component, we can arrive at *maximum and minimum limits of size* for each part by applying the tolerance in the required direction.

(1) *Housing.* Using a normal boring process we can achieve, let us say, an accuracy of 0·025 mm. Thus, if the minimum diameter of the hole is 25·00 mm, the maximum diameter will be 25·025 mm.

(2) *Outside Diameter of Bush.* We should be able to turn this to a tolerance of 0·025 mm. To give a minimum interference of 0·050 mm with the hole, the minimum outside diameter must be 25·075 mm. Therefore the maximum outside diameter will be 25·100 mm.

(3) *Inside Diameter of Bush.* If this is reamed we may well achieve an accuracy of 0·025 mm. If the minimum diameter is 16·00 mm, the maximum diameter will be 16·025 mm.

100

(4) *Shaft Diameter*. If we grind the shaft we should be able to hold a tolerance of 0·012 mm but the minimum clearance is to be 0·025 mm, so the maximum diameter of the shaft will be 15·975 mm and the minimum will be 15·963 mm. Summarising this data we get:

Dimension	PART			
	Housing	Bush O.D.	Shaft O.D.	Bush I.D.
Maximum Dia.	25·025 mm	25·100 mm	15·975 mm	16·025 mm
Minimum Dia.	25·00 mm	25·075 mm	15·963 mm	16·000 mm
Tolerance	0·025 mm	0·025 mm	0·012 mm	0·025 mm
Limiting conditions	Max. interference 0·100 mm Min. interference 0·050 mm		Max. clearance 0·052 mm Min. clearance 0·025 mm	

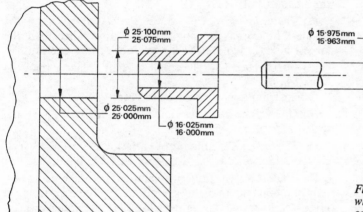

Fig. 5.20. Housing, bush and shaft with limits on dimensions. These parts can now be made

These limited dimensions are shown in fig. 5.20. Note that by comparing the maximum and minimum conditions, as shown in the above table, we hold our original minimum values but, due to the tolerances, maximum values which far exceed these are to be allowed. This condition cannot be avoided and the designer must produce a compromise in which the worst conditions still allow correct functioning of the assembly.

The above example illustrates two types of fit, clearance and interference. There is a third, the transition fit, which can be clearance or interference in cases where a 'large' hole mates with a 'small' shaft or a 'small' hole mates with a 'large' shaft. This fit is used for locations, dowels etc. so that parts can be easily assembled without undue pressure, and is sometimes known as a 'push' fit. The three types of fit can be clearly defined as follows, fig. 5.21 illustrating them diagrammatically.

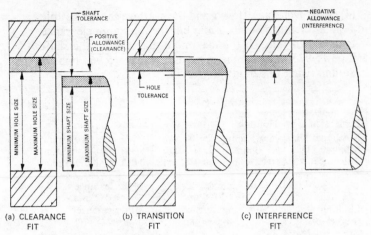

Labels in figure:
SHAFT TOLERANCE
POSITIVE ALLOWANCE (CLEARANCE)
NEGATIVE ALLOWANCE (INTERFERENCE)
HOLE TOLERANCE
MINIMUM HOLE SIZE
MAXIMUM HOLE SIZE
MINIMUM SHAFT SIZE
MAXIMUM SHAFT SIZE

(a) CLEARANCE FIT   (b) TRANSITION FIT   (c) INTERFERENCE FIT

Fig. 5.21. Three basic types of fit, hole-base system. Note that the hole limits are the same in each case

(1) *Clearance Fit:* The largest shaft must be smaller than the smallest hole.

(2) *Transition Fit:* The largest shaft is larger than the smallest hole and the smallest shaft is smaller than the largest hole (in fig. 5.21(b) the tolerance zones overlap).

(3) *Interference Fit:* The smallest shaft is larger than the largest hole.

Other definitions which are used are:

(4) *Limits:* The maximum and minimum sizes of the part, which must not be exceeded.

(5) *Tolerance:* The amount of variation in part size which can be tolerated, i.e., the difference between the limits.

(6) *Allowance:* The prescribed amount between the mating pair in the maximum metal condition. A positive allowance gives clearance and a negative allowance gives interference.

SYSTEMS OF LIMITS AND FITS

If a designer had to perform the computation shown on page 100 for every fit he required, he would hardly get any work done. Systems of limits and fits have therefore been developed in which the limits and tolerances for mating parts are set out in tabular form. The standard system in Britain is the British Standard 4500, an extract from which is shown in Appendix I. Here we shall attempt to analyse the thinking behind such systems and the student should refer to these tables to see how they support this reasoning.

Two distinct bases can be used in producing a system of limits and fits. These are:

(1) Hole-basis system;   (2) Shaft-basis system.

(1) HOLE-BASIS SYSTEM   For a given size, the limits on the hole are always the same and a series of fits is obtained by applying different limits to the shafts. Thus, for a

102

nominal dimension of 25·00 mm diameter, all holes will be, say, $25·00^{+0·025}_{-0·000}$ mm diameter, and in conjunction with this common hole we obtain fits as follows:

(a) *Interference fit:* Shaft size $25^{+0·075}_{+0·025}$ mm diameter, giving maximum and minimum interference of 0·075 mm and 0·025 mm respectively.

(b) *Transition fit:* Shaft size $25·00^{+0·001}_{-0·000}$ mm, giving maximum clearance *and* maximum interference of 0·025 mm.

(c) *Clearance fit:* Shaft size of $25·00^{-0·025}_{-0·050}$ mm, giving maximum and minimum clearances of 0·075 mm and 0·025 mm respectively.

Fig. 5.22. Shaft-basis system of obtaining different fits. Note that the shaft limits are the same in each case

VARIATION IN HOLE LIMITS

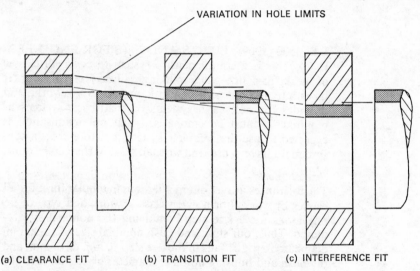

(a) CLEARANCE FIT   (b) TRANSITION FIT   (c) INTERFERENCE FIT

(2) SHAFT-BASIS SYSTEM For a given size, the limits on the shaft are always the same and a series of fits is obtained by varying the size of the holes.

These two systems are shown diagramatically in figs. 5.21 and 5.22. The hole basis is most commonly used since many holes are made with fixed-size tooling, i.e., drills, reamers etc. If a shaft-basis system with 12 different fits was used we might need 12 different reamers at each nominal size, which would be very expensive apart from problems of identification. Shafts, however, are made with adjustable tooling, i.e., lathes, grinding machines etc., and a range of different-sized shafts can readily be produced.

TYPES OF HOLE Even with a hole-basis system, it is found that just one class of hole is not practicable. If one class only was used it would have to be to the finest tolerance required, say for fine grinding and lapping, and be specified for all work. It would be ridiculous if we applied a tolerance of 0·001 mm to a hole that was to be flame-cut! Thus, even with a hole-basis system, a range of holes is required to permit economic methods of manufacture.

Examine the extract from B.S. 4500 in the Appendices and see how many types of hole are used.

SIZE OF WORK As the work size increases it is not possible, nor usually necessary to hold the same tolerances; larger limits are provided on larger work sizes.

Do the tolerances increase with work size in B.S. 4500?

B.S. 4500 (1969): LIMITS AND FITS FOR ENGINEERING This is a comprehensive system to cover all classes of work from fine gauge making to heavy engineering. It takes into account size of work and class of work, and provides for hole-basis systems or shaft-basis systems as required. It must be emphasised that no organisation is expected to use the complete system, but to extract a subsystem for its own use, and we shall see how this can be done.

Size of Work
The tolerances are set out in size steps in tabular form for all classes of work. For a given class of work and type of fit, one looks for a size step containing the nominal size required. Thus, our shaft and bush nominal size of 16·00 mm diameter on p. 101 falls in the size step 10 mm to 18 mm, and the bush and housing nominal diameter of 25 mm is in the size step 18 mm to 30 mm.

Class of Work
Eighteen grades of tolerance are quoted, designated from 00, 0, 1 to 16 by numbers, and suit the types of work shown below.

Grade of Tolerance	Class of Work
00, 0, 1	Gauge blocks.
2	High quality gauges. Plug gauges.
3	Good quality gauges. Gap gauges.
4	Gauges. Precise fits produced by lapping.
5	Ball bearings. Machine lapping. Fine boring and grinding.

6	Grinding. Fine boring.
7	High quality turning. Broaching. Boring.
8	Centre-lathe turning and boring. Reaming. Capstan lathes in good condition.
9	Worn capstan or automatic lathes. Boring machines.
10	Milling, slotting, planing, rolling, extrusion.
11	Drilling, rough turning and boring. Precision tube drawing.
12	Light press work. Tube drawing.
13	Press work. Tube rolling.
14	Die casting or moulding. Rubber moulding.
15	Stamping.
16	Sand casting. Flame cutting.

Type of fit

The position of the tolerance zone relative to the nominal size is indicated by a letter, capital letters being used for holes and small letters for shafts. Twenty-eight holes and 28 shafts are specified, their positions relative to the nominal size being shown below.

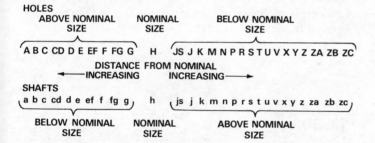

Class **H** is most important since one of its limits is the nominal size and the other above it. It follows that, when used in conjunction with a class **H** hole, shafts of class **a** to **g** give clearance fits, classes **h**, **j** and **k** give transition fits and classes **m** to **z** give interference fits.

Each of these classifications may be associated with a given grade of tolerance and a hole may be designated **H 7**, **H 11**, **H 14** etc. All these holes have a low limit of $+0\cdot0000$, the high limit increasing as the number increases. Similarly, shafts may be designated **a 10**, **e 8**, **p 9** etc. If associated with a class **H** hole, a shaft **a 10** would give a clearance fit, **e 8** a closer clearance fit, and **p 9** an interference fit. A typical fit is therefore designated **H 7/p 9** or **H 7—p 9**.

Practical Application of B.S. 4500

Let us consider a light machine shop doing grinding, turning, milling and shaping, i.e., general machining, for which a system is to be extracted from B.S. 4500. It is decided to use a *hole-basis system* and this means that all holes will be of class **H**. The grades of tolerance used, according to the class of work, will be, say, **H 7** and **H 8**, which should cover most cases. The work will require press fits using class **p** shafts, a transition fit using class **k** and three clearance fits, **e** for loose clearance, **f** for medium running and **g** for precise location.

Analysing this further, close limits would not be used for class **e**, so all **e** shafts will be of grade **8** and all loose clearance fits will be **H8/e8**.

Medium-running fits will use an **H 9** hole in conjunction with an **f 8** shaft and precise location **H 7/g 6**.

A similar type of analysis is made for transition and interference fits, and a complete system suitable for the class of work can be reproduced in a similar form to that of Appendix I, which is a data sheet extracted from B.S. 4500 to cover general engineering work.

Using B.S. 4500 let us now dimension our housing, bush and shaft assembly from p.101 and calculate tolerances and maximum and minimum clearances, the results being shown below in tabular form. Those for the interference fit would require machining to much tighter tolerances than the previous example on page 101.

Dimension	H7 Housing Bore	p6 Bush O.D.	H8 Bush I.D.	f7 Shaft O.D.
Maximum dia.	25·021	25·035	16·027	15·984
Minimum dia.	25·000	25·022	16·000	15·950
Tolerance	0·021	0·013	0·027	0·034
Limiting conditions	Maximum interference 0·035 Minimum interference 0·001		Max. clearance 0·077 Min. clearance 0·016	

Finally, the terminology of **H 7/p 6** etc. is only intended for use by the designer. For workshop drawings, the draughtsman then usually converts such specifications into dimensions, from the data sheet. A drawing which showed a hole diameter as 30·00 mm **H 11**, sent to the workshop, might

106

result in a swift trip to the drawing office with a demand in no uncertain terms for more information.

LIMIT GAUGES When a part is made it usually has to be checked or inspected. For a single dimension this can be done in two ways:

(1) *By measurement:* The size of the part is determined by means of a measuring instrument, such as a micrometer, dial gauge, gauge blocks etc. This requires a degree of skill and is slow and sometimes laborious.

(2) *By gauging:* A limit gauge is used to ensure that the size of the part does not exceed either of the designed limits of size. Gauging is quick and simple, and requires little skill.

For a hole, the gauge would simply be a plug gauge as shown in fig. 5.23. If the small or 'GO' end enters, the hole is above the low limit, and if the large or 'NOT GO' end will not enter, the hole is below the top limit and therefore acceptable.

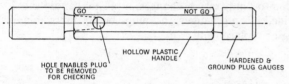

HOLE ENABLES PLUG TO BE REMOVED FOR CHECKING

HOLLOW PLASTIC HANDLE

HARDENED & GROUND PLUG GAUGES

(a) DOUBLE-ENDED PLAIN PLUG GAUGE

Fig. 5.23. Two types of plain plug limit gauge

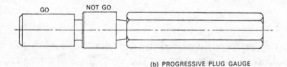

(b) PROGRESSIVE PLUG GAUGE

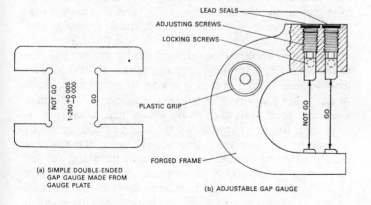

Fig. 5.24. Gap gauges

LEAD SEALS
ADJUSTING SCREWS
LOCKING SCREWS

PLASTIC GRIP

FORGED FRAME

NOT GO   1·250 +0·005 −0·000   GO

NOT GO   GO

(a) SIMPLE DOUBLE-ENDED GAP GAUGE MADE FROM GAUGE PLATE

(b) ADJUSTABLE GAP GAUGE

107

Similarly, gap gauges can be used to check outside diameters and sizes. They may be either fixed gauges, made from gauge plate, or adjustable gauges, as shown in fig. 5.24. The adjustable type can be reset, by gauge blocks or other methods, to correct any error or to meet a change in size. Note that a plug gauge has a fixed size but an adjustable gap gauge can readily be changed; this is another reason for using a hole-basis system of limits and fits.

Tolerances are also needed on gauges and are given in B.S.969, Plain Limit Gauges: Limits and Tolerances, but if this is not available for reference the gauge tolerance should normally be about one-tenth of the work tolerance. The tolerance grades shown on p. 105 progress in sets of five, so that grade 6 has a tolerance ten times that of grade 1, grade 7 a tolerance ten times that of grade 2 and so on. Thus, if a workpiece is made to grade 8, the gauge tolerance will be grade 3. However, B.S. 969 should be referred to for precise information.

The working faces of gauges should be made hard to resist wear, and of good finish. The gauge can be made from a good quality high-carbon steel and hardened, or from case-hardening mild steel carbonised and hardened. To avoid errors due to temperature changes, a plastic handle should be provided in plug gauges, the plugs being removable for checking or replacement.

SUMMARY

In this Chapter we have discussed the rudiments of measurement in relation to the engineer on the shop floor. This can only be a précis of the subject, starting with the standards of measurement, through the working tools of measurement to the tolerances and limits necessary, and to simple gauges which ensure that these limits are held. All the safety notes in this Chapter refer to the safety of the *instruments* and not of the operator. It is difficult for an engineer to hurt himself with a gauge block but it is very easy to damage the block or any other measuring instrument. Engineers should take a pride in their tools and, above all, in their measuring instruments, for it is on these that the accuracy and continued correctness of their work depend. However, the engineer should never be carried away by over-enthusiasm for his measuring equipment. None of it can be used to measure exactly, however good it is. Furthermore, excessive accuracy costs a great deal of money. Where limits are being decided, work to a published system of limits and fits and, if this is not possible, always ask the question—'Can I make the tolerance greater?' If the answer is yes, the part will usually cost less.

6
Metal Cutting

If a piece of hardened tool steel is ground so that its end is square, with all corners and edges sharp, and it is pressed against a piece of soft steel with a force of P N, as shown in fig. 6.1(a), and if a force of F N is then applied parallel to the surface so that the tool is moved against friction, the tool will not cut. The heel of the tool will foul the work and prevent the leading edge from entering it. The only effect will be for the tool to rub on the work.

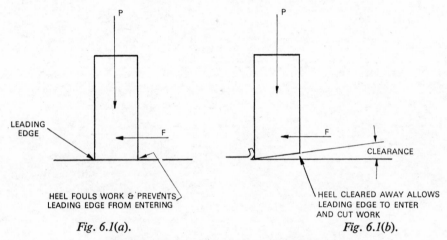

Fig. 6.1(a).   Fig. 6.1(b).

Clearance necessary to allow cutting to take place

For cutting to take place, the heel of the tool must be cleared away, by grinding, to form a *clearance angle* as shown in fig. 6.1(b). The efficiency of cutting can be improved by grinding the face of the tool to give a *rake angle*, and further, by modifying the shape of the tool in plan profile.

All these important features are affected by the conditions of cutting, the work material, the tool material, the coolant used and the condition of the machine, and will now be considered in turn.

CLEARANCE   The clearance angle may be defined as the angle between the flank face of the tool and a tangent to the work surface originating at the cutting edge.

All cutting tools must have clearance to allow cutting to take place, but an excessive clearance angle will not increase the cutting efficiency and will merely weaken the tool. The clearance angle is therefore affected only by the shape of the

110

work, and there are only three basic shapes, as shown in fig. 6.2. These are:

    (a) external cylinders (turning):
    (b) flat surfaces (shaping):
    (c) internal cylinders (boring).

In (a), turning, the surface falls away from the tool flank, tending to create clearance. In (b), a flat surface, the work has no effect on the clearance and in (c), boring, the work curves towards the tool flank and tends to reduce the clearance.

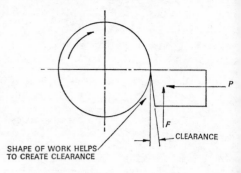

SHAPE OF WORK HELPS TO CREATE CLEARANCE

(a) EXTERNAL CYLINDER

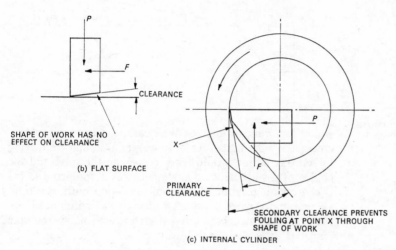

SHAPE OF WORK HAS NO EFFECT ON CLEARANCE

(b) FLAT SURFACE

PRIMARY CLEARANCE

SECONDARY CLEARANCE PREVENTS FOULING AT POINT X THROUGH SHAPE OF WORK

(c) INTERNAL CYLINDER

The clearance angle required generally increases as follows:

    (a) external cylinder: 5° to 7°
    (b) flat surface: 6° to 8°
    (c) internal cylinder: 8° upwards, with secondary clearance depending upon the work diameter.

Note the similarity between the boring tool in (c) and a tooth of a milling cutter. Both work on the inside of a cylindrical surface and have a similar job to do, and both have a secondary clearance angle.

Fig. 6.2. Effect of shape of work on clearance angle

RAKE   Rake is the angle between the top face of the tool and the normal to the work surface at the cutting edge, as shown in fig. 6.3.

As the tool is forced into the work by the combined action of forces P and F, it causes the chip produced to ride up the tool face, a continuous shearing action taking place in the zone ahead of the tool (see fig. 6.3). If we consider the tool to be a wedge, forced into the work by the resultant R of forces P and F, it is clear that reducing the angle of the wedge would make the tool more effective. To do this, since

111

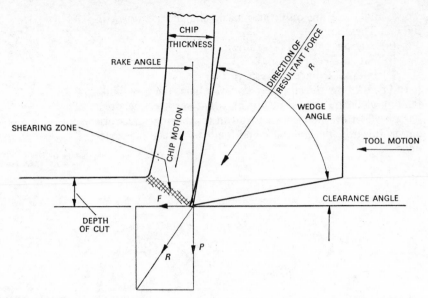

CHIP THICKNESS

RAKE ANGLE

DIRECTION OF RESULTANT FORCE

R

WEDGE ANGLE

SHEARING ZONE

CHIP MOTION

TOOL MOTION

DEPTH OF CUT

F

CLEARANCE ANGLE

R

P

Fig. 6.3. Tool considered as a wedge forced into work by resultant force 'R'

we do not want to increase the clearance angle, we must increase the rake angle. This, however, although improving the cutting action would tend to weaken the tool, and the choice of a suitable rake angle becomes a compromise between adequate strength of tool and good cutting action. Generally, for work materials which give a continuous chip, the greater the work-material strength, the smaller the rake angle, as shown in the following table.

Work Material	Rake Angle*
Aluminium	40°
Copper	30°
Mild steel	27°
Medium-carbon steel	14°
High-carbon and alloy steels	8°

During the cutting process, the metal removed undergoes considerable deformation and, if the material is brittle, fracture of the chip takes place before it is completely formed. Thus, with cast iron, cast brass and other materials giving a discontinuous chip, the cutting process is a series of cycles of chip formation, breakdown, chip formation, breakdown, and so on. This imposes higher loads on the tool and to give adequate strength a zero rake angle is often used.

A third type of chip is called a continous chip with built-up edge. Due to extreme conditions of temperature and pressure, small particles of the work material become welded to the tool face at the cutting edge, forming a built-up edge

* These values are for roughing cuts with high-speed steel tools.

112

on the tool. This becomes very hard and abrasive, due to work-hardening, and is continually breaking down and being reformed. When it breaks down, the pieces of the built-up edge are carried across the tool face, causing rapid wear, and at the same time the surface finish of the work is marred.

The built-up edge can be avoided by reducing the friction between the chip and tool face, by improving the surface finish of the tool face and by using the correct cutting speed and cutting fluid.

CHIP BREAKERS In high-speed cutting it is often inconvenient and dangerous to have continuous chips producing long streamers of swarf. These can be avoided by grinding a step in the tool face just behind the cutting edge. The step causes a greater amount of deformation than the work-hardened chip can take, and the chip thus breaks into small segments. A tool with a chip breaker is shown in fig. 6.4.

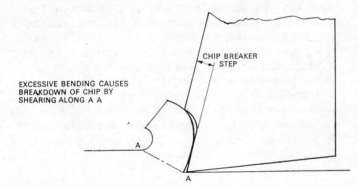

Fig. 6.4. Use of chip breaker

Fig. 6.5. Different lengths of cutting edge for the same depth of cut, due to different plan approach angles

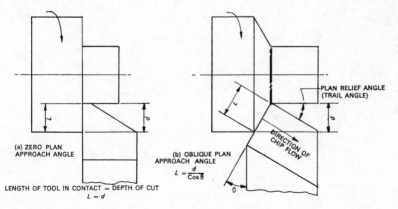

113

PLAN PROFILE OF TOOL The plan shape of the tool is often dictated by the shape of the work, but it also has an effect on the tool life and the cutting process. Fig. 6.5 shows two tools, one used where a sharp corner is desired and the other where the step in the work ends with a chamfer or angle. The diagram shows that, for the same depth of cut, the angled tool has a much greater length of cutting edge in contact with the work and thus the load per unit length of the edge is reduced. The angle at which the edge approaches the work should in theory be as large as possible but, if too great an approach angle is used, chatter may occur. The *plan approach angle* should therefore be as large as possible without causing chatter, which will depend to a large extent on the condition of the machine.

The trailing edge of the tool is ground backwards to give clearance and prevent rubbing, and a good general guide is to grind the trailing edge at 90° to the cutting edge, where the tool has an approach angle. Thus the *trail angle*, or *plan relief angle*, will depend upon the approach angle. If it is made too great the tendency is again to weaken the tool.

A further point is that much of the heat generated in cutting must be conducted away from the tool edge by the tool itself. A slender tool has less body to absorb and conduct the heat, and a smaller plan relief angle, giving more tool metal, allows the heat to disperse more readily.

A small nose radius on the tool improves the cutting and reduces tool wear. If a sharp point is used it gives poor surface finish and wears rapidly, and if the nose radius is too large the chip, tending to flow at right angles to the edge all round the curve, is crowded and does not flow freely. The

Fig. 6.6. Features of a single point cutting tool

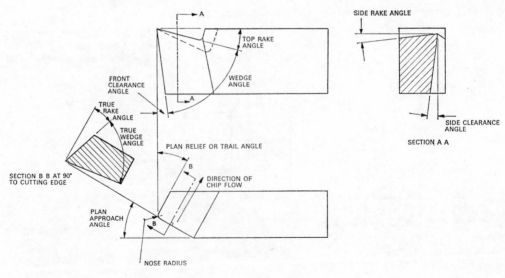

114

chip pressure is also concentrated and tends to produce rapid wear on the tool face. The nose radius should therefore be the smallest that gives adequate surface finish and long tool life.

If a cutting tool is ground with a top, or front-to-back, rake as shown in figs. 6.3 and 6.4, and also with a side rake, the actual or true rake is a combination of the two. The true rake may be defined as the rake angle measured in the direction of chip flow at the cutting edge, and will normally be measured at 90° to the cutting edge. Thus its value may be determined by drawing a section of the tool at 90° to the cutting edge as shown in fig. 6.6. This drawing of a cutting tool shows all the features mentioned, and should be studied and understood so that in any discussion on cutting tools we all speak the same language.

THE STRAIGHT-EDGED CUTTING TOOL

In the previous section we have discussed a tool which has both top rake and side rake. If it is agreed that for a given work material there is a best-rake angle, and those on p. 112 have been found over the years to be best by experience, verified by experiment, it follows that ideally the rake angle should be constant for the full cut.

Fig. 6.7. Difference in rake angle at nose and back of tool, due to top rake

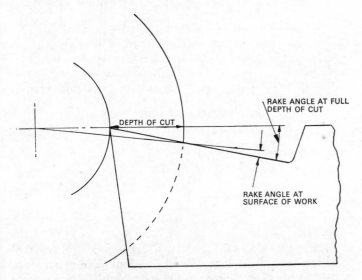

If the tool has top rake the angle is not constant, as is shown in fig. 6.7; the rake angle at the back of the cutting edge is less than at the front. If the idea of top rake with side rake is abandoned, and the true rake is ground with the cutting edge kept horizontal, this error is avoided, and the rake angle is constant over the whole length of the cutting edge. Fig. 6.8 is a drawing of such a tool.

115

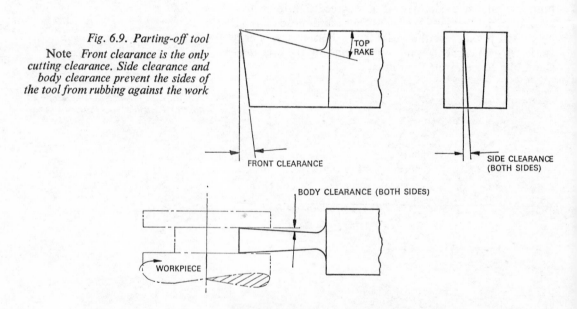

Fig. 6.8. Tool given zero top rake by grinding the rake angle in a direction at right angles to the cutting edge

TRUE RAKE

SECTION A A

CLEARANCE

HORIZONTAL CUTTING EDGE GIVING ZERO TOP RAKE

A

DIRECTION OF CHIP FLOW

A

Fig. 6.9. Parting-off tool

Note *Front clearance is the only cutting clearance. Side clearance and body clearance prevent the sides of the tool from rubbing against the work*

TOP RAKE

FRONT CLEARANCE

SIDE CLEARANCE (BOTH SIDES)

BODY CLEARANCE (BOTH SIDES)

WORKPIECE

THE PARTING-OFF TOOL This is a special form of cutting tool used for parting-off a workpiece from bar stock held in the chuck. To keep the full length of front cutting edge in operation, the tool is given body clearance, i.e., it is made thinner at the back than at the cutting edge in plan, as shown in fig. 6.9, so that the sides do not rub against the groove being cut. Such a tool must be set on or very slightly above centre, but never below centre, or the work will climb on top of the tool just before it is parted off. The tool is naturally rather weak and can easily be broken if this happens.

116

It should be noted that this principle of body clearance applies to any tool which works in a hole or slot and cuts only at the bottom of the hole or slot. Examine a hacksaw blade, woodsaw blade and crosscut chisel to see how body clearance is applied to these tools.

TOOL SETTING   The setting of a cutting tool can have a marked effect on the cutting angles. The correct setting for a lathe tool in the horizontal position is with the cutting point at centre height, and four incorrect conditions can occur. The tool can be too high or too low or, if a tool post with a boat-shaped packing is used, the correct height may have been achieved by inclining the tool up or down. These effects can be seen in fig. 6.10 and are as follows:

Fig. 6.10. Various effects of incorrect tool settings

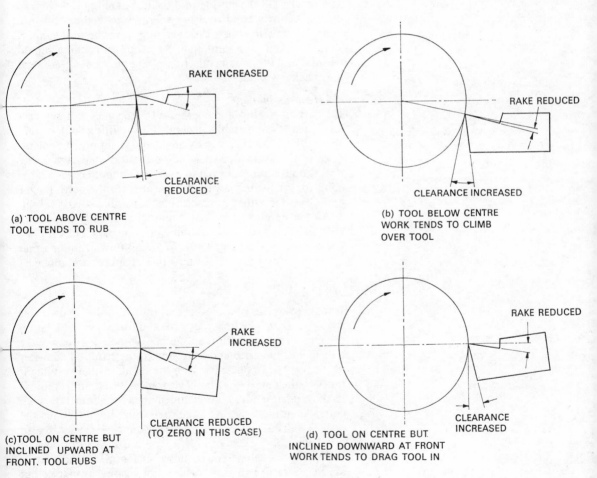

(a) TOOL ABOVE CENTRE
TOOL TENDS TO RUB

(b) TOOL BELOW CENTRE
WORK TENDS TO CLIMB
OVER TOOL

(c) TOOL ON CENTRE BUT
INCLINED UPWARD AT
FRONT. TOOL RUBS

(d) TOOL ON CENTRE BUT
INCLINED DOWNWARD AT FRONT
WORK TENDS TO DRAG TOOL IN

(a) tool high: rake increased and clearance reduced:

(b) tool low: rake reduced and clearance increased:

(c) tool inclined up at front: rake increased and clearance reduced:

(d) tool depressed at front: rake reduced and clearance increased.

Other factors worthy of attention in the care and use of cutting tools are:

(1) *Finish of tool face*
If the rake face over which the chip passes is lightly stoned after grinding, its surface finish will be improved. This will improve the cutting action by reducing the chip-to-face friction and the amount of heat generated.

(2) *Tool rigidity*
The more rigid the cutting tool the less likelihood there is of chatter. Thus a solid tool is preferable to a small bit in a holder and, with either, the overhang from the tool support should be kept to a minimum. Any support packing should be solid and flat, not a collection of old pieces of sheet metal and hacksaw blades!

(3) *Heat dissipation*
If a carbon steel tool is overheated it becomes soft and useless. Heat is inevitably generated by cutting and should generally be carried away by an adequate supply of coolant. Heat is also generated in grinding the tool and, again, the tool should not be allowed to overheat. In both cases a large solid tool will carry away more heat from the cutting edge and absorb it without overheating than will a small tool bit.

All the statements in the Chapter are basically true for all cutting tools. All tools require clearance to cut and the correct rake to cut efficiently. We shall now examine other types of cutting tool to see how these features are applied.

DRILLS

If we take a piece of tool steel bar, rather smaller in diameter than the size of the hole required, and forge a central flat on the end larger in width than the bar diameter, we can make a drill. The flattened end is ground to the required diameter at the front and concentric with the shank, with a very slight taper to the rear to give body clearance. The point is ground to the shape required, an included angle of about 120° with equal lengths of cutting edge and equal angles about the drill axis. These edges must have clearance and we can also grind lips to give a rake angle. Such a drill, which must be hardened and tempered, is shown in fig. 6.11. These drills are very useful if a twist drill is not readily available, but they have a limited number of regrinds and are usually made of plain carbon steel, so the cutting speed must be kept low.

118

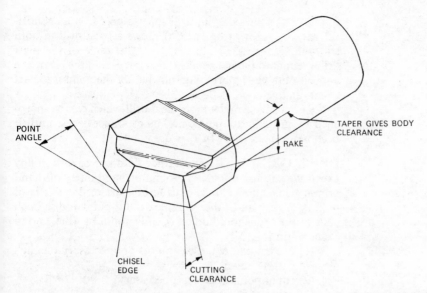

Fig. 6.11. Flat or spade drill

Note *The spade has been shown thicker than normal to enable features to be seen more clearly*

The speed can be increased by using a high-speed steel drill but a higher number of regrinds can only be achieved by using the logical extension of the flat drill, the *twist drill*.

If we now superimpose our flat drill on a cylindrical bar of the same diameter and carry the rake angle around the cylinder, it forms a helix. The flat section is not very rigid but we can leave a central web of the same thickness as the flat drill and build up the thickness towards the outside where, incidentally, the stress due to twisting is greater.

Fig. 6.12. Development of twist drill from flat drill

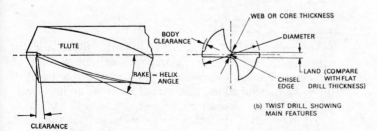

119

Fig. 6.12(a) shows the flat drill superimposed on a cylindrical bar and below it fig. 6.12(b) shows a twist drill in both end and side views. Note that the rake angle of the twist drill is equal to the helix angle of its flutes, and the clearance angle is obtained by grinding each half of the point into part of an oblique cone.

We now have a much more rigid drill which can be sharpened by grinding its point, i.e., its clearance faces, until it becomes too short for further use.

DRILL GRINDING   The author does not believe in any expensive cutting tool being ground by hand on an off-hand grinding machine. This is as true of twist drills as it is of milling cutters and other complex multi-point tools. Each edge of the drill should do an equal amount of work and in order to do this:

   (1) correct and equal clearances are necessary on each
       cutting edge:
   (2) equal point angles are necessary:
   (3) equal edge lengths are necessary.

A skilled man can grind a twist drill correctly *sometimes* but his overall performance will never be as consistent as that obtained from a drill-grinding machine. There will be no discussion here on the hand grinding of drills—only of the effects of faults produced by incorrect grinding and extremely likely to occur in hand grinding.

EFFECTS OF INCORRECT DRILL GRINDING

(1) *Clearance angle too small*
The drill will rub and not cut. Excessive heat will be generated, particularly at the periphery, which will soften and rapidly wear away.

(2) *Clearance angle too great*
This weakens the cutting edge and may cause early failure. The drill also tends to cut an irregularly-shaped, non-circular hole.

(3) *Edges of unequal angle*
In this case, shown in fig. 6.13, one lip does most of the work, the other merely cleaning up at the extreme edge because of the unequal thrust. This produces rapid wear of one edge and an oversize hole.

(4) *Edges of unequal length*
This condition is shown in fig. 6.14.

The point of the drill is not in line with the axis of the drill and unless the work is clamped, it will move about on the machine table, following the movement of the point. If the work is clamped then the lateral stress set up may break the drill. The hole produced will be oversize, with a diameter equal to twice the radius of the longer edge from the point.

120

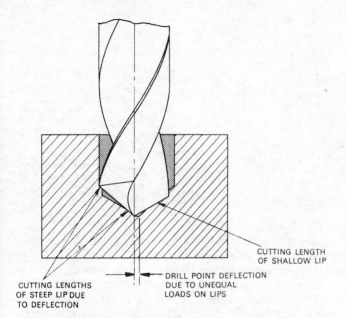

Fig. 6.13. Action of drill ground with edges of equal length but unequal angle
(by courtesy of Brooke Tools Limited)

CUTTING LENGTH
OF SHALLOW LIP

CUTTING LENGTHS
OF STEEP LIP DUE
TO DEFLECTION

DRILL POINT DEFLECTION
DUE TO UNEQUAL
LOADS ON LIPS

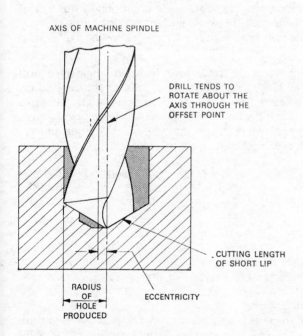

AXIS OF MACHINE SPINDLE

Fig. 6.14. Action of drill ground with cutting edge of unequal length
(by courtesy of Brooke Tools Limited)

DRILL TENDS TO
ROTATE ABOUT THE
AXIS THROUGH THE
OFFSET POINT

CUTTING LENGTH
OF SHORT LIP

RADIUS
OF
HOLE
PRODUCED

ECCENTRICITY

POINT MODIFICATIONS   Under certain circumstances the point of a drill can be modified after it has been machine-ground. The main changes which can be made are to the helix angle, point angle and the thickness of the point.

121

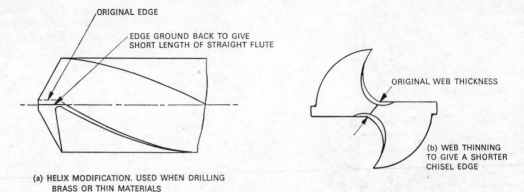

ORIGINAL EDGE

EDGE GROUND BACK TO GIVE
SHORT LENGTH OF STRAIGHT FLUTE

ORIGINAL WEB THICKNESS

(b) WEB THINNING
TO GIVE A SHORTER
CHISEL EDGE

(a) HELIX MODIFICATION. USED WHEN DRILLING
BRASS OR THIN MATERIALS

Fig. 6.15. Drill point modifications

(1) *Helix Angle*

A standard twist drill has a helix angle suitable for most purposes but drills can be obtained with a 'quick' or 'slow' helix to suit particular materials to be cut. However, it may be necessary to grind a short length of straight flute at the point of a standard drill, as shown in fig. 6.15(a), when drilling brass, which normally requires a smaller rake angle, and particularly when drilling thin material, to prevent the drill 'corkscrewing' as soon as the point breaks through. If this happens with the work unclamped, the work rides up the drill and rotates with it, often breaking the drill.

(2) *Point Angle*

For many years the traditional inclusive angle of a drill point was 118°, i.e., 59° on either side of the centre line. Recent research has shown that the point angle should be different for different materials, and the table below shows these angles, together with the type of helix angle and the lip clearance angle to be used.

Material	Helix Angle	Point Angle	Lip Clearance
Aluminium alloy	Quick	140°	12°—15°
Magnesium alloy	Standard	100°	12°—15°
Brass	Slow	130°	10°—12°
Copper	Quick	125°	12°—15°
Bakelite	Slow	30°	12°—15°
Manganese steel	Slow	130°	7°—10°

(*Reproduced by courtesy of Brooke Tools, Ltd.*)

(3) *Point Thinning*

The web thickness increases towards the back end of a drill. Thus, as the drill is ground back, the thickness of the point increases, as the length of the chisel edge shows, and excessive pressure is required to feed the drill into the metal. This can be reduced by thinning the point as shown in fig. 6.15(b), which also shows helix modification at the point to give reduced rake.

122

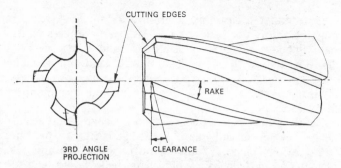

CUTTING EDGES

RAKE

3RD ANGLE PROJECTION

CLEARANCE

Fig. 6.16. Four-flute core drill

CORE DRILLS Two-flute twist drills should normally not be used for opening out existing holes but if they have to be used the helix angle should be reduced by grinding (see p. 122). Core drills are specially designed for this work and have three or four flutes, with three or four short conical cutting edges, as shown in fig. 6.16.

Three-flute drills are to be preferred for opening out cored holes in castings; the amount of chatter is reduced since no two edges are diametrically opposite.

REAMERS Whereas a drill is used to make a hole, a reamer is used to finish it accurately to size and to give it a surface finish of high quality. The reamer is a side or periphery-cutting tool, whereas the drill is an end-cutting tool. Since the teeth of a reamer require rake and clearance, as with any other cutting tool, these are provided on its side-cutting edges, as shown in fig. 6.17.

Fig. 6.17. Reamers
(a) Machine reamer with short bevel lead and left-hand helix for right-hand rotation
(b) End view showing rake and clearance angles
(c) Hand reamer with straight flutes and long tapered lead

Note *Hand reamers may also have left-hand helical flutes: the main difference is in the lead*

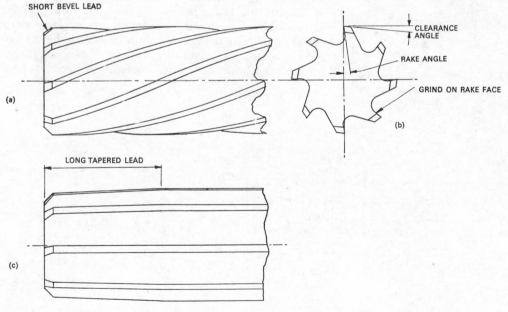

SHORT BEVEL LEAD

CLEARANCE ANGLE

RAKE ANGLE

GRIND ON RAKE FACE

(a)

(b)

LONG TAPERED LEAD

(c)

Note that the clearance angle is very small. A reamer must obviously not be ground on its clearance faces or its size will be destroyed, and it is ground on its rake faces, i.e., along its flutes. The flutes have a wide land and a small clearance angle, so that the size reduction caused by regrinding is minimized and the width of the land allows a number of regrinds.

Reamers may have either straight or helical flutes, and helical reamers usually have a left-hand helix to prevent 'corkscrewing' in use. A reamer removes only a small amount of material and if it had a right-hand helix would tend to follow the helix and reproduce its own form in the hole.

The hole to be reamed must be undersize, and to enter it initially the reamer must have a taper, or lead, at the front end, where most of the cutting is done. Hand reamers have a long lead to allow a considerable entry at the start of the operation and to align the reamer with the hole. Machine reamers have a much shorter bevel lead of about 45° and the tools should not be confused. It will be found difficult to start a machine reamer by hand.

The stock allowance for reaming should be about 0·015 in per inch of diameter, although this is a general guide and may be reduced for hand reaming. Softer materials may be given a greater allowance, and hard materials a lesser one.

TAPS AND DIES

Taps. A tap is essentially a screw which has been given cutting edges and hardened so that when it is screwed into a hole of its core diameter it will cut and reproduce its own thread. All the cutting is done by the front portion of the tap, on which the clearance is ground, the remainder of its thread performing the two functions of feeding the tap forward and finishing the cut thread. Fig. 6.18 is a diagram of a tap, showing how the cutting action is obtained.

Fig. 6.18. Details of taper tap. Plug and second taps are similar but with reduced taper lead.

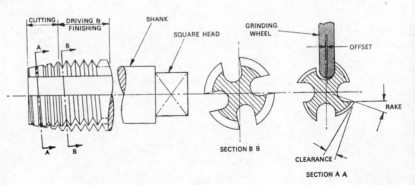

124

There are three types of tap: taper, second and plug. The taper tap is used for starting the thread and, indeed, if tapped right through the hole can be used to finish the thread. The second and plug taps are used in sequence to cut the thread to the bottom of a blind hole; they have reduced cutting portions and greater lengths of full-form thread.

In use, the tap must be set accurately in line with the hole axis and if the hole, as is usual, is square to the work face, the tap wrench can be removed when the tap has been started and the squareness of the tap can be checked with a try square. Methods of tapping in a drilling machine or a lathe, to ensure squareness, are discussed in Chapters 7 and 8 respectively.

TAPPING-SIZE HOLES Ideally, the diameter of the hole drilled prior to tapping should be equal to the minor, or root, diameter of the thread. In practice, the torque required to cut the thread to a full form may be excessive, resulting in a broken tap, and a slightly larger tapping hole is generally used. It must be appreciated that this procedure reduces the depth of form of the thread and the size of the tapping hole must not be too large or the thread will strip when the screw is tightened in it. A useful guide is to use 90% of the nominal thread depth and the tapping hole size can then be calculated as follows:

For I.S.O. Metric form threads:
Depth of thread $= 0.54 \times$ pitch.
Thus for a 48 mm fine thread with 3 mm pitch:

Depth of thread $\quad = 0.54 \times 3\,\text{mm} = 1.62\,\text{mm}$

90% depth of thread $= \dfrac{1.62 \times 90}{100} = 1.46\,\text{mm}$

Tapping size $\quad = 48 - (2 \times 1.46)\,\text{mm}$
$\quad\quad\quad\quad\quad\quad = 45.08\,\text{mm diameter}$

The next convenient drill size *above* this should be used.

In tapping a hole, a suitable lubricant should be used. The tap should be rotated a full turn forwards and then turned backwards until the cut chip breaks off. This prevents the chips from filling the flutes and clogging the cutting action.

A blind hole does not allow the chip to fall clear, so the tap should be removed and the chips cleared out occasionally or they will become jammed in the bottom of the hole.

DIES Just as a tap is a hardened screw provided with cutting edges, a die is a hardened nut provided with cutting edges which have rake and clearance as shown in fig. 6.19. The length of thread available for a lead, and hence the length of primary cutting edge, is more limited than in a tap and it is not advisable to cut the full depth of thread in one cut. The die is therefore split and is sprung open slightly

125

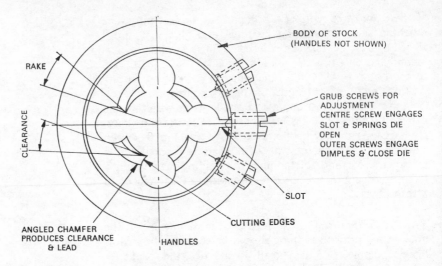

RAKE

CLEARANCE

BODY OF STOCK
(HANDLES NOT SHOWN)

GRUB SCREWS FOR
ADJUSTMENT
CENTRE SCREW ENGAGES
SLOT & SPRINGS DIE
OPEN
OUTER SCREWS ENGAGE
DIMPLES & CLOSE DIE

SLOT

CUTTING EDGES

HANDLES

ANGLED CHAMFER
PRODUCES CLEARANCE
& LEAD

Fig. 6.19. Split screwing die showing cutting angles and adjustments

for the first pass, by adjustment of the grub screws in the die stock. The thread is finished by a second or third pass with the die closed, the grub screws being adjusted to suit.

To reduce the load on the die a suitable lubricant should be used, and after each complete rotation the die should be turned back until the chip cut can be felt to break off. As in tapping, this helps to clear the chips and prevents them from clogging the die.

Solid die-nuts are available but these are normally used only for finishing a thread, or for running down a damaged thread to clean it up and permit free passage of its nut.

MILLING CUTTERS The tooth of a milling cutter can be likened to a boring tool in that both work on the inside of a curved surface. A major difference for milling cutters of disc type when they are cutting a slot is that the chips cannot escape until the tooth in front of them is well clear of the slot. Thus the space between the teeth is important

Fig. 6.20. Teeth of a milling cutter, showing main features

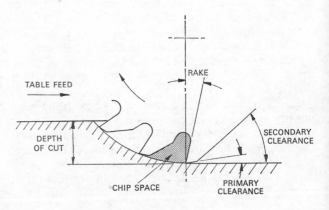

TABLE FEED

DEPTH
OF CUT

RAKE

SECONDARY
CLEARANCE

CHIP SPACE

PRIMARY
CLEARANCE

126

since it must adequately contain the chip produced. Secondary clearance is provided to increase this space and other angles are similar to those of a boring tool. If figs. 6.2(c) and 6.20 are compared, the similarity is obvious.

For a given size of cutter the number and size of teeth depend upon:

    (1) tooth load—what will be the maximum load the tooth must bear in service?

    (2) chip clearance—will the space between the teeth contain the chip produced at maximum load?

These two factors depend upon each other. For instance, if the chip clearance is too small it can be increased either:

    (a) by retaining the same tooth size but reducing the number of teeth. For a given depth of cut and rate of feed, each tooth then has to do more work and the load on each tooth is increased; or

    (b) by retaining the same number and depth of teeth but increasing the gap by making the tooth thinner. This reduces the load which the tooth can take and means a lower maximum depth of cut and feed, but these in turn will mean that less chip space is required. Thus the size, shape and number of teeth are a carefully thought-out compromise between tooth strength and chip space, and the necessary proportions must be maintained. If a cutter is ground excessively on the clearance face so that the tooth space is considerably reduced, the cutter should be re-gashed to restore the original tooth shape and give adequate chip space.

TYPES OF MILLING CUTTER

(1) *Slitting Saws and Slot Cutters*
These cutters have no side-cutting teeth and cut only on the periphery. To give side clearance and prevent binding in

Fig. 6.21. Slot milling cutters. Note how body clearance is obtained and compare with parting-off tool in Fig. 6.9

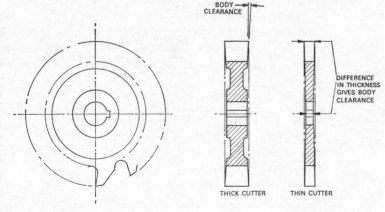

BODY CLEARANCE

DIFFERENCE IN THICKNESS GIVES BODY CLEARANCE

THICK CUTTER   THIN CUTTER

the slot which they cut, they are dished, or made wider at the cutting edge than at the centre, as shown in fig. 6.21. Note that the dishing serves the same purpose as the front-to-back clearance on a parting-off tool for a lathe.

It is important that there should be no side thrust on these cutters; they should not be used to cut on one side but only in a slot, to give a balanced load.

Fig. 6.22. Side-and-face cutter. Note that the side cutting edges have zero rake

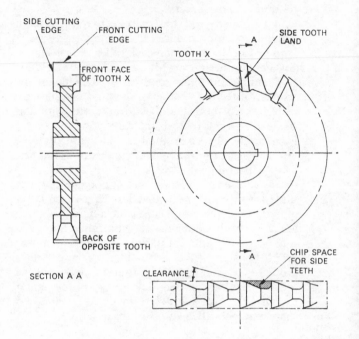

Plan view. Note this is not a true plan but a view of a straight line of teeth as if the cutter had been unrolled

Side-and-Face Milling Cutters

These cutters have side cutting edges as well as the normal front cutting edges. Consequently they can be used to cut on the side as well as on the face. They are usually wider than slot cutters and more able to withstand side loads. Fig. 6.22 shows such a cutter and that the side cutting edges have

    (1) zero rake angle:
    (2) little chip space.

Fig. 6.23. Extended plan view of staggered tooth side-and-face cutter showing rake on side cutting teeth

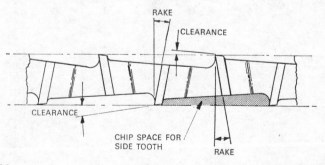

These faults can be overcome by removing alternate side-cutting teeth on opposite sides. This increases the chip clearance and allows the teeth to be angled in opposite directions to give rake to the side-cutting edges, producing the staggered-tooth side-and-face cutter shown in fig. 6.23.

Slab or Roller Milling Cutters
These are large cylindrical cutters used for machining horizontal surfaces. It should be noted that the shape of the workface is determined by the shape of the cutter, and if the teeth do not lie on a true cylinder the work will not be milled flat or parallel.

The teeth may be straight or helical but helical teeth are preferred. When straight teeth are used, each tooth bites into the work with its complete width, creating shock loads and vibrations, and the chips pile up on the work face in front of the cutter.

Fig. 6.24. Slab or rolling milling cutter and forces set up during its action

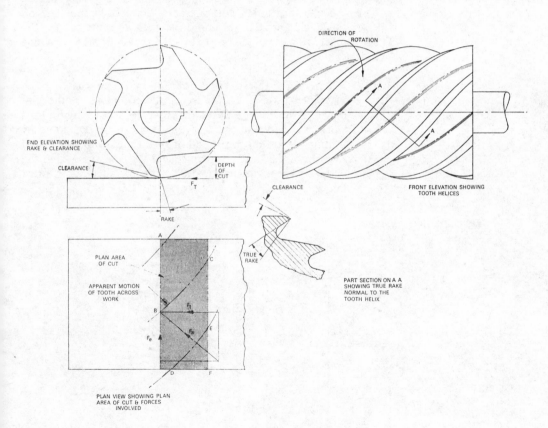

A cylindrical cutter with a steep helix angle is shown in fig. 6.24. The end elevation and front elevation show the general appearance of the cutter, but the plan view is a view of the work during cutting with the lines of the teeth super-imposed, and shows two effects of such a cutter.

The forces involved in plan are shown. They are:

Fn, the force normal to the tooth:

Ft, ,, ,, tangential to the cutter:

Fe, the end thrust.

The lines of the teeth show that the cut is taken up and relinquished gradually by each tooth. Compared with a straight-toothed cutter, the number of teeth in operation is increased and the length of tooth in operation is reduced. At A, a tooth is starting to cut at a point; at BC it has pro-gressed to its maximum width of cut and at DE the cut has started to reduce, to run out gradually at F. All these factors produce a much smoother cutting action, a better surface finish and a more even distribution of tooth load.

It should be noted that the action produces an end thrust on the cutter, and the steeper the helix the greater will be this end thrust. The cutter should therefore be mounted on the machine so that the end thrust is *towards* the body of the machine, and not tending to pull the arbor out of the machine spindle.

FACE MILLING   The width of end face that can be machined by a side-and-face cutter is limited by the dia-meter of the cutter and the fact that the arbor may foul the work, as shown in fig. 6.25(a). This can be overcome by putting the cutter on the end of the arbor, so to speak, and recessing its clamping arrangement. At the same time the cutter can be made broader and more able to support thrust loads.

Fig. 6.25. Face milling

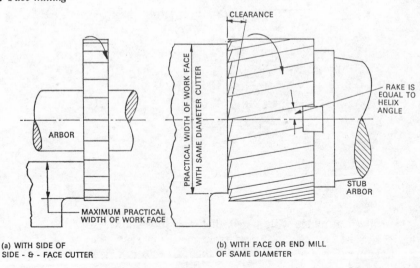

(a) WITH SIDE OF
SIDE - & - FACE CUTTER

(b) WITH FACE OR END MILL
OF SAME DIAMETER

As the cutter will be used only on one end, the teeth can be given a rake angle by making the flutes helical as shown in fig. 6.25(b). The angle of the helix gives rake angle to the teeth on the end of the cutter, not to those on the periphery.

END MILLS AND SHELL END MILLS These cutters may be relatively small and made from solid bar, when they are known as *end mills*. With larger cutters the cost of a solid cutter and shank, all of high-speed steel, would be prohibitive and such cutters are therefore made separately from their shanks, which may be made of plain carbon steel. Since they are shaped like a cylindrical shell, they are called *shell end mills* and are mounted on their shanks as shown in fig. 6.26. Note that the shank takes the place of the usual

Fig. 6.26. Exploded assembly of shell end milling cutter and arbor

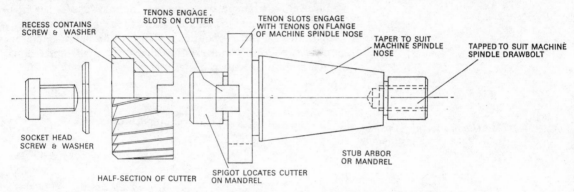

Fig. 6.27. Types of end mill and their cutting angles

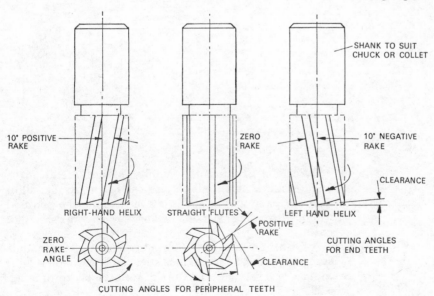

131

arbor in the machine spindle and is positively driven by tenons, and that the cutter is located on the shank by a spigot and in turn has a positive drive by other tenons. Fig. 6.27 shows three small solid-shank end mills, all with the same direction of rotation but with different helix angles. Note the effect of the helix on the rake angle of the end cutting teeth.

FLY CUTTERS If a very large width of face is to be machined a face-milling cutter capable of machining it in one pass may not be available. Under these circumstances, a single-point tool can be mounted in a disc or bar at the required radius. A disc is preferable since it is more rigid and less likely to distort under load, thus reducing vibration. However, the bar or arm type is sometimes used since it is more economical in material and can be readily adjusted for radius of cut. It requires a shank to fit the machine or may be made to fit an existing shank for a shell end mill. Such a cutter is shown in fig. 6.28.

Fig. 6.28. Use of fly cutter for face milling

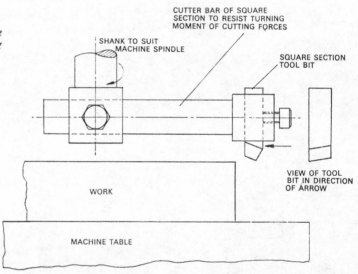

By careful adjustment, a number of such teeth can be fitted in a disc cutter, all at the same height, so that all of them share the cutting load, when the feed may be increased without increasing the tooth loading or impairing the surface finish.

A further advantage of a fly cutter is that, if the tooth is accurately ground and set, the cutter can be used to machine circular grooves and tracks in flat surfaces as shown in fig. 6.29.

132

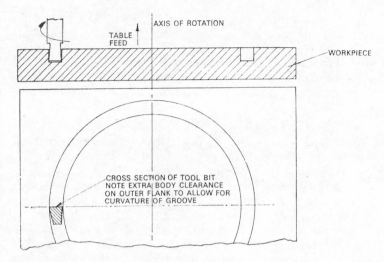

AXIS OF ROTATION

TABLE FEED

WORKPIECE

CROSS SECTION OF TOOL BIT
NOTE EXTRA BODY CLEARANCE
ON OUTER FLANK TO ALLOW FOR
CURVATURE OF GROOVE

Fig. 6.29. Use of fly cutter to cut a circular groove

COPYING AND GENERATING ON THE MILLING MACHINE

If a surface is dependent for its shape on the shape of the cutter it is said to be *copied*.

If the shape of the surface is independent of the shape of the tool but depends on the relative motions of work and tool, it is said to be generated. Thus, the surface produced by a slab mill or by a gang milling set-up is copied but that produced by a fly cutter or end mill is generated. As long as the fly cutter or end mill axis is at right angles to the table motion the surface produced is flat, and bears no resemblance to the shape of the cutting tool.

If the cutter axis is inclined, however, the cutter generates a curved surface across the workpiece, the curve being a portion of an ellipse, in accordance with the view of the cutter motion as seen along the work face. This effect is shown in fig. 6.30.

Fig. 6.30. Concave surface generated by inclining axis of fly cutter or end mill

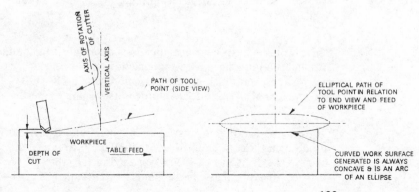

AXIS OF ROTATION OF CUTTER

VERTICAL AXIS

PATH OF TOOL POINT (SIDE VIEW)

DEPTH OF CUT

WORKPIECE

TABLE FEED

ELLIPTICAL PATH OF TOOL POINT IN RELATION TO END VIEW AND FEED OF WORKPIECE

CURVED WORK SURFACE GENERATED IS ALWAYS CONCAVE & IS AN ARC OF AN ELLIPSE

133

In practice, the cutter axis is slightly inclined so that the far side of the tool passing over the surface already cut clears the work by 0·05 to 0·10 mm. This avoids an unsightly criss-cross surface finish and improves the tool life by preventing rubbing. The amount of curvature produced is too small to be of any account in practical terms.

HAND TOOLS

Little or no mention has been made of hand cutting tools in this Chapter. However, an examination of hand tools will show that they follow the same principles, as indeed do all cutting tools. The student should examine hacksaw blades, files, chisels, scrapers, non-engineering tools such as safety razors, woodworking tools and, indeed, any edge used for a cutting action (as distinct from a shearing action) to find the clearance and rake angles, and to estimate the kind of force required to produce cutting. All the tools will be found to have a similar action. At the dentist's, ask if you may examine some of his 'drills'. Look closely and you will see that they are miniature end mills and die-sinking tools with the same characteristics as cutters described in this chapter.

CUTTING FLUIDS

In the cutting process, heat is generated in two ways:
- (1) By the deformation of the material in two places, in the zone of deformation ahead of the tool and in the chip as it bends over the rake face.
- (2) By friction at the tool point and where the chip rubs over the rake face.

The frictional heat can be reduced by using a lubricant to decrease the coefficient of friction between the tool and the work. The heat from deformation cannot be reduced but must be carried away by the cutting fluid. Thus a cutting fluid should be a good lubricant and have a high specific heat. At the same time it should have a good 'wetting action' and form a film instead of settling out into droplets. Fluids available are:

(1) *Water*
This has a high specific heat but is a poor lubricant and, strangely enough, has little wetting action: it also encourages rusting and is suitable only as a coolant during tool grinding. An addition of washing soda improves its wetting properties.

(2) *Soluble Oils*
Oil will not dissolve in water but can be made to form an intimate mixture, or emulsion, with it by adding emulsifying agents. The oil is in fact then suspended in the water in the form of tiny droplets. These fluids—often called 'suds'—

134

have some lubricating action and good cooling properties. They are very fluid and give good wetting of the surface, while the oil prevents rusting. Soluble oils are suitable for light cutting operations on general-purpose machines where high rates of metal removal are often not of first importance.

(3) *Mineral Oils*
These are used for heavier cutting operations because of their much better lubricating properties, and are commonly found in production work where high rates of metal removal are employed. Where extreme pressures are involved, sulphur compounds are added to the oils to prevent the chip welding to the rake face and forming a built-up edge. Mineral oils should not be used on copper and its alloys since they have a corrosive effect on them, but are suitable for steels.

(4) *Vegetable Oils*
These are good lubricants but are little used since they are liable to decompose and smell, and may become a health hazard.

The oil companies which market cutting oils have produced some very good literature on them, an outstanding book being published by the Esso Petroleum Co. Ltd., which provides a useful basis for further study.

CUTTING SPEEDS AND FEEDS
The cutting speed and feed used depend mainly on the type of work material, the type of tool material, the coolant, and the type and condition of machine. It must be realised that, in cutting metal, work is done and this work or energy is converted into heat which must be dissipated before the tool overheats and becomes soft. Thus a plain-carbon steel tool, which softens at a temperature of about 300°C to a point where it will not cut, must be run at a lower speed than a high-speed steel tool which retains its hardness up to about 450°C. Later developments such as 'Stellite', cemented carbide and ceramic tools cut at much higher speeds, but their action is rather different and is dealt with in more advanced books on the subject.

A strong material requires higher cutting forces than a weak one and at a given speed more work is done on the stronger material and greater heat is generated. Thus, to bring the heat produced down to manageable proportions the cutting speed must be reduced. It follows that weak materials are generally cut at high speeds and strong materials at lower speeds.

If a coolant is used the speed may be increased, and a light cut can be taken at higher speed than a finishing cut. The speeds given in the table opposite are for a roughing cut with a high-speed steel tool under toolroom conditions, and may be increased by 10% to 15% for light finishing cuts. In all cases the use of a coolant is assumed.

The feed rate depends largely on the surface finish required, and for roughing-out soft material a feed of up to about 0·25 mm per revolution, or 40 cuts per cm may be used. With tough, stronger materials this would be reduced to a maximum of 0·10 mm per revolution (80 cuts per cm) for roughing. Finishing requires a finer feed and about half the feed in mm per revolution, or double the cuts per cm, is a useful guide.

Milling cutters must be treated rather differently, since the cut is interrupted and vibratory in nature, and the speed must be reduced by 10% to 15%. The feed rate is normally based on the table feed per tooth of the cutter, in inches per tooth, and can be calculated from the number of teeth and the speed of the cutter. For roughing, a coarse feed to the limit of the cutter and machine should be used.

Finishing feeds are about 0·125 mm/tooth for helical slab mills to 0·250 mm/tooth for face mills.

The example below, based on a 100 mm diameter helical slab mill with 5 teeth and a cutting speed of 30 m/min, will clarify the position.

$$\text{Rev/min} = \frac{\text{Cutting speed in m/min}}{\text{Circumference of cutter in m}}$$

$$= \frac{30 \text{ m/min}}{\pi \times 100/1000 \text{ m}}$$

$$= \frac{300}{\pi}$$

$$= 95 \text{ rev/min}$$

$$\begin{aligned}
\text{Feed} \quad &= 0\cdot125 \text{ mm/tooth} \\
&= 0\cdot125 \times 5 \text{ mm/rev} \\
&= 0\cdot125 \times 5 \times 95 \text{ mm/min} \\
&= \underline{59\cdot4 \text{ mm/min}}
\end{aligned}$$

Rounding these figures would give a table feed of 60 mm/min. Note from the above that cutting speeds are quoted as surface speeds and can therefore be used for all sizes of work, cutter and types of machine.

Thus for cylindrical work:

$$\begin{aligned}
\text{Cutting speed} &= \text{Circumference} \times \text{rev/min} \\
&= \pi D \times N \quad \text{where } N = \text{rev/min} \\
N &= \frac{\text{Cutting speed}}{\pi D} \quad \begin{array}{l} D = \text{work} \\ \text{diameter} \end{array}
\end{aligned}$$

Note that the work diameter and the cutting speed must be in similar units. Therefore taking π as approximately 3

136

$$N = \frac{\text{Cutting speed (m/min)}}{3 \times \dfrac{D \text{ mm}}{1000}}$$

$$= \frac{1000 \times \text{Cutting speed (m/min)}}{3D \text{ mm}}$$

where D = work diameter

This is a good enough approximation, for the machine is not likely to give this precise speed, but since the approximation gives a slightly excessive speed choose the next *lower* speed available.

The table below quotes surface speeds in metres per minute for high-speed steel tools with a soluble oil coolant under roughing conditions, but not for mass-production work.

Material	Cutting speed m/min
Aluminium alloys	130
Brass	70
Mild steel	30
Medium-carbon steel, bronze, and cast iron	20
High-carbon and alloy steels	10

SAFETY NOTES *Metal cutting is a perfectly safe operation as long as a few simple and commonsense rules are observed. There is nothing glamorous about hospitalisation through stupidity, or about hands without fingers, or about scalps not attached to heads. Bearing this in mind it is no hardship to observe the following points, which may save considerable pain and loss of work.*

(1) *Always keep your hands away from the cutting zone.*

(2) *Always wear safety glasses.*

(3) *Always keep your hair cut reasonably short, or, if fashion dictates that you must wear long hair, wear a safety cap. The author once saw a portion of scalp just after its long-haired owner had lost it, and there was nothing handsome about it. This rule applies particularly to drilling machines.*

(4) *Always feed coolant to the work through pipes. Brushes can get caught up and carry your hand into the cutting zone.*

(5) *Always observe the regulations regarding the use of guards.*

(6) *Never wear loose clothing or a hanging necktie—this might strangle you.*

(7) *Never touch swarf with your bare hands, or with anything else while the machine is running. Swarf is sharp and very dangerous.*

No doubt this list could be extended, and its tone may shock some people. If so, remember that an accident is much more shocking, particularly to the victim, than to read a few rules. These rules should be acted upon and not just read and laughed off—it CAN happen to you.·

7
The Drilling Machine

We have seen that in order to cut metal successfully any cutting tool must overcome the resistance of the metal. In the case of a drill, two forces are required, a torque to provide the tangential cutting force and a direct thrust normal to the work surface to feed in the drill. Thus any drilling machine must provide two motions to the drill:

(1) A rotary motion whose speed is adjustable to give the required cutting speed and whose power is sufficient to provide the necessary tangential force for cutting.

(2) A linear motion for the feed.

If the machine is to produce accurate holes without exerting bending forces on the drill:

(a) the drill must rotate on its own axis, i.e., 'run true' without eccentricity, which demands an accurate drill-holding device:

(b) the drill must cut equally on both cutting edges:

(c) the feed motion must be along the line of the axis of the drill.

Furthermore, a rigid base or table must be provided on which the work can be fixed for the drilling operation. This table must normally be at right angles to the axis of rotation of the drill and therefore at right angles to the direction of feed.

These requirements are called the basic alignments of the machine and are illustrated in fig. 7.1. They are common to all drilling machines, and machines differ only in size, power and the way the drill is positioned over the work.

Fig. 7.1. Main alignments of a drilling machine

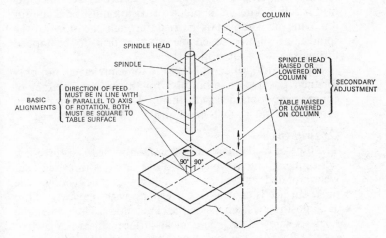

139

DRILL-HOLDING DEVICES

(1) *Taper shanks and sockets*

Drills, and indeed other tools requiring similar mounting, can be obtained with straight shanks, to be gripped in a chuck, or with taper shanks which fit in a taper socket in the end of the machine spindle. The straight-shank drills are driven by friction between the shank and the chuck jaws and may slip if the torque required is greater than that provided by the frictional grip.

Taper-shank drills, on the other hand, have a positive drive. The shank of the drill is made as shown in fig. 7.2, with a shallow taper of approximately $\frac{5}{8}$ in per foot on dia-

Fig. 7.2. End of drilling machine spindle and taper shank of drill

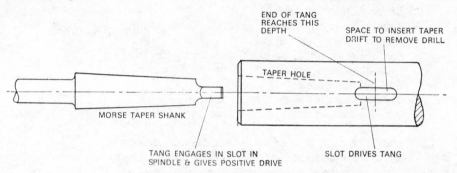

meter. This is known as a *self-locking taper* because when the drill is pushed into a mating taper hole it stays in position and a considerable force is required to loosen it. However, this alone would provide only a friction drive, so the end of the taper bears a *tang*, as shown, which fits in a corresponding slot at the end of the tapered hole in the spindle. The tang thus provides a positive drive. Since the drill is self-locking in its taper, provision must be made for removing it. The slot is carried through the sides of the spindle, as shown, to enable a taper drift to be tapped through to force the drill out.

Taper shank drills are generally to be preferred, not only for their positive drive but also for the greater accuracy of concentricity obtained with them. However, they are more expensive than straight-shank drills.

(2) *Drill Chucks*

The type of drill chuck most commonly used is a three-jaw self-centring one in which the outer sleeve is threaded and, when rotated, moves axially along the chuck body. The inner surface is conical to correspond with the jaws, whose axial position is fixed inside the chuck body. Thus, when the sleeve is screwed up, the conical surface causes the jaws to

140

close on the drill, and vice versa. Closing and releasing the chuck may be either by hand, on smaller sizes of chuck or, more commonly, by means of a key which carries a small bevel gear which engages with similar teeth on the chuck.

If frequent drill changes are required, for example when a radial drilling machine is used to drill a large number of different-sized holes in one component, a quick-change chuck may be used. In this case the outer sleeve of the chuck is freely rotating and when it is moved up the chuck body the drill is released. The drill is fitted with a collet to suit the chuck and a positive drive is obtained by a tang on the collet engaging a driving slot in the chuck.

THE MACHINE SPINDLE The spindle must not only rotate but must also provide a linear feed motion with the necessary thrust for the feed. The drive to the spindle does not normally move down with the feed so provision must be made for transmitting the drive regardless of the movement of the spindle downwards and upwards.

A simple machine spindle is shown in fig.7.3. This has a ball thrust bearing at top and bottom, any end play being taken up by adjusting a pair of locknuts at the top. The radial bearings are a pair of plain phosphor-bronze bushes and the complete spindle is carried in a sleeve. The sleeve slides axially in the spindle housing, which is attached to the machine frame or column. A gear or pinion mounted in the spindle housing engages with a rack, or length of teeth, cut in the back of the sleeve. The operating, or feed, lever is attached outside the spindle housing to the shaft of the pinion, and movement of the lever turns the pinion, thus moving the sleeve and the spindle downwards or upwards.

The spindle drive pulleys or gears are mounted in bearings in a fixed part of the frame above the spindle housing, and drive the spindle by a sliding key or splines, so that the spindle can move axially and still be driven in any position.

This technique is common to almost all drilling machines. Various refinements in the bearings are used, and power feed is commonly provided in addition to manual feed, but the basic features are the same.

TYPES OF DRILLING MACHINE

A simple method of classifying drilling machines is to consider two categories, all machines having the basic alignments already mentioned:

(1) those in which the work is moved into position under a fixed drill axis, which are the most common:

(2) those in which the work is fixed and the drill axis is moved into position over the hole.

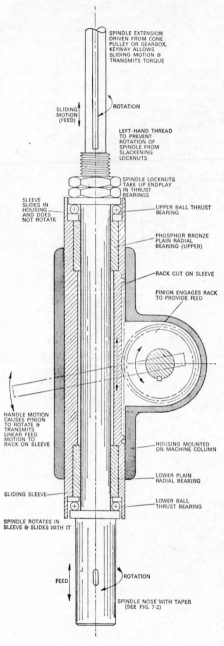

SPINDLE EXTENSION
DRIVEN FROM CONE
PULLEY OR GEARBOX.
KEYWAY ALLOWS
SLIDING MOTION &
TRANSMITS TORQUE

ROTATION

SLIDING
MOTION
(FEED)

LEFT-HAND THREAD
TO PREVENT
ROTATION OF
SPINDLE FROM
SLACKENING
LOCKNUTS

SPINDLE LOCKNUTS
TAKE UP ENDPLAY
IN THRUST
BEARINGS

SLEEVE IN
HOUSING AND
DOES NOT ROTATE

UPPER BALL THRUST
BEARING

PHOSPHOR BRONZE
PLAIN RADIAL
BEARING (UPPER)

RACK CUT ON SLEEVE

PINION ENGAGES RACK
TO PROVIDE FEED

HANDLE MOTION
CAUSES PINION
TO ROTATE &
TRANSMITS
LINEAR FEED
MOTION TO
RACK ON SLEEVE

HOUSING MOUNTED
ON MACHINE COLUMN

LOWER PLAIN
RADIAL BEARING

SLIDING SLEEVE

LOWER BALL
THRUST BEARING

SPINDLE ROTATES IN
SLEEVE & SLIDES WITH IT

FEED

ROTATION

SPINDLE NOSE WITH TAPER
(SEE FIG. 7·2)

Fig. 7.3. Cross section of drilling
machine spindle assembly showing how
both rotary cutting motion and sliding
feed motion are obtained

Fig. 7.4. Outline of sensitive drilling
machine

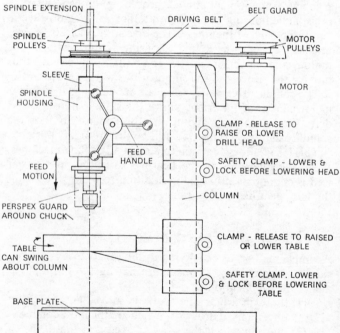

SPINDLE EXTENSION

DRIVING BELT

BELT GUARD

SPINDLE
POLLEYS

MOTOR
PULLEYS

SLEEVE

MOTOR

SPINDLE
HOUSING

CLAMP - RELEASE TO
RAISE OR LOWER
DRILL HEAD

FEED
HANDLE

SAFETY CLAMP - LOWER &
LOCK BEFORE LOWERING HEAD

FEED
MOTION

COLUMN

PERSPEX GUARD
AROUND CHUCK

CLAMP - RELEASE TO RAISED
OR LOWER TABLE

TABLE
CAN SWING
ABOUT COLUMN

SAFETY CLAMP. LOWER
& LOCK BEFORE LOWERING
TABLE

BASE PLATE

FIXED-AXIS MACHINES

(1) THE SENSITIVE DRILLING MACHINE These machines are usually bench mounted, although pedestal machines are available. They are of small capacity, i.e., maximum size of drill, and do not have power feed. Thus the operator, by hand feeding, can 'feel' the drill cutting, particularly as it breaks through—hence the name 'sensitive'.

An outline of such a machine is given in fig. 7.4, and the adjustments available are as follows.

   (a) speed adjustment by changing the belt on the pulleys:
   (b) table height adjustment to accommodate different work heights within the spindle feed range. In some machines, as in the one shown, the position of the drill head and spindle housing on the column can also be adjusted:
   (c) table position adjustment about the column. This enables the table to be swung clear to accommodate larger workpieces:
   (d) spindle feed stop to allow holes to be drilled to a set depth (see drilling operations, p. 148).

(2) THE PILLAR DRILLING MACHINE This is simply a much more robust version of the sensitive drill, floor-mounted and provided with power feed, usually at three rates, and with a wide range of spindle speeds provided by a gearbox rather than by cone pulleys. As an example let us consider a machine with a drill-size range from 6 mm diameter to 25 mm diameter, to be used for all materials from brass, requiring a cutting speed of 70 m/min, to high-carbon steel, requiring a cutting speed of 10 m/min.

Obviously the fastest speed will be required when drilling brass with the smallest drill and therefore:

$$\text{Maximum rev/min} = \frac{\text{Cutting speed}}{\text{Drill circumference}}$$

$$= \frac{70}{\pi \times \dfrac{6}{1000}}$$

$$= 3700 \text{ rev/min}$$

The lowest speed will be used when drilling high-carbon steel with the largest drill and similarly:

$$\text{Minimum rev/min} = \frac{10}{\pi \times \dfrac{25}{1000}}$$

$$= 127 \text{ rev/min}$$

Thus the speed range needs to be from 127 to 3700 rev/min and would usually be provided in nine steps.

Note that the table can be swung clear of the base to allow large castings to be accommodated, as with a sensitive drilling machine. This has the disadvantage that although the machine is more massive it loses rigidity since the table cannot be supported from underneath. A similar machine using a box column is much more rigid, since the table moves on slides on the front of the column as shown in fig. 7.5, and is supported under the point of drill thrust by the table-raising screw. However the table cannot be moved, to position the work under the drill, nor swung clear.

Fig. 7.5. Vertical drilling machine of the box column type. Compare this machine with a sensitive drill or pillar drill for rigidity

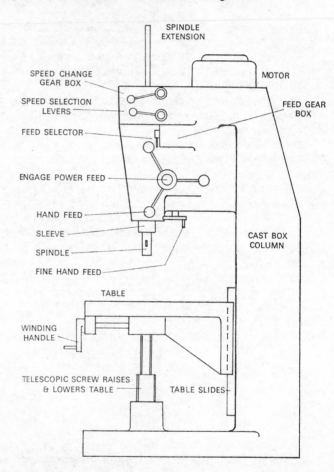

SPINDLE
EXTENSION

SPEED CHANGE
GEAR BOX

MOTOR

SPEED SELECTION
LEVERS

FEED GEAR
BOX

FEED SELECTOR

ENGAGE POWER FEED

HAND FEED

SLEEVE

CAST BOX
COLUMN

SPINDLE

FINE HAND FEED

TABLE

WINDING
HANDLE

TELESCOPIC SCREW RAISES
& LOWERS TABLE

TABLE SLIDES

(3) THE COMPOUND-TABLE DRILLING MACHINE

This is a development of the box column machine, with a table mounted on two slideways to give horizontal motions at 90° to each other and controlled by lead screws, as shown in fig. 7.6. The work is clamped to the compound table which can then be accurately adjusted to bring each hole centre under the spindle axis in turn for drilling.

144

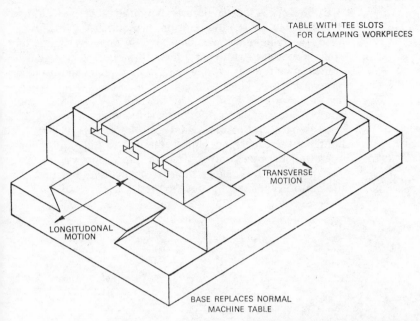

Fig. 7.6. *Compound table for drilling machine. This is particularly useful where a large number of holes is to be drilled in a single component. Operating lead screws not shown*

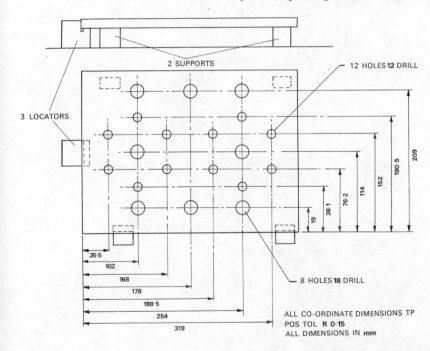

Fig. 7.7. *Typical component for drilling on a compound table machine. The 12 mm holes could have been specified twice as '6 holes 12 drill equi-spaced on 152·5 PCD' but, for this method of drilling, co-ordinate dimensions are necessary*

If the work is located accurately on the table, by locators in the tee slots, once the position of the first hole has been fixed, the remaining holes can be positioned by means of table movements without recourse to marking-out.

Ideal jobs for this type of machine are plates requiring a large number of holes whose coordinate centres are specified, as shown in fig. 7.7. The method is used where the number of components does not justify making a special jig.

Looking ahead to more advanced work, it is worthy of note that these machines lend themselves to fully-automatic operation by tape control. The operator simply loads the workpiece on the table at the correct location and presses the button. The machine does the rest.

Fig. 7.8. Radial drilling machine: note that all controls are on the spindlehead within easy reach of the operator

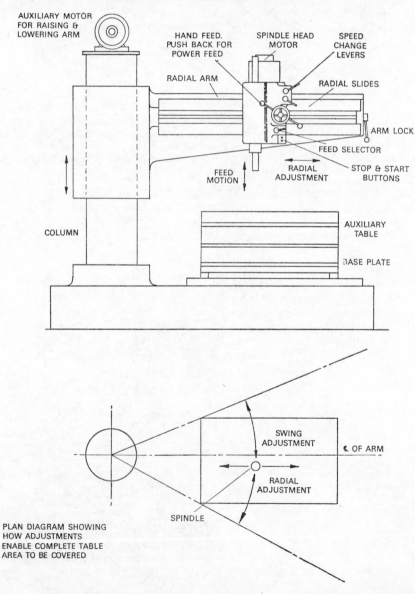

AUXILIARY MOTOR FOR RAISING & LOWERING ARM

HAND FEED. PUSH BACK FOR POWER FEED

SPINDLE HEAD MOTOR

SPEED CHANGE LEVERS

RADIAL ARM

RADIAL SLIDES

ARM LOCK

FEED SELECTOR

FEED MOTION

RADIAL ADJUSTMENT

STOP & START BUTTONS

COLUMN

AUXILIARY TABLE

BASE PLATE

SWING ADJUSTMENT

℄ OF ARM

RADIAL ADJUSTMENT

SPINDLE

PLAN DIAGRAM SHOWING HOW ADJUSTMENTS ENABLE COMPLETE TABLE AREA TO BE COVERED

MOVING-AXIS MACHINES

The only common machine of this type is the radial drilling machine, so called because the drilling head is mounted to move on slides along a radial arm which itself can be swung about the end column.

Such a machine is shown in outline, in front elevation and plan, in fig. 7.8, so that the adjustments can be shown. The base of the machine itself is the work table and is provided with tee-slots for clamping large workpieces. An auxiliary table is usually provided to which smaller workpieces can be clamped and in some cases, where utilisation is high, two such tables are used. One is placed on the machine while drilling is in progress and the other is at one side, having the previous work removed and new parts positioned. When the work is completed the tables are interchanged by hoist, the radial arm being swung clear for the purpose.

DRILLING OPERATIONS

The obvious purpose of a drilling machine is to drill holes but, in fact, the machine is much more versatile than this and is used for other operations. However, drilling itself is worthy of comment since there are several points to be made clear for correct and safe procedures to be followed.

DRILLING   The machine table is machined flat and accurately mounted square to the axis of rotation and feed. Dirt or burrs will destroy this alignment and the table must therefore be kept clean and in good condition. Great care must be taken never to drill into the table surface.

WORK-HOLDING   The holding of work by hand is dangerous. If the drill 'picks up' the workpiece, a bad cut may result as the workpiece rotates with it. Work should always be held in a vice or clamped to the table. In some cases work is best clamped to an angle plate as shown in fig. 7.9. Note that it should then normally be clamped on the inner face of the plate so that the feed force does not tend to tilt the plate.

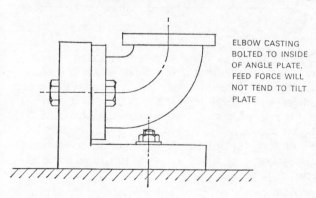

ELBOW CASTING
BOLTED TO INSIDE
OF ANGLE PLATE.
FEED FORCE WILL
NOT TEND TO TILT
PLATE

Fig. 7.9. Use of angle plate in holding workpiece for drilling

147

Details were given in Chapter 6 of modifications to a drill point for opening out a hole or drilling thin material. As stated, a core drill is preferable to a twist drill for the former operation.

DRILLING A HOLE TO A SET DEPTH If a blind hole is to be drilled, some means other than guessing is required to gauge its depth. The drill sleeve motion is usually provided with adjustable stops which can be set in two ways.

(1) The stationary drill is brought down lightly on to a pile of workshop-grade gauge blocks of the correct height, as shown in fig. 7.10(a), with protective blocks top and bottom, to give the total depth of hole. With the drill in this position, the feed stop is appropriately adjusted and locked.

Fig. 7.10(a). Setting total depth of hole by gauge blocks

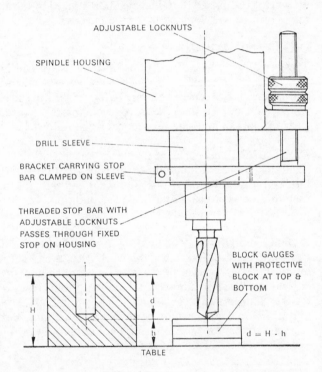

ADJUSTABLE LOCKNUTS

SPINDLE HOUSING

DRILL SLEEVE

BRACKET CARRYING STOP
BAR CLAMPED ON SLEEVE

THREADED STOP BAR WITH
ADJUSTABLE LOCKNUTS
PASSES THROUGH FIXED
STOP ON HOUSING

BLOCK GAUGES
WITH PROTECTIVE
BLOCK AT TOP &
BOTTOM

$d = H - h$

TABLE

(2) If the depth of full diameter is specified, drilling is started until full diameter is just obtained and the machine is then stopped. The stationary drill is brought down until it contacts the conical depression, and the feed stop is set so that the drill penetrates only to the depth required. This method is shown in fig. 7.10(b).

In both cases the drill should be withdrawn as soon as the stop is reached since, if it is allowed to rub, rapid overheating and wear will result.

148

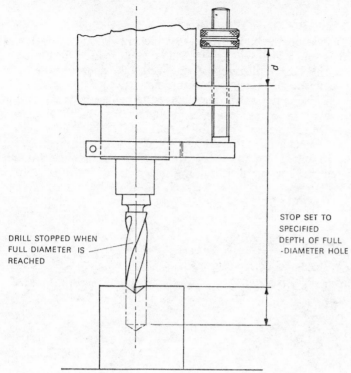

Fig. 7.10(b). Setting depth of full-diameter hole

d

STOP SET TO
SPECIFIED
DEPTH OF FULL
-DIAMETER HOLE

DRILL STOPPED WHEN
FULL DIAMETER IS
REACHED

CORRECTING HOLE POSITIONS DURING DRILL-ING In Chapter 5 the technique of 'boxing' holes when marking them out for drilling was recommended. However accurately the central punch mark is made the drill may not position itself quite correctly, which can be detected by comparing the initial cone cut by the drill with the box *before the drill has attained its full diameter*. If the cone is off-centre a groove is chipped down the side of the cone to the apex, as shown in fig. 7.11. This draws the drill in the direction of the groove so that, with care, it is brought back to cut centrally.

Note: This 'drawing' of the drill cannot be done once the drilled cone has reached full diameter.

Fig. 7.11. Correcting hole centre position after initial error in starting drill

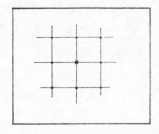

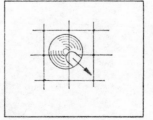

GROOVE CUT WITH
ROUND-NOSED CHISEL
DRAWS HOLE BACK
TO CENTRE

ORIGINAL MARKING SHOWING
BOXING OF HOLE

EXAMINATION BEFORE FULL DIAMETER
IS REACHED SHOWS DRILL TO HAVE
WANDERED

SPOT-FACING When a bolt hole is drilled in a boss on a casting the boss surface, on which a bolt has to pull down, is rough and does not provide a good seating for the bolt. The boss is therefore cleaned up, or machined flat, by a spot-facing cutter as shown in fig. 7.12(a).

The cutter is an interchangeable blade fitted in a cutter bar whose nose diameter is slightly less than that of the drilled hole, in which the nose acts as a pilot for the cutter. The blade can also be fitted in the reverse position and used to spot-face an inside face after the bar has been fed through a previously drilled hole, as shown in fig. 7.12(b).

Fig. 7.12. Spot-facing with blade-type spot-facing tool

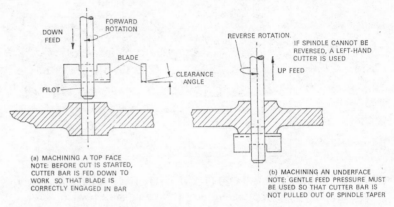

(a) MACHINING A TOP FACE
NOTE: BEFORE CUT IS STARTED, CUTTER BAR IS FED DOWN TO WORK SO THAT BLADE IS CORRECTLY ENGAGED IN BAR

(b) MACHINING AN UNDERFACE
NOTE: GENTLE FEED PRESSURE MUST BE USED SO THAT CUTTER BAR IS NOT PULLED OUT OF SPINDLE TAPER

COUNTERBORING If a hole has to take a socket-head screw it must be opened out to a depth slightly greater than the depth of the screw head. This operation is performed with an end-cutting tool similar to an end mill but with a pilot to guide the tool and keep it concentric with the hole, as shown in fig. 7.13. Larger counterboring tools are sometimes used for spot-facing.

Fig. 7.13. Counter boring tool. A large counter boring tool can be used to spot-face top surfaces

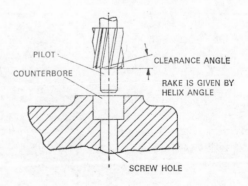

150

TAPPING Unless the machine has special equipment for power tapping, the tapping of screw threads by it is still a hand operation, but the machine alignments are used to ensure that the tap is correctly aligned with the hole. When the hole to be tapped has been drilled, a centre is fitted in the drill spindle. The tap is entered into the hole and the spindle is fed down until the centre engages with the centre hole in the shank of the tap. The tap is then turned by hand in the normal way to produce the thread and is kept square to the work by maintaining the contact of the centre.

Many sensitive drilling machines have the spindle weight counterbalanced by spring loading. If the spring loading is disconnected, the spindle will follow and support the tap by its own weight, leaving both hands of the operator free for the tapping operation. The counterbalance must be reconnected when the tapping has been completed.

REAMING Reaming may be performed on a drilling machine with a machine reamer (see p. 124). A very slow speed must be used, with a plentiful supply of cutting fluid, mainly to wash away the swarf which might mar the surface finish if allowed to build up in the hole.

SAFETY NOTES *Many accidents occur on drilling machines but the machines themselves are rarely to blame. The fault usually lies with the operator, but the causes of the accidents are easily enumerated and knowledge of the dangers enables them to be avoided.*

(1) *Work picked up and revolving with the drill*
The drilling machine is one of only two machines in general use (the other is the off-hand grinder) on which the operator can work without clamping or fixing the workpiece. No one thinks of holding work by hand in a shaping or milling machine, yet similar cutting forces are at work in a drilling machine. If work picks up and is torn from the operator's grasp at 360 rev/min, he has one-sixth of a second to remove his hand before it comes round again and strikes him. Since human reaction times are of the order of two-fifths of a second, the odds are in favour of an accident.

Work should always be clamped, or a stop should be fixed on the table to resist the torque set up by the drilling.

(2) *Scalping*
Never bend the head close to the drill to see what is happening, or blow away swarf. The rotating spindle can pick up hair and tear away a part of the scalp with very painful results. When the drill is held in a chuck, the chuck should be covered by a guard attached to the spindle sleeve so that the guard screens all but the drill itself. This reduces the danger but does not eliminate it. Keep your head out of the way.

151

(3) Swarf cuts

A well-ground drill will produce two equal-length spirals of swarf, one from each flute, which rotate with it and tend to fly outwards under centrifugal force. If these become too long and lash the back of the hand, bad cuts can result. Before the swarf streamers become too long, ease the feed so that they break off. Never try to break them off with a brush or piece of wire.

(4) Coolant brushes

These are an abomination, for they can easily be picked up by the drill and cause an accident. If no coolant feed is available use a pressure oilcan to squirt the coolant into the work area.

Like any other machine tool, the drilling machine is quite safe as long as the operator is its master. It can, however, exact swift retribution from the careless and the foolish.

8
The Centre Lathe

A centre lathe is basically a machine tool used to produce cylindrical, flat and conical surfaces by a generating process and the use of a single-point tool. From a previous discussion on cutting tools (p. 133) it will be recalled that the shape of surface produced by a generating process depends entirely on the relative motion between tool and work, not on the shape of the tool. In generating a surface, two motions are required, plus a further one to adjust the depth of cut, this adjustment remaining fixed while each cut is in progress.

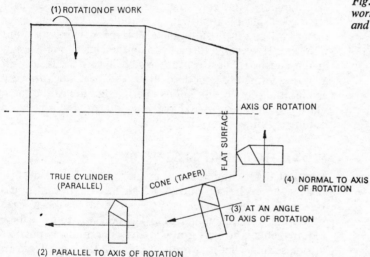

Fig. 8.1. Relative motions of tool and work for generating cylindrical, flat, and conical surfaces on a lathe

For the application of this principle to the lathe, the motions shown in fig. 8.1 must be provided. These are:

(1) rotary motion of the work about a fixed axis, with
either (2) linear motion of the tool parallel to the axis, to generate a cylindrical surface:
or (3) linear motion of the tool at right angles to the axis, to generate a flat surface:
or (4) linear motion of the tool at an intermediate angle to the axis, to generate a conical surface or taper.

The generating motions for a cylinder are the rotary work motion and the parallel tool motion, with right-angled motion of the tool to set the cut. For a flat surface, the right-angled tool motion generates the surface, with parallel motion to set the cut. In generating a taper, the right-angled motion is most frequently used to set the depth of cut. Thus if work is to be produced to a high order of accuracy and

153

surface finish, the following physical requirements must be met:

(1) Provision for work holding must be so made that the work rotates but is not moved in any other way by the applied cutting forces. This implies support to prevent the work from deflecting during cutting.

(2) The feed motions must have a constant speed to produce a uniform and good surface finish. This demands power feed for all feed motions, if possible, and certainly for the longitudinal and transverse feeds.

(3) The depth of cut must be controllable to a high degree of accuracy.

These basic alignments and physical requirements were realised many years ago, and an early lathe built a century ago is basically little different from the modern machine except in power and robustness. In those days, rates of metal removal, using plain carbon-steel tools, were much lower than today and the resulting loads on the machine structure were less. However, a turner who finished his apprenticeship at the end of the last century would have no difficulty in adapting himself to a modern lathe. The techniques are very similar and most of the knobs and handles are in the same places—a few new ones have been added, but the basic outline is still as shown in fig. 8.2.

WORK-HOLDING METHODS

It is a general requirement of cylindrical work that all diameters should be concentric and all faced surfaces should be square to the cylinder axis. (This is what we mean when we talk of work 'running true'.) The best way to meet these requirements is to perform as many operations as possible at one setting, that is, without removing the work from its setting in the machine. This is not always practicable, so a number of work-holding methods have been devised to suit various types of job and to enable the accuracy requirements to be met.

(1) THE SELF-CENTRING CHUCK Undoubtedly the most convenient, and therefore most used, method of holding work is the three-jaw self-centring chuck. This takes a wide range of work diameters, and with the provision of a second set of 'outside' jaws its range can be increased, as shown in fig. 8.3. The chuck consists of a cylindrical body, across the face of which the three jaws move in equally-spaced radial slots, driven by a scroll plate inside the body. This plate has a spiral groove, or 'thread', cut across its face in the form of a scroll, which mates with similar 'threads' cut on the back of each jaw, so that when the scroll plate is rotated the scroll moves all three jaws in or out. The jaws

154

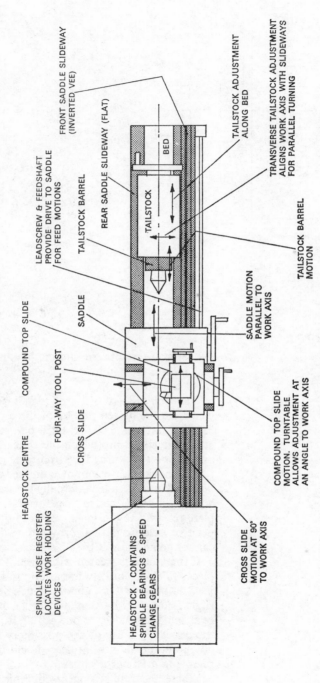

SPINDLE NOSE REGISTER
LOCATES WORK HOLDING
DEVICES

HEADSTOCK CENTRE

COMPOUND TOP SLIDE

FOUR-WAY TOOL POST

SADDLE

CROSS SLIDE

LEADSCREW & FEEDSHAFT
PROVIDE DRIVE TO SADDLE
FOR FEED MOTIONS

TAILSTOCK BARREL

REAR SADDLE SLIDEWAY (FLAT)

FRONT SADDLE SLIDEWAY
(INVERTED VEE)

TAILSTOCK ADJUSTMENT
ALONG BED

TRANSVERSE TAILSTOCK ADJUSTMENT
ALIGNS WORK AXIS WITH SLIDEWAYS
FOR PARALLEL TURNING

BED

TAILSTOCK

TAILSTOCK BARREL
MOTION

SADDLE MOTION
PARALLEL TO
WORK AXIS

COMPOUND TOP SLIDE
MOTION. TURNTABLE
ALLOWS ADJUSTMENT AT
AN ANGLE TO WORK AXIS

CROSS SLIDE
MOTION AT 90°
TO WORK AXIS

HEADSTOCK - CONTAINS
SPINDLE BEARINGS & SPEED
CHANGE GEARS

*Fig. 8.2. Plan view diagram of lathe showing how motions shown in fig. 8.1 are obtained.
Shaded parts are slideways used to guide moving parts*

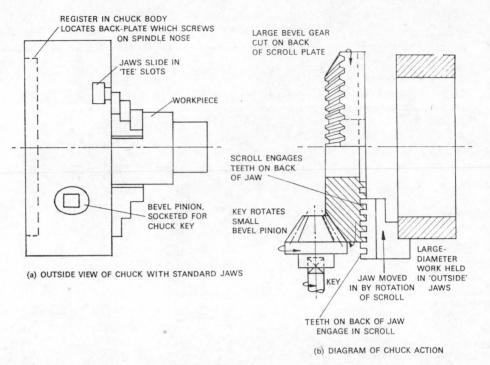

REGISTER IN CHUCK BODY
LOCATES BACK-PLATE WHICH SCREWS
ON SPINDLE NOSE

LARGE BEVEL GEAR
CUT ON BACK
OF SCROLL PLATE

JAWS SLIDE IN
'TEE' SLOTS

WORKPIECE

SCROLL ENGAGES
TEETH ON BACK
OF JAW

BEVEL PINION,
SOCKETED FOR
CHUCK KEY

KEY ROTATES
SMALL
BEVEL PINION

LARGE-
DIAMETER
WORK HELD
IN 'OUTSIDE'
JAWS

KEY

JAW MOVED
IN BY ROTATION
OF SCROLL

(a) OUTSIDE VIEW OF CHUCK WITH STANDARD JAWS

TEETH ON BACK OF JAW
ENGAGE IN SCROLL

(b) DIAGRAM OF CHUCK ACTION

Fig. 8.3. Self-centring three-jaw chuck

and slots are numbered and the jaws must be assembled in sequence in their individual slots or they will not centralise correctly.

The back plate of the scroll plate forms a large bevel gear which can be driven by any of three pinions which are let into the rim of the chuck. Each pinion has a square socket at its outer end into which the chuck key fits. Rotation of any pinion thus turns the scroll plate and moves the jaws.

The chuck body is mounted on the back plate, which may be bored and threaded internally to screw on the nose of the lathe spindle. A better form of attachment has the back plate recessed to engage a register on the spindle nose, and positive holding is then provided by four bolts. This type cannot come loose if the machine stops suddenly.

If the chuck is treated with care, it will centralise workpieces fairly accurately for a long time, but the scroll and jaws do become worn and the chuck becomes inaccurate. A slight inaccuracy is often immaterial, e.g., when parts are to be machined all over at one setting from bar stock held in the chuck. Because of the possibility of inaccurate setting all operations on a workpiece should be completed without removing it from the chuck.

Where accurate setting or concentricity with an existing diameter is required a self-centring chuck should *not* be used.

156

(2) THE INDEPENDENT FOUR-JAW CHUCK   This chuck has four jaws, each working independently of the others in its own slot in the chuck body and actuated by its own separate square-thread screw. By suitable adjustment of the jaws, a workpiece can be set to run either true or out of truth, as required. If it is removed for any reason, it can be replaced and reset to run concentrically by checking with a dial gauge and adjusting each jaw as necessary. The check on the workpiece should be carried out near the chuck and repeated as far from it as the workpiece permits, to ensure that the work is not held in the chuck at an angle to the axis of rotation.

Fig. 8.4. Setting of independent four-jaw chuck for turning an eccentric crank pin

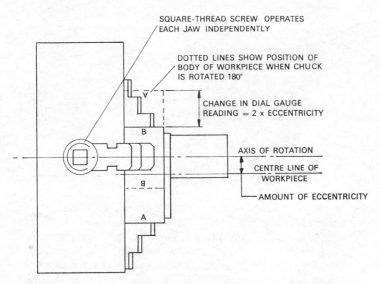

The independent adjustment also provides the facility of deliberately setting work off-centre to produce an eccentric workpiece, as shown in fig. 8.4. The concentric diameters are turned first and the chuck is then adjusted for eccentricity by a dial gauge which, for accuracy, must register at a radial position. Note that the dial gauge readings must vary by *twice* the amount of eccentricity required.

(3) THE COLLET CHUCK   A collet is a chuck which is tightened through being drawn into a tapered socket in the spindle nose by a draw tube which bears against the back end of the spindle. Each collet is made for a single diameter and a set of collets is provided for standard diameters of work. Apart from this limitation, collets give a high repeatability of position and work can be removed and replaced in them with the knowledge that any resulting eccentricity will be very slight. Furthermore, work of very small diameter can be held and, since it is gripped round

157

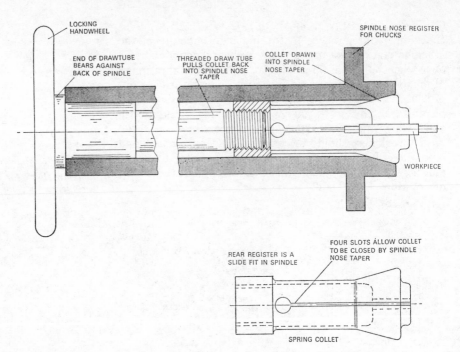

LOCKING
HANDWHEEL

END OF DRAWTUBE
BEARS AGAINST
BACK OF SPINDLE

THREADED DRAW TUBE
PULLS COLLET BACK
INTO SPINDLE NOSE
TAPER

COLLET DRAWN
INTO SPINDLE
NOSE TAPER

SPINDLE NOSE REGISTER
FOR CHUCKS

WORKPIECE

REAR REGISTER IS A
SLIDE FIT IN SPINDLE

FOUR SLOTS ALLOW COLLET
TO BE CLOSED BY SPINDLE
NOSE TAPER

SPRING COLLET

Fig. 8.5. Collet chuck. The rear register and taper are ground concentric with the gripping chuck bore to ensure true running of workpiece and concentricity of machining

virtually its full circumference, no damage is done to its surface.

A collet chuck with a typical workpiece is shown in fig 8.5; the workpiece has a small diameter and requires machining at both ends, and the ends are to be concentric. It is too small to grip in a four-jaw chuck and would be difficult to turn between centres, so that it is ideal for collet work, particularly if a number of workpieces is required. A further point to note is that the absence of rotating jaws, as found on three- and four-jaw chucks, makes it possible to cut close to the collet with minimum length of work protruding, deflections due to tool loads thus being minimized.

The collet is made from medium-carbon steel and is hardened and spring-tempered so that when unlocked it will spring open and release the workpiece. To enable it to close on the workpiece three or four narrow slots are cut from the body to the gripping end. The outer taper of the gripping end matches the taper bore of the machine spindle nose and as the collet is drawn into the spindle its gripping end is closed on the workpiece. The draw tube and the back end of the collet are hollow to permit bars to be fed through the spindle for repetition turning and parting-off of workpieces.

After the collet has been hardened and tempered its rear register in the spindle, its grip taper, and its gripping bore are fine-ground to size so that they are concentric, to ensure true running of workpieces and concentricity of machining.

158

(4) HOLDING WORK BETWEEN CENTRES If a workpiece is solid, i.e., not bored, and can have a centre hole in each end, it can be supported between a running centre in the headstock spindle and a fixed centre in the tailstock spindle or barrel. Provided the headstock centre (live centre) is running true, the work can be removed and replaced at will, and the repeatability of position will be virtually exact. Thus one end can be machined, the work turned round in position and the other end machined with matching concentricity.

It is, of course, necessary to drive the work, so a 'catch' plate with a driving pin is fitted on the spindle nose and a work carrier or 'driving dog' is attached to the work as shown in fig. 8.6.

Fig. 8.6. Work held between centres. Note requirements for parallelism and concentricity

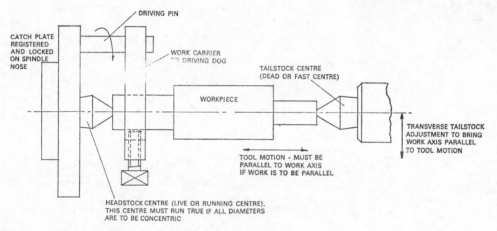

Parallelism in turning can be achieved only if the axis of rotation, i.e., the line between centres, is parallel with the tool motion. The transverse position of the tailstock across the bed can be adjusted to correct any error which may exist in this alignment.

The headstock centre must 'run true' for concentricity to be realised, and the centres must be clean and free from damage.

Since the headstock centre does not rotate relative to the work it need not be hard and, if the taper of the spindle nose is for any reason out of truth, a soft centre can be fitted and turned in position to the correct point angle. It will then be concentric and remain so as long as it is not removed. However, soft centres are prone to damage and should not be used unless necessary. It is better to maintain the spindle in good condition so that a normal hard centre runs true.

The tailstock centre is stationary and does not affect the concentricity, but it must be hard to resist wear and kept

159

lubricated to reduce overheating by friction. The tailstock, i.e., the position of the tailstock centre, must be adjusted so that the work is free to rotate but has no end play. After some running the work heats up and expands, so the tailstock barrel requires periodic adjustment.

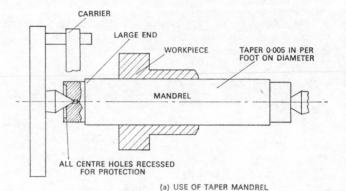

Fig. 8.7. Workpieces mounted on mandrels between centres

(a) USE OF TAPER MANDREL

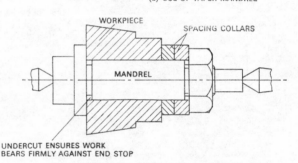

(b) USE OF PARALLEL MANDREL WITH LOCKING NUT

If the work has been bored or reamed to a standard diameter it can be mounted on a mandrel as shown in fig. 8.7(a) and the outside diameters then turned. As long as the mandrel is straight and runs true on its centres the work will be concentric. Standard plain mandrels are made to standard sizes and have a very slight taper, of 1 in 2000 on diameter, so that workpieces can be driven tightly on them. If a taper mandrel is used, the feed force of the tool should normally be towards the large end, otherwise the work may be pushed along the mandrel and freed.

Fig. 8.7(b) shows a parallel mandrel in which the work is gripped between a shoulder at one end of the mandrel and a nut on a screw thread at the other. The concentricity of machining will depend upon the closeness of fit between the mandrel and the bore in the work. However, the grip is more positive than with a taper mandrel, and the part is always located in the same place along the axis of the machine.

160

(5) THE FACEPLATE The faceplate is simply a circular worktable, mounted on the spindle nose, to which large or awkwardly shaped work is bolted or clamped by the slots provided. Work of awkward shape is then usually out of balance and it is generally necessary to fit a balance weight at an appropriate point on the faceplate to stop vibration.

SAFETY NOTE *The forces which cause vibration due to an out-of-balance weight* are not removed *by balancing— they are simply balanced by an equal and opposite force. Thus the stresses due to the out-of-balance weight are still present and since the force, and hence the stress, increases with the* square of the speed, *the speed must be kept low.*

The method of setting the work on the faceplate depends largely on the accuracy required. If we consider the flanged tee-piece shown in fig. 8.8(a), in which dimension Y is important but dimension X is not critical, we can examine two methods of setting the workpiece, to suit these conditions.

As dimension Y is important it would be as well to machine flange A and its associated bore first to give us a datum from which we can work. The casting is first marked-out, establishing the centres of the cored holes as accurately as is practicable and ensuring that there is enough metal on each face to allow for machining, i.e., that all faces will clean up.

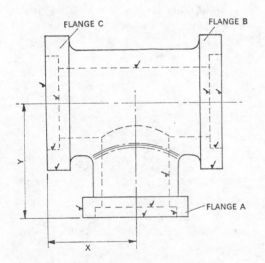

Fig. 8.8(a). Workpiece suitable for machining on faceplate

The hole in flange A is plugged with a piece of wood or lead, and its centre marked in the plug. An angle plate is lightly bolted to the faceplate in the approximate position and the tee-piece is set up on it as shown in fig. 8.8(b). The setting is adjusted until the marked centre is stationary when the faceplate is rotated slowly. Checking with the point of a

161

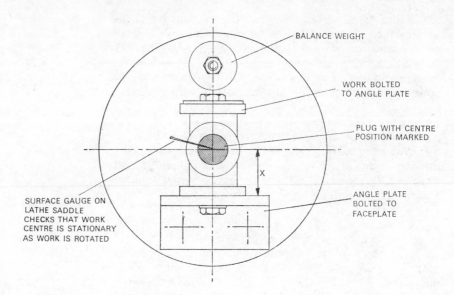

Fig. 8.8(b). Checking setting of workpiece to a marked centre for dimension X

surface gauge against the marked centre is accurate enough for this dimension. The bolts holding the angle plate and the bolts or cramps holding the tee-piece to the angle plate are tightened and the setting given a final check. The lathe spindle is put in a free position so that the balance of the faceplate can be tested as a suitable balance weight is fixed in the appropriate position on it. The balance weight is secured firmly. The hole plug is removed and flange A and its associated bore are then machined, with the facing taken to its marked line so that the distance Y is approximately correct.

Fig. 8.8(c) Pre-setting angleplate to give precise dimension Y

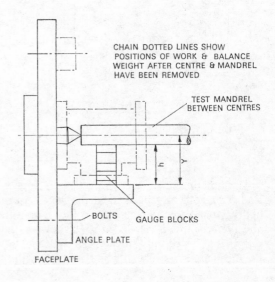

To set for flange B, a test mandrel is placed between the lathe centres and the distance between the angle plate and the mandrel is set with the aid of workshop-grade gauge blocks as shown in fig. 8.8(c). The height h of the gauge blocks is given by:

$$h = \text{Dimension Y} - \tfrac{1}{2} \text{ diameter of mandrel}$$

Whatever other setting may be necessary, dimension Y is now fixed accurately. The workpiece is clamped to the angle plate on the machined datum face of flange A and adjusted sideways until a surface gauge indicates that the outside diameters of flanges B and C are running approximately true. Note that setting an unmachined surface of a casting with a surface gauge is adequate; a dial gauge should never be used on the rough surface of a casting.

A suitable balance weight is mounted in the appropriate position and the tightness of all bolts and cramps is checked. Flange B and its associated bore are then machined, the tee-piece is removed, and the angle plate and balance weight are dismantled. Flange B can now be clamped to the face plate and set true by checking the machined bore with a dial gauge. Flange C and its recess can then be machined. Alternatively, flange B can be held in a four-jaw chuck for the machining of flange C.

The accuracy of work such as this depends very largely on the care taken in setting up. This is unavoidably time-consuming but not nearly so expensive as working in a slapdash way and scrapping an expensive casting.

THE USE OF TOOLMAKERS' BUTTONS

If a workpiece is to be bored on the faceplate and its hole centre is to be positioned in both directions, e.g., from two edges, to a high degree of accuracy, toolmakers' buttons will enable this positional accuracy to be obtained. Consider the part shown in fig. 8.9(a), where the hole centre is to be to a positional tolerance of 0·008 mm diameter from the true position (TP). Assuming the part to be machined accurately all over, apart from the hole, then the procedure would be as follows:

(1) Mark-out the hole centre position with a height gauge:

(2) At the marked centre position, drill and tap a no. 4 BA hole:

(3) Fit a toolmakers' button over the hole but do not fully tighten the screw.

A toolmakers' button is a small, hardened and ground cylinder of steel, usually 10 mm diameter, whose end is accurately square to its cylindrical axis. The hole in the button is well in excess of 5 mm diameter to give ample clearance around the no. 4 BA screw which holds the button in place, so that the button can be adjusted into

163

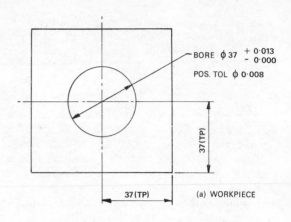

BORE φ37 $^{+\ 0\cdot013}_{-\ 0\cdot000}$

POS. TOL φ 0·008

37 (TP)

37 (TP)

(a) WORKPIECE

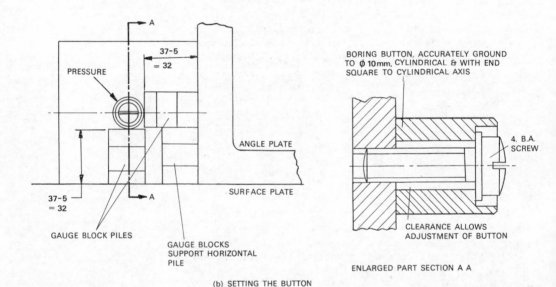

A

37-5
= 32

PRESSURE

ANGLE PLATE

SURFACE PLATE

37-5
= 32

GAUGE BLOCK PILES

GAUGE BLOCKS
SUPPORT HORIZONTAL
PILE

A

BORING BUTTON, ACCURATELY GROUND
TO φ 10mm, CYLINDRICAL & WITH END
SQUARE TO CYLINDRICAL AXIS

4. B.A.
SCREW

CLEARANCE ALLOWS
ADJUSTMENT OF BUTTON

ENLARGED PART SECTION A A

(b) SETTING THE BUTTON

Fig. 8.9. Use of toolmakers' buttons

the correct position even though the drilled hole and screw are slightly out of correct position, as is likely.

(4) Adjust the button position by piles of gauge blocks equal to the TP dimensions minus 5 mm (button radius) as shown in fig. 8.9(b).

(5) When the button position is correct, lock the screw and check that the button position has not changed.

(6) Mount the work on the faceplate (or in a four-jaw chuck) and adjust the position of the work, not the button, until the button runs true as shown by a 0·002 mm dial gauge.

As the button has been positioned accurately on the axis of the required hole the work is now rotating on this axis.

164

(7) Remove the button and drill out the tapped hole, which will probably be eccentric, to a convenient size for boring.

(8) Bore the hole to size.

In practice, a faceplate is better for this work than a four-jaw chuck, since its face can usually be relied upon to be square to the axis of rotation, so that the problem of setting the workface square to the axis of rotation does not arise.

This technique of button boring is not, of course, limited to one hole per workpiece. A job may require a number of holes whose centre distances are critical to be bored in the same workpiece and the correct centres can all be preset with boring buttons and bored one at a time. Such a job could be carried out much more quickly on a jig boring machine, or even on a vertical-spindle milling machine, but it can be done on a lathe by this method.

EXTERNAL WORK SUPPORTS

Apart from gripping and driving the work in a chuck, it is also necessary to ensure that the work is not deflected during cutting through the cutting forces. Work with a large over-hang is usually supported by the tailstock centre but if it is long and slender it requires additional support close to the tool to prevent it from bending. In this case a *travelling steady* is used, as shown in fig. 8.10, bolted to the cross-slide on the saddle and travelling with the tool as it feeds along the work. Note that the steady rests are positioned to withstand the two forces which would bend the work, i.e., the tangential cutting force F_T and the radial force F_R set up by the cutting action.

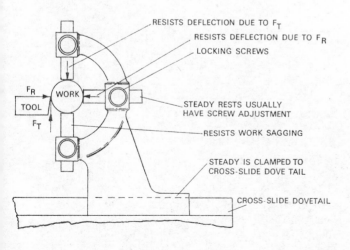

RESISTS DEFLECTION DUE TO F_T
RESISTS DEFLECTION DUE TO F_R
LOCKING SCREWS
F_R
WORK
TOOL
F_T
STEADY RESTS USUALLY HAVE SCREW ADJUSTMENT
RESISTS WORK SAGGING
STEADY IS CLAMPED TO CROSS-SLIDE DOVE TAIL
CROSS-SLIDE DOVETAIL

Fig. 8.10. Travelling steady: used with long slender work to prevent deflection by cutting forces

Consider now a tube 5 ft long in which one end has to be bored to size. Obviously the tailstock cannot be used as an end support, so a *fixed steady* is used, bolted to the bed near the end of the tube. The tube must be set to run true at the chuck end and the fixed steady must be adjusted to support the tube parallel to the lathe bed and parallel to the tool motion, or tapered work will result. These adjustments are carried out with the aid of a dial gauge or a surface gauge, first to ensure that the headstock end is running true and then to check that the gauge reading remains constant in both planes along the length of the tube. A fixed steady is illustrated in fig. 8.11.

The pads or rests of both types of steady act as bearings and are usually made of brass. Like any other bearing they require lubricating from time to time to avoid excessive wear and overheating.

Fig. 8.11. Fixed steady: used for supporting long work which cannot be supported by the tailstock

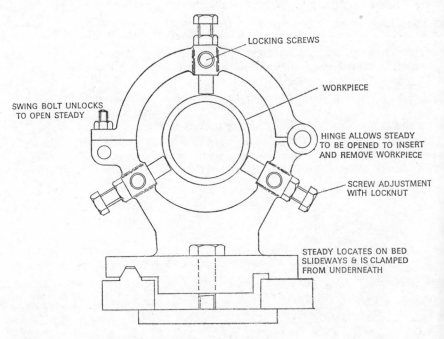

LOCKING SCREWS

WORKPIECE

SWING BOLT UNLOCKS TO OPEN STEADY

HINGE ALLOWS STEADY TO BE OPENED TO INSERT AND REMOVE WORKPIECE

SCREW ADJUSTMENT WITH LOCKNUT

STEADY LOCATES ON BED SLIDEWAYS & IS CLAMPED FROM UNDERNEATH

TAPER TURNING

In order to produce a taper, the tool must be caused to move at an angle to the work axis in the horizontal plane. One method is to set the tailstock off-centre, where a fine taper is required and the work is mounted between centres. However, the main purpose of the tailstock adjustment is to enable the tailstock to be set to give truly parallel work, and to have to reset it after adjustment to produce a taper is

166

often more trouble than it is worth. The two other methods of taper turning both cause the tool direction to be adjusted, not the axis of rotation.

(1) TAPER TURNING WITH THE COMPOUND TOP SLIDE   The top slide on a lathe saddle is normally set parallel to the axis of the work and is used for setting the depth of cut when facing. However, it is mounted on a rotary base, graduated in degrees, and can be swung to produce a taper as shown in fig. 8.12. Note that the slide is swung through the semi-angle of taper, not the included angle.

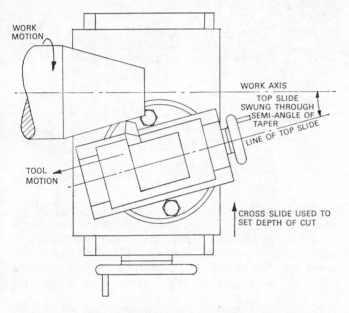

WORK
MOTION

WORK AXIS

TOP SLIDE
SWUNG THROUGH
SEMI-ANGLE OF
TAPER

LINE OF TOP SLIDE

TOOL
MOTION

CROSS SLIDE USED TO
SET DEPTH OF CUT

Fig. 8.12. Generating a taper with the compound top slide

This method has the advantage that it can be used for any angle and direction of taper, but the length of travel is limited and hand feed must be used. The angular scale is of comparatively small diameter and the unit graduations of degrees are therefore small, so the accuracy of setting by the angular scale is somewhat limited. If a test bar or specimen component of the correct taper is first mounted in the lathe, however, the top slide can easily be set to it without reference to the angular scale and will then reproduce the same taper.

(2) THE TAPER-TURNING ATTACHMENT   Many modern lathes have a taper bar fitted at the back of the bed, which can be adjusted through a range of angles to the spindle axis. The bar carries a sliding block which, during taper turning, is attached by a link to the back of the cross-slide, as shown in fig. 8.13. The lead screw of the cross slide

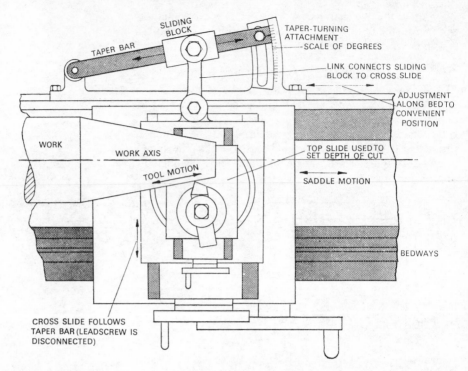

Fig. 8.13. Generating a taper with a
taper-turning attachment

is released so that it no longer controls the depth of cut setting, and the slide is thus freed. When the saddle is moved along the bed the cross-slide now follows the taper bar, so that the tool moves parallel to the bar and a taper is produced. The top slide is swung through 90° to lie at right angles to the work axis so that it can be used to apply the cut.

The length of the taper bar allows large degree divisions on its degree scale, which enable accurate setting to be carried out, an angle vernier often being incorporated. The taper is produced by the movement of the saddle under power feed, giving improved and controllable surface finish, and a long taper is possible. It is, however, limited to semi-angles of taper of about 15° (30° included angle).

THE EFFECT OF INCORRECT TOOL SETTING ON TAPER TURNING For cutting a taper it is important that the tool height should be set correctly to the spindle axis. If the tool is set low, two faults will occur:

    (1) the angle of taper will be incorrect:

    (2) the taper will not be straight but will be a hollow
          curve of complex mathematical shape.

Both effects can be demonstrated by deliberately setting a tool too low. Let us assume that the tool has been set 2·0

168

mm low, and the machine is set to produce a taper whose radius increases by 5 mm for each 10 mm traversed (taper of 0·5 mm per mm on radius, or 1 mm per mm on diameter).

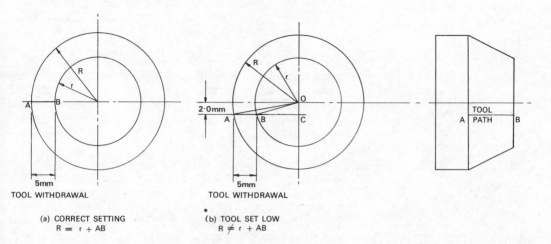

(a) CORRECT SETTING
$R = r + AB$

(b) TOOL SET LOW
$R \neq r + AB$

Fig. 8.14. Effect of incorrect tool setting on taper turning

However high or low the tool has been set, it will still move away from the machine centre line by 5 mm for each 10 mm traversed. Thus in figs. 8.14(a) and (b) the distance AB is 5 mm for each 10 mm traversed. In fig. 8.14(a) the outside radius $R = r + AB$, but in fig. 8.14(b) this statement is not true. Let $r = 20$ mm, and the tool be set 2·0 mm low. The machine is traversed 10 mm, so the tool withdraws a distance AB = 5 mm.

$$\text{In } \triangle \text{ OBC, } (BC)^2 = r^2 - (OC)^2$$
$$= (20)^2 - (2·0)^2$$
$$(BC)^2 = 396 \text{ mm}^2$$
$$BC = 19·9 \text{ mm}$$
$$AC = AB + BC$$
$$= 5 + 19·9 \text{ mm}$$
$$= 24·9 \text{ mm}$$
$$R^2 = (AC)^2 + (OC)^2$$
$$= (24·9)^2 + (2·0)^2$$
$$= 620·01 + 4·0$$
$$= 624·01 \text{ mm}^2$$
$$R = \sqrt{624·01} = 24·98 \text{ mm}$$

But for a correct taper R should be $(r + 5·0)$ mm or 25 mm. Thus there is an error of 0·02 mm per mm length on radius, or 0·04 mm per mm length on diameter simply due to setting the tool low.

The straightness of the taper can easily be checked by sighting it against a straight edge, and if the tool has been set too low the resulting curve is readily seen.

169

SCREWCUTTING IN THE LATHE

Generating processes have already been discussed and copying processes mentioned. The screwcutting process is a combination of the two in which:

(1) the thread form is copied from the tool shape:

(2) the thread helix is generated from the machine motions.

SCREWCUTTING TOOLS The form of thread is copied from the tool, which must therefore be ground to the correct shape, i.e., to the correct thread angle and nose radius. It must also be set correctly, square to the work and at the correct height, and must not have top rake, or the thread form will be incorrect.

TOOL GRINDING The tool shape can be ground by hand to give cutting clearance and the correct angles can be obtained by comparing them with a screwcutting plate gauge. The same gauge is used for setting the tool square to the work surface, as shown in fig. 8.15. It is important to note that a hand-ground single-point cutting tool must not have a rake angle or the form will not be reproduced correctly.

Fig. 8.15. Setting a screwcutting tool in the lathe

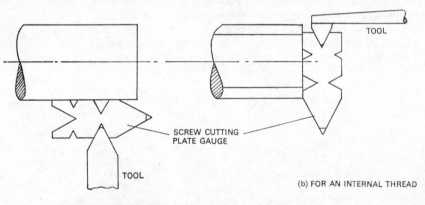

SCREW CUTTING PLATE GAUGE

TOOL

(a) FOR AN EXTERNAL THREAD

(b) FOR AN INTERNAL THREAD

Fig. 8.16 shows, greatly exaggerated, the effect of grinding top rake on a screwcutting tool.

The tool has been fed in an amount AB, giving a depth of cut of D in. But due to the top rake angle the tool actually contacts the work surface at C, not at B. Projecting these points down on to a plan view of the tool we see that the tool flanks contact the work surface at C and C, giving a width of form W. This however is produced at a distance D backwards from the point, and the angle produced, which is

170

the angle actually cut, is shallower than that of the tool itself.

If a screwcutting tool is to be given top rake it must be

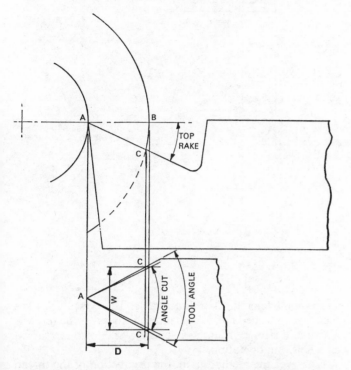

Fig. 8.16. Effect of top rake on thread form

'form ground', that is, the tool form must be corrected for the rake angle. Circular form-tools of the type shown in fig. 8.17 are made by Johansson Ltd., and are corrected for rake angle, and also for the clearance effect of a circular tool. They must be set accurately with the tool centre a specified height above the work centre, and the cutting edge on centre, for the correct form to be produced. That shown in fig. 8.17 bears the inscription $\frac{W \times 8}{3-10°}$. This means that it is of Whitworth form of 8 threads per inch and if the tool centre is 3 mm above the work centre, the cutting edge being on centre, the clearance angle and form will be correct and the rake angle will be 10°. A special toolholder is required so that the tool can be tilted into the line of the helix angle of the thread. If these tools are set and used correctly a much more accurate screw thread form results, with a better surface finish than can be produced by a single-point tool.

A further advantage of this type of tool is that it produces the correct crest radius on the Whitworth-form thread (the crest radius is optional on the Metric series) and with a

171

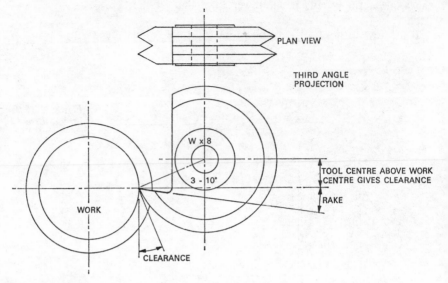

PLAN VIEW

THIRD ANGLE PROJECTION

W x 8

3 - 10°

TOOL CENTRE ABOVE WORK CENTRE GIVES CLEARANCE

RAKE

WORK

CLEARANCE

Fig. 8.17. Circular form-tool for screwcutting

single-point tool this is impracticable. The crest radius has then to be finished either by hand chasing or, if the screw is a standard size, by running a solid die-nut down the thread as a finishing operation.

Whatever the method used, the production of the thread form is a copying process, so that any errors in the tool or in its setting will be reproduced or reflected in the thread form.

GENERATING THE THREAD HELIX A screw thread takes the form of a *helix*, which is a geometric shape defined as the path of a point which moves around a cylinder and at the same time moves along the cylinder so that the linear movement is proportional to the angular movement around the cylinder. If therefore we wish to generate a true helix on a lathe we must arrange for the tool to advance along the bed at a constant speed while the work rotates at a constant speed.

The *pitch* of a screw thread is defined as the distance from a point on one thread to a similar point on the next thread, measured parallel to the axis. Thus, if we measure the length containing a certain number of threads:

$$\text{Pitch} = \frac{\text{length}}{\text{No. of threads}} \text{ in units of mm per thread}$$

Note: Metric threads usually only quote pitch in mm.

172

In screwcutting, the saddle is driven by the leadscrew of the lathe and this in turn is driven from the machine spindle through a gear train, shown in diagrammatic form in fig. 8.18. Note that the idler has no effect on the gear ratio, but is provided to give the DRIVEN gear on the leadscrew the same direction of rotation as the DRIVER gear on the spindle. The gear ratio between the DRIVER gear and the DRIVEN gear clearly affects the speed of rotation of the leadscrew in relation to that of the spindle. It thus affects the traverse of the saddle and, in fact, controls the pitch and the helix of the thread being cut. To determine the pitch, therefore, we are concerned about the numbers of teeth on the driver and driven gears.

Fig. 8.18. Simplified diagram of drive train from work to tool for screw cutting

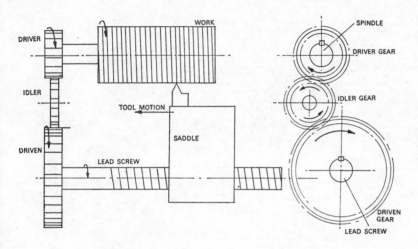

Consider a lathe whose leadscrew is of 5 mm pitch cutting a thread of 1 mm pitch, and let the tool move along the work 50 mm. For these conditions the work must make 50 revolutions and the leadscrew 10.

Thus: $\dfrac{\text{Revs of work}}{\text{Revs of leadscrew}} = \dfrac{50}{10}$

As the spindle is rotating faster than the leadscrew it will have the smaller gear, and therefore

$\dfrac{\text{No of teeth on DRIVER gear}}{\text{No of teeth on DRIVEN gear}} = \dfrac{10}{50} = \dfrac{1}{5}$

or

$\dfrac{\text{Driver}}{\text{Driven}} = \dfrac{1}{5}$

Considering the 1 mm pitch thread and the 5 mm pitch leadscrew we find that:

$\dfrac{\text{Driver}}{\text{Driven}} = \dfrac{\text{Pitch of Work}}{\text{Pitch of Leadscrew}}$

173

It is not practicable to use a gear with less than 20 teeth, and a gear larger than 120 teeth becomes unwieldy, so most machines are provided with gears ranging from 20 teeth to 120 teeth in steps of 5 teeth, the 20-tooth gear being duplicated. We must therefore find a pair of gears which give us the ratio $\frac{1}{5}$ out of those available.

Fig. 8.19. Simple train of screwcutting gears showing adjustments for correct mesh

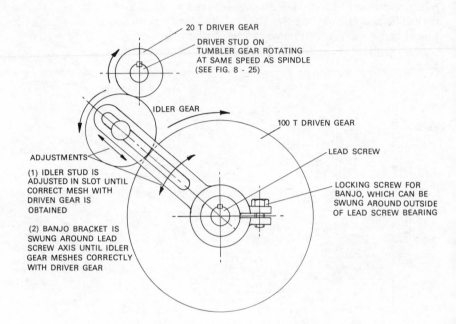

20 T DRIVER GEAR

DRIVER STUD ON TUMBLER GEAR ROTATING AT SAME SPEED AS SPINDLE (SEE FIG. 8 - 25)

IDLER GEAR

100 T DRIVEN GEAR

LEAD SCREW

ADJUSTMENTS

(1) IDLER STUD IS ADJUSTED IN SLOT UNTIL CORRECT MESH WITH DRIVEN GEAR IS OBTAINED

(2) BANJO BRACKET IS SWUNG AROUND LEAD SCREW AXIS UNTIL IDLER GEAR MESHES CORRECTLY WITH DRIVER GEAR

LOCKING SCREW FOR BANJO, WHICH CAN BE SWUNG AROUND OUTSIDE OF LEAD SCREW BEARING

In calculations of this nature it is important to remember that the fraction must remain unchanged and that whatever is done to the numerator of the equation must also be done to the denominator.

$$\text{Thus } \frac{\text{DRIVER}}{\text{DRIVEN}} = \frac{1}{5} \times \frac{20}{20} = \frac{20}{100}$$

so we can use a 20-tooth driver and a 100-tooth driven gear set up as shown in fig. 8.19. This is a *simple train* in which the idler gives the leadscrew the same direction of rotation as the machine spindle, so that a right-hand thread, like that of the leadscrew, is cut.

Now consider a thread of 0·7 mm pitch to be cut on a lathe with a 3 mm leadscrew.

$$\frac{\text{DRIVER}}{\text{DRIVEN}} = \frac{0·7}{3} \times \frac{50}{50} = \frac{35 \text{ teeth}}{150 \text{ teeth}}$$

We do not have a 150-tooth gear, so a *compound train* with two pairs of gears is required. The gears can be found by factorising the fraction into:

174

$$\frac{\text{DRIVER}}{\text{DRIVEN}} = \frac{35}{150} = \frac{5 \times 7}{10 \times 15}$$ Multiplying top and bottom by 5×5 we get

$$= \frac{5 \times 7}{10 \times 15} \times \frac{5 \times 5}{5 \times 5}$$

$$= \frac{25 \times 35}{50 \times 75}$$

These gears are set up as shown in fig. 8.20.

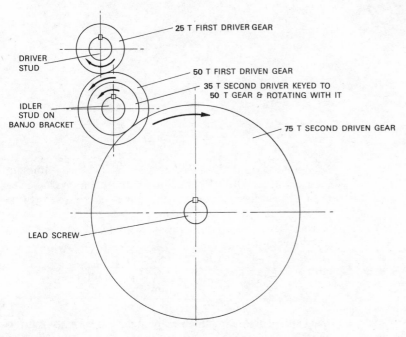

Fig. 8.20. Compound screwcutting train to cut 27 T.P.I. thread on lathe with leadscrew of 4 T.P.I.

25 T FIRST DRIVER GEAR

DRIVER STUD

50 T FIRST DRIVEN GEAR

35 T SECOND DRIVER KEYED TO 50 T GEAR & ROTATING WITH IT

IDLER STUD ON BANJO BRACKET

75 T SECOND DRIVEN GEAR

LEAD SCREW

Such a train may not be convenient on account of the large size difference between the gears, and in fact, they would not mesh if the arrangement were $\frac{25}{75} \times \frac{35}{50}$. It is always wise to put the largest driven gear on the leadscrew. Note that in fig. 8.20 the second 35-tooth gear and the 50-tooth gear on the idler stud are not idlers but are keyed together and part of the gear ratio.

If we wish to change these gears, we can do anything to suit our convenience so long as we do not change their overall ratio, and any of the following trains will give the same result.

$$\frac{25}{100} \times \frac{70}{75}; \frac{20}{60} \times \frac{70}{100}; \frac{25}{60} \times \frac{70}{125} \text{ etc.}$$

From these, the most convenient train should be selected, bearing in mind that trains of larger gears tend to give a smoother traverse to the saddle and a more uniform screw thread than trains of smaller gears.

175

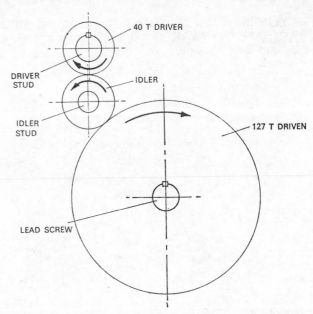

Fig. 8.21. Simple train for cutting metric thread of 2 mm pitch on lathe with leadscrew of ¼ in pitch (4 T.P.I.)

METRIC THREADS ON INCH LATHES. Although industry in the United Kingdom is proceeding to change to the metric system, it is likely that for many years it will be necessary to cut threads on lathes having inch pitch lead-screws. Let us assume a thread of 2 mm pitch is to be cut on a lathe with a leadscrew of ¼ in pitch.

$$\frac{DRIVER}{DRIVEN} = \frac{\text{Pitch of work}}{\text{Pitch of leadscrew}}$$

$$= \frac{2 \text{ mm}}{\frac{1}{4} \text{ in}}$$

We cannot divide millimetres by inches so we must convert the 2 mm to inches.

Now 1 in = 25·4 mm or 1 mm $= \dfrac{1}{25\cdot4 \text{ in}}$

Therefore 2 mm $= \dfrac{2}{25\cdot4} \text{ in}$

$$\frac{DRIVER}{DRIVEN} = \frac{\frac{2 \text{ in}}{25\cdot4}}{\frac{1}{4} \text{ in}} = \frac{8}{25\cdot4} \times \frac{5}{5}$$

$$= \frac{40 \text{ teeth}}{127 \text{ teeth}}$$

This ratio is set up in fig. 8.21.

The number 127 is a prime number, i.e., its only factors are 1 and 127, and it cannot be subdivided. Thus to cut an accurate metric thread on a lathe which has a leadscrew whose pitch is based on inches we require 127-tooth gear in the gear train.

Any gear larger than 120 teeth is rather unwieldy, but if

176

we divide the ratio by two we get $\dfrac{20 \text{ teeth}}{63\frac{1}{2} \text{ teeth}}$, and a gear with an odd half tooth is an apprentice's joke! If we approximate and use a 63-tooth gear we get an error of 1 in 127 or approximately 8 parts per 1000. Thus the pitch would be in error by about 8 mm in each metre of length.

If, however, the 63-tooth gear is used as a driver in the example worked out above, we get:

$$\frac{\text{DRIVER}}{\text{DRIVEN}} = \frac{8}{25\cdot4}\ \text{Substituting 63 for the driver we get}$$

$$\therefore \frac{63}{\text{DRIVEN}} = \frac{8}{25\cdot4}$$

$$\therefore \text{DRIVEN} = \frac{25\cdot4 \times 63}{8}$$

$$= \frac{1600\cdot2}{8}$$

Dropping the fraction $0\cdot2$ gives us an error of only 1 in 8000 and therefore:

$$\text{DRIVEN} = \frac{1600}{8} = 200$$

$$\therefore \frac{\text{DRIVER}}{\text{DRIVEN}} = \frac{63}{200}$$

$$= \frac{9 \times 7}{10 \times 20}$$

$$= \frac{4\cdot5 \times 3\cdot5}{5 \times 10} \times \frac{10 \times 10}{10 \times 10}$$

$$\therefore \frac{\text{DRIVER}}{\text{DRIVEN}} = \frac{45 \times 35}{50 \times 100}$$

This ratio is shown set up in fig. 8.22.

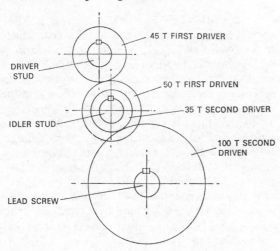

45 T FIRST DRIVER

DRIVER STUD

50 T FIRST DRIVEN

35 T SECOND DRIVER

IDLER STUD

100 T SECOND DRIVEN

LEAD SCREW

Fig. 8.22. Approximate gear train for metric thread of 2 mm pitch giving a pitch error of 1 part in 8000. This is based on a 63T driver, which is not in fact used (see text)

Thus, we now do not need the 63-tooth gear and the approximation used gives an error of only 1 part in 8000, which is negligible for most screw threads.

SAFETY NOTE *One of the most efficient devices for crushing fingers is a gear train driven by a powerful motor.* Never *start up a lathe after changing the screwcutting gears without replacing the guard.*

MODERN SCREWCUTTING LATHES

THE NORTON GEARBOX Most modern lathes do not require a new gear train to be fitted for each thread pitch to be cut. They are fitted with a quick-change type of gearbox, often known as a Norton gearbox, which covers all the ratios likely to be wanted.

As shown in fig. 8.23, it has an input shaft driven from the headstock which drives a long roll gear R. Through the tumbler gears T_1 and T_2, shown in the end view, gear R can be engaged with any one of the gears numbered 1 to 9 in the 'cone cluster' of gears. A sliding cluster of three gears a, b and c is engaged with gears 10, 11 and 9 respectively on the cone cluster shaft to give three alternative output ratios.

Since this three-speed output gearbox is compounded with the nine speeds from the cone cluster, the gearbox provides a total of 27 different gear ratios which cover a very wide range of screw pitches and satisfy most needs.

In the engagements shown in fig. 8.23, the drive is from R to cluster gear no. 1, and from gear no. 11 to gear b and the overall gear ratio is:

$$\frac{\text{Roll gear R}}{\text{Gear 1}} \times \frac{\text{Gear 11}}{\text{Gear } b}$$

ENGAGEMENT OF SADDLE The saddle feed for normal turning is produced by a feed shaft which is geared to the leadscrew and drives through a worm and wheel arrangement at the saddle. The revolutions of the feed shaft are thus in a constant ratio with those of the leadscrew, and the sliding feeds, which are expressed in cuts per inch or inches per revolution of work, are in a fixed ratio to the number of threads per inch obtained when the same gear train is used for screwcutting rather than sliding.

In screwcutting, the leadscrew is engaged by a split-nut arrangement at the saddle. The phosphor-bronze nut which engages the leadscrew is split and the two halves slide vertically in dovetail slides. The half nuts are moved to the engaged or disengaged position by a cam plate, shown in fig. 8.24, which is turned by the operating lever on the outside of the saddle apron.

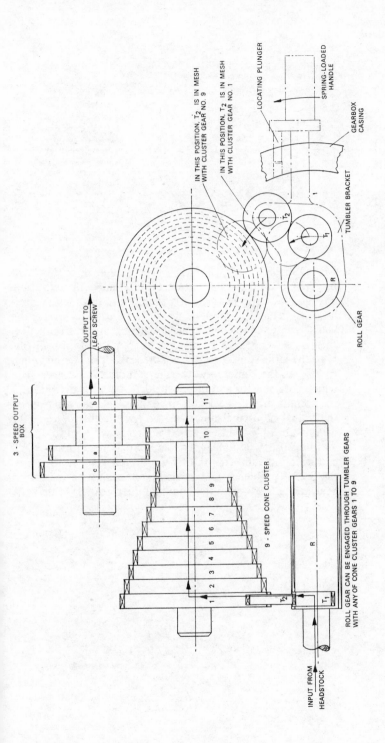

Fig. 8.23. Layout of Norton-type screwcutting gearbox

IN THIS POSITION, T_2 IS IN MESH WITH CLUSTER GEAR NO. 9

IN THIS POSITION, T_2 IS IN MESH WITH CLUSTER GEAR NO. 1

LOCATING PLUNGER

SPRING-LOADED HANDLE

GEARBOX CASING

TUMBLER BRACKET

ROLL GEAR

END VIEW OF CONE CLUSTER & TUMBLER GEAR ARRANGEMENT
(3 - SPEED GEARS, a, b AND c NOT SHOWN)

OUTPUT TO LEAD SCREW

3 - SPEED OUTPUT BOX

9 - SPEED CONE CLUSTER

ROLL GEAR CAN BE ENGAGED THROUGH TUMBLER GEARS WITH ANY OF CONE CLUSTER GEARS 1 TO 9

INPUT FROM HEADSTOCK

Fig. 8.24. Split-nut method of engaging leadscrew, shown disengaged

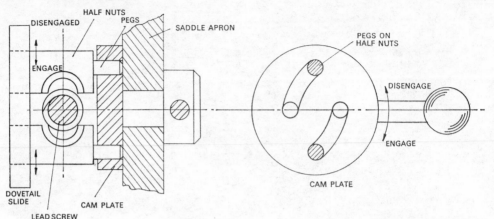

LEADSCREW REVERSAL   The tumbler gear shown in fig. 8.23 is used to allow gears of different diameters to be engaged with another gear at a fixed centre distance. A similar arrangement of tumbler gears can be used to reverse the leadscrew, to enable left-hand threads to be cut. In practice, the first driver gear of a screwcutting train is not fitted directly to the lathe spindle but is mounted on a driver stud which rotates at the same speed as the spindle. The driver gear which rotates with and drives the driver stud is driven from the spindle driving gear and since they have the same speed they must be of the same size. To reverse this driven gear we must be able to insert an extra idler at will and to do this we interpose two tumbler gears, mounted on a bracket which can swing around the axis of the driven gear as shown in fig. 8.25. Tumbler gear A is always in mesh with the driven gear and in mesh with its fellow tumbler gear B. In fig. 8.25

Fig. 8.25. Tumbler gearbox for reversing direction of rotation of leadscrew

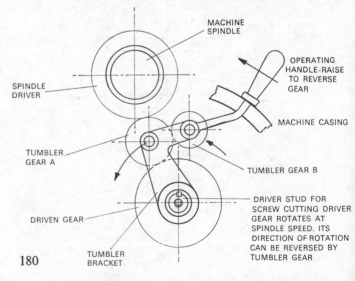

180

the drive is direct through tumbler gear A and tumbler gear B is idle. If the tumbler bracket is moved upwards, tumbler gear A rolls around the driven gear until it is out of mesh with the driver gear, and tumbler gear B moves into mesh with the driver, reversing the direction of the driven gear. Thus the two trains available are:

$$\text{B not engaged}$$

Forward: Driver——→A——→Driven
Reverse: Driver——→A——→B——→Driven

THE CHASING DIAL When a screw thread is being cut in the lathe, the traverse of the saddle is caused by the engagement of the leadscrew by the split-nut device described on page 180 and shown in fig. 8.24.

Once the first cut has been taken and a helix produced on the work, the leadscrew must subsequently be engaged in such a way that the tool always picks up the same helix on successive cuts until the thread is completed. The *chasing dial*, fitted usually at the left-hand end of the saddle, enables this to be done correctly. It consists of a disc which rotates when the saddle is stationary but stops rotating when the saddle is traversed by the leadscrew. The disc has four equi-spaced marks numbered 1 to 4 with intermediate marks, giving eight in all.

With leadscrews of 5 mm pitch, it is driven by a 16-tooth worm wheel which engages the leadscrew and makes $\frac{1}{16}$ of a turn for each turn of the leadscrew. The leadscrew can thus be engaged as each mark passes the index on the saddle and

Fig. 8.26. Chasing dial for screw cutting

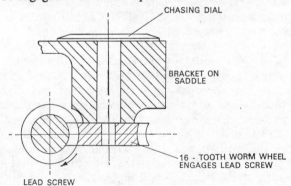

CHASING DIAL

BRACKET ON SADDLE

16 - TOOTH WORM WHEEL ENGAGES LEAD SCREW

LEAD SCREW

2

3

1 REV. OF DIAL REQUIRES
16 REV. OF LEAD SCREW

INDEX MARK ON SADDLE

4

PLAN VIEW OF DIAL

181

also halfway between each mark, giving sixteen positions on the dial where the leadscrew can be engaged. The plan view and drive to the dial are shown in fig. 8.26. As each successive cut is taken, the tool must be dropped in, i.e., the leadscrew must be engaged, only when the work thread and the leadscrew thread coincide. Since it takes 16 revolutions of the leadscrew to give one revolution of the chasing dial, one revolution of the dial represents an 80 mm length of leadscrew moving past a fixed point or index mark. If we lay off this 80 mm length of leadscrew, with its 16 threads to scale, against a length of 2·50 mm pitch work thread as shown in fig. 8.27, we see that each leadscrew thread, representing a position on the dial at which the leadscrew can be engaged, coincides with a work thread and that this is true for all work threads which divide exactly into 5. This means that for such threads we can engage the leadscrew at any point.

If we now compare the leadscrew scale with a thread whose pitch will divide exactly into 10 mm (two marks), we find that only every other point coincides, so we can only drop in at every other position, i.e., at every mark on the dial but not at intermediate positions.

Comparing a scale representing a thread pitch which will only divide exactly into 20 mm (four marks), we find coincidence at each fourth position, i.e., every second mark on the chasing dial, so we can drop in at every numbered mark but not at intermediate marks or unmarked places on the dial.

If the pitch will only divide exactly into 40 mm, e.g., 8 mm, we find that we can engage at only two positions, i.e., every alternate number on the dial. If we start cutting on number 2 we can only engage on number 2 or number 4, and if we start on 1 we can continue on 1 or 3. A thread which will only divide exactly into 80 mm, e.g., 16 mm pitch, allows only one engaging position on the dial, since it does not coincide anywhere on our scales except at each end. Other threads will not coincide anywhere on the scales except at the single position at which they were engaged. This means that if the leadscrew is disengaged it will not 'pick up' the work thread again. Therefore such threads should be cut without disengaging the leadscrew; the tool is withdrawn with the leadscrew still engaged and the machine reversed to traverse the tool back to the beginning of the thread.

All these scales are shown in fig. 8.27 which refers to a 5 mm pitch leadscrew and a 16 tooth wormwheel with an eight-mark (16-position) dial.

A little thought will show that a rule for finding the divisions of a dial suitable for 'dropping in' is:

The pitch to be cut must exactly divide into the length of leadscrew represented by the fraction of a revolution of the dial at which it may be dropped in.

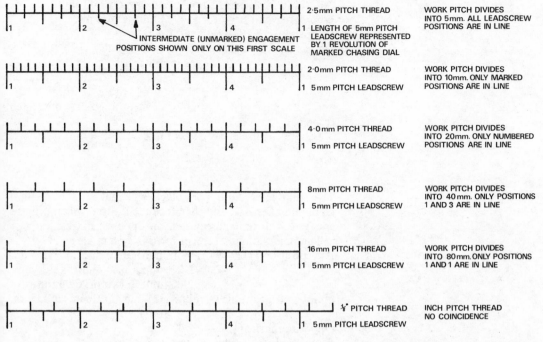

The figure shows six horizontal scales with the following labels:

- 2·5mm PITCH THREAD — LENGTH OF 5mm PITCH LEADSCREW REPRESENTED BY 1 REVOLUTION OF MARKED CHASING DIAL — WORK PITCH DIVIDES INTO 5mm. ALL LEADSCREW POSITIONS ARE IN LINE
- INTERMEDIATE (UNMARKED) ENGAGEMENT POSITIONS SHOWN ONLY ON THIS FIRST SCALE
- 2·0mm PITCH THREAD — 5mm PITCH LEADSCREW — WORK PITCH DIVIDES INTO 10mm. ONLY MARKED POSITIONS ARE IN LINE
- 4·0mm PITCH THREAD — 5mm PITCH LEADSCREW — WORK PITCH DIVIDES INTO 20mm. ONLY NUMBERED POSITIONS ARE IN LINE
- 8mm PITCH THREAD — 5mm PITCH LEADSCREW — WORK PITCH DIVIDES INTO 40mm. ONLY POSITIONS 1 AND 3 ARE IN LINE
- 16mm PITCH THREAD — 5mm PITCH LEADSCREW — WORK PITCH DIVIDES INTO 80mm. ONLY POSITIONS 1 AND 1 ARE IN LINE
- ¼″ PITCH THREAD — 5mm PITCH LEADSCREW — INCH PITCH THREAD NO COINCIDENCE

Fig. 8.27. Scales showing coincidence between a leadscrew thread of 5 mm pitch and work threads of various pitches as indicated by marked positions on chasing dial

In fact the suitable fractions are $1/n$; $\frac{1}{8}$; $\frac{1}{4}$; $\frac{1}{2}$; and $1/1$ revolutions of the dial, where n is the number of teeth on the wormwheel and hence the number of possible positions for engagement.

This rule can be written as a mathematical expression:

$$\frac{\text{Length of leadscrew per rev. of dial}}{\text{pitch to be cut}} \times \frac{1}{N} = I$$

where I must be the smallest whole number (integer) obtainable if $1/N$ is one of the above fractions. E.g., if a 16 tooth, 8 mark dial, is used with a 5 mm pitch leadscrew find the positions on the dial at which the leadscrew may be engaged when cutting a thread having a pitch of 4 mm.

Length of leadscrew per rev of dial $= 5 \text{ mm} \times 16 = 80 \text{ mm}$

$$\frac{80}{4} \times \frac{1}{N} = I$$

The value of $1/N$ which will make I the smallest whole number is $\frac{1}{4}$. Thus the leadscrew may be engaged every $\frac{1}{4}$ turn or, from fig. 8.27, every numbered mark.

Working from this principle, the pitches that can be cut by engaging the leadscrew at various positions of this chasing dial-leadscrew system are:

Any position (1/16 rev.): 0·25 mm; 0·5 mm; 1·0 mm; 1·25 mm; 2·50 mm; 5·0 mm

183

Alternate positions ($\frac{1}{8}$ rev.): 2·00 mm; 10·00 mm
Numbered marks ($\frac{1}{4}$ rev.): 4·00 mm; 20·00 mm
Opposite marks ($\frac{1}{2}$ rev.): 8·00 mm
Same mark always (1/1 rev.): 16·00 mm

For other threads the leadscrew must not be disengaged.

Another combination of leadscrew and chasing dial in use is a 6 mm pitch leadscrew used with a 20 tooth wheel and a 20 mark dial. Again consider a thread of 4 mm pitch to be cut.

Length of thread per rev. of dial $= 20 \times 6$ mm $= 120$ mm

$$\frac{120}{4} \times \frac{1}{N} = I$$

The suitable fraction $1/N$ which will make I the smallest whole number is $\frac{1}{2}$, and therefore the leadscrew can only be engaged with the chasing dial on opposite marks.

The points of engagement for this system are:
Any position (1/20 rev.): 0·50 mm; 0·60 mm; 0·75 mm; 1·00 mm; 1·20 mm; 1·50 mm; 2·00 mm; 3·00 mm; 6·00 mm
Numbered positions ($\frac{1}{4}$ rev.): 1·25 mm; 2·50 mm; 5·00 mm; 10·00 mm
Opposite marks ($\frac{1}{2}$ rev.): 4·00 mm
Same mark each time (1/1 rev.): 8·00 mm

For other pitches the leadscrew must not be disengaged.

If the pitches available in either of these systems are compared with the pitches specified in the ISO Metric thread series, it will be seen that only about half of those specified are catered for. To overcome this problem lathe manufacturers have adopted various solutions which allow the length of leadscrew per revolution of the dial to be changed. One manufacturer supplies interchangeable wormwheels to fit the chasing dial. Another drives the dial from the leadscrew and wormwheel via a small gearbox built into the saddle. It may well be that this is a case where adoption of the metric system will increase rather than decrease complexity due to the small number of factors of 10.

SCREWCUTTING WITHOUT THE CHASING DIAL
If a screw is to be cut on a lathe without a chasing dial some other means must be adopted to ensure that the tool always engages the thread correctly after the first cut has been taken. Two methods are available.

(1) At the end of each cut the leadscrew is not disengaged but the tool is withdrawn and the lathe is reversed until the tool is back at the tailstock end of the bed. The tool is then advanced to the correct depth for the next cut and the machine restarted forwards.

SAFETY NOTE *Always traverse back well beyond the start of the cut so that, when the tool starts to cut, any backlash in the leadscrew has been taken up.*

(2) Marking the machine. The tool will only re-engage the thread correctly if:
- (a) the position of the saddle,
- (b) the angular (rotational) position of the work and
- (c) the angular position of the leadscrew are all three exactly the same as they were for the start of the original cut.

These requirements can be met if, before the first cut is taken, the leadscrew is engaged and a mark is made or a stop is fitted on the bed so that the saddle can always be returned to its original starting position. At the same time the leadscrew is marked against a convenient datum on the saddle and the work-holding device is marked relative to the headstock. The first cut is taken and the saddle is returned to its starting position. The machine is now pulled over by hand until the other two marks coincide and the leadscrew is engaged. The tool can then be advanced to the correct depth for the next cut and the machine started in the sure knowledge that the tool will re-engage the first cut, cut correctly on this and, with the same preliminaries, on successive cuts.

TAILSTOCK OPERATIONS

The hole in the front end of the tailstock barrel is bored to a Morse taper, so that the tailstock can be used in performing all the operations that can be carried out on a drilling machine. The tailstock centre is simply replaced by a drill chuck, drill, spot-facing tool or counterbore etc., while the workpiece is rotated at the headstock.

The commonest operation is drilling, and the barrel is usually marked with a scale so that the depth of the drilled hole can be controlled by noting the scale reading when the drill touches the work and continuing to drill until the required depth is reached. A drill tends to wander and cannot always be relied on to produce a straight concentric hole, and if the geometry of the hole is important, the hole should be bored out to ensure concentricity and straightness.

Reaming can be carried out from the tailstock but a reamer will only bring a hole to size and will not necessarily correct its geometry. Thus, where possible, the hole should be bored to correct its alignment before reaming. If the hole has not been bored and is out of true, the side loads on the reamer may result in an oversize hole or even break the reamer. The reamer should therefore be supported in a holder which allows it to 'float', or by the tailstock centre, so that it can follow the hole. In the latter case the work is kept stationary and the reamer is rotated by a wrench.

When a hole is to be tapped, the tap can also be supported by the tailstock centre to ensure that it is kept square to the work. The tap is turned by a tap wrench and followed up by the centre to ensure continued support to the tap.

SUMMARY

This Chapter has made no attempt to explain in detail how to operate a lathe but has tried rather to cover the principles involved. The only way to become proficient in the operation of any machine tool is to understand its underlying principles and then use it. For the student, this practical experience is normally provided during off-the-job training at work, and the principles are explained and demonstrated in College workshops.

The principles involved in the centre lathe will be found to apply in other machines used for large work, such as a vertical boring machine, which is basically a lathe standing on its headstock, and on high-production machines such as capstan and turret lathes, single-spindle and multi-spindle automatic lathes, chucking automatics etc. None of these machines will produce work of correct geometry unless the basic alignments are correct. Parallel work is produced only when the tool motion is parallel to the axis of rotation. Flat facing occurs only when the tool moves at right angles to the axis of rotation, and a true taper is produced only when the tool is set correctly.

SAFETY NOTE *The workpiece on a lathe rotates, usually at high speed and with a considerable amount of power behind it. All rotating and moving parts represent a hazard, and the hands should be kept clear. Loose clothing can be picked up and drawn in, and a necktie in a rotating mechanism is as efficient as, if slower than, a hangman's noose. Do not be tempted to touch swarf, stationary or moving, with the bare hands or a deep cut can result; stop the machine and use a swarf-hook. Coolant should be fed to the job through pipes, not brushed on, and the machine should be allowed to stop itself —hands are too delicate and precious to use as brake bands on the chuck. Eyes need protection; swarf is hot and sharp, and if it gets into the eye can cause damage. A man with a lot of luck and quick reflexes catches the swarf particle between his eyelids where it sticks and blisters them, which is most painful.* Wear safety glasses.

9
The Shaping Machine

THE GENERATING PROCESS IN SHAPING

The shaping machine may be defined as a machine tool designed to produce flat surfaces by a generating process which uses a reciprocating single-point tool. These surfaces may be horizontal, vertical or at some angle between the two.

The essential motions for the machine to fulfil this function are as shown in fig. 9.1 and are as follows.

(1) *Reciprocating motion of tool*
This motion supplies the power for cutting and must be adjustable for speed, length of stroke and position of stroke over the workpiece.

(2) *Feed motion for horizontal surfaces*
This is the motion of the table across the front of the machine, which may be hand or power fed.

(3) *Feed motion for vertical surfaces*
This is normally a hand-fed motion of the toolpost in a head slide mounted on the front of the ram head, but it may be power fed.

(4) *Feed motion for inclined surfaces*
This is a variant of (3) above; the head slide is set over at the angle of inclination required and the tool feeds down at this angle.

(5) *Vertical table adjustment*
This is an additional motion not normally used for feed purposes but to adjust the height of the table to accommodate wide variations in the height of the work.

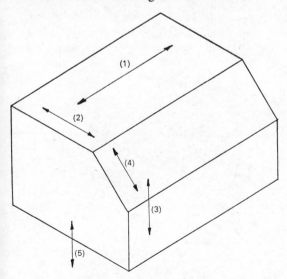

Fig. 9.1. Basic motions of tool and work on a shaping machine

The flat horizontal surfaces generated by the machine must normally be parallel with opposite surfaces, and vertical surfaces must normally be at right angles to adjacent horizontal surfaces. If these conditions are to be realised, other requirements in the alignments of the basic motions must be satisfied. For flat, parallel surfaces, motions (1) and (2) must be straight and parallel to the table surface. If the vertical surfaces are to be square then motion (3) must be at right angles to the table surface. This statement presumes that the work-holding methods adopted ensure that the underside of the work rests on or is parallel to the surface of the table, and we shall discuss how this is ensured in a later section. Basically, the motions and alignments listed are built into the machine.

As was emphasised in Chapter 8 on the lathe, a generating process requires two motions, the cutting motion and the feed motion, with all other adjustments locked while the cutting proceeds. In the case of horizontal surfaces, motions (1) and (2) produce the surface, and motion (3) provides adjustment for depth of cut. Vertical surfaces are produced by motions (1) and (3), and motion (2) provides adjustment for depth of cut. Inclined surfaces use motion (1) and motion (3) inclined to give motion (4), and the depth of cut is again adjusted by motion (2).

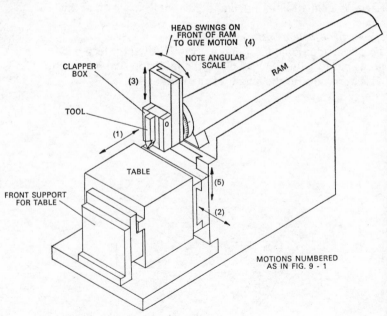

Fig. 9.2. Block diagram of shaping machine indicating basic features and motions. Note slideways provided for motions

Fig. 9.2 shows how these alignments are produced on the actual machine. The ram, which carries the head slide at the front, moves forwards and backwards in long slideways which are at right angles to the vertical slide in the front of the machine. The head slide gives the vertical tool feed for motion (3) and is mounted on a rotary head so that it can be inclined to give motion (4). The table is mounted on a horizontal feed slide, which in turn is mounted across the main vertical slide, so that the table surface is parallel to the ram slide in both directions. The horizontal feed motion (2) is provided by moving the table across the horizontal slide, which is parallel to its own upper surface (this requirement for parallelism is also found in the milling machine; see Chapter 10).

Finally, the vertical adjustment of the table, motion (5), is provided by the vertical slide but this is an adjustment, not normally used for feeding.

TESTING ALIGNMENTS

The shaping machine is a notable example of the advantage of checking the machine alignments before starting to use the machine, rather than checking machined work and finding too late that it is in error. Two of the important alignments for parallelism and squareness can be adjusted and may therefore be incorrect.

(a) *Parallelism*

The cross-slide motion of the table cannot normally be adjusted, but the work will only be parallel in a fore-and-aft

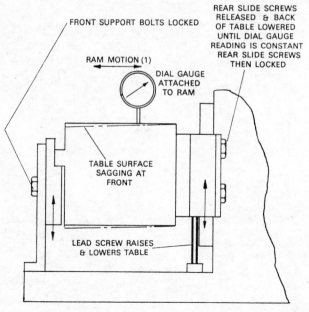

Fig. 9.3. *Checking and correcting table sag after height adjustment*

189

direction if the table surface is parallel to the ram motion. Through wear in the front vertical slide and the weight of the table, there is a tendency for the table to sag at the front every time the vertical adjustment (5) is used. The amount of sag can be checked by mounting a dial gauge in the tool post and noting the reading as it is traversed over the table. If the front is low the bolts on the front table support should be locked and the rear of the table lowered by the vertical adjustment until the reading on the dial gauge is constant. This alignment error and its correction are shown in fig. 9.3.

(b) *Squareness*

When adjacent horizontal and vertical faces are to be shaped at one setting, the vertical face will be machined square only when the vertical feed motion (3) of the head slide is truly square to the table surface. When this slide has been 'set over' to machine an inclined surface, it can be readjusted to the perpendicular position with the aid of a dial gauge and try square, as shown in fig. 9.4.

A mistake sometimes made is to run a dial gauge over a surface, in position, after it has been machined and then

Fig. 9.4. Motion of head slide for squareness to table. The dial gauge reading will remain constant only when the tool-slide motion is perpendicular to the table surface

Note: A cylindrical square may be used instead of an engineer's square as shown

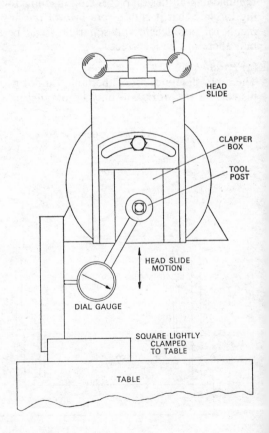

HEAD SLIDE

CLAPPER BOX

TOOL POST

HEAD SLIDE MOTION

DIAL GAUGE

SQUARE LIGHTLY CLAMPED TO TABLE

TABLE

190

wonder why, although the dial gauge reading is constant, the surface is later found to be not parallel or square to other surfaces previously machined. The offending surface was, of course, parallel with the tool motion, and since the dial gauge had the same motion as the tool this 'test' shows nothing except that the operator does not realise or know what he is doing. Too many people believe that a dial gauge has magic powers and give the advice 'Clock it up' with complete abandon and disregard for what may be involved.

THE DRIVE MECHANISM OF THE SHAPING MACHINE

For its reciprocating motion the ram of the shaping machine must have:

(a) a speed adjustment to cater for different materials and lengths of stroke;
(b) an adjustment for length of stroke;
(c) an adjustment for position of stroke;
(d) a quick-return action.

(b) and (c) are necessary to reduce the time spent in 'cutting air'. The tool does no useful work on the return stroke and the drive is arranged so that the return stroke is quicker than the forward stroke. The quick-return mechanism is incorporated in the drive, which is shown in fig. 9.5.

(a) *Speed of stroke*

Common with many reciprocating motions, the linear ram motion is obtained from the rotary motion of a driving wheel or *bull wheel* which rotates once per stroke. The number of strokes per minute therefore depends on the revolutions per minute of the bull wheel, which are controlled by a gear box driven from the motor.

(b) *Length of stroke*

The drive from the bull wheel to the ram is by means of a *slotted link*, as shown in fig. 9.5. A driving pin in the bull wheel engages a block which slides in the slotted link so that, as the wheel rotates, the link is caused to rock about its pivot in the base of the machine. The top end of the slotted link moves forwards and backwards in an arc and thus cannot be connected directly to the ram, so a *compensating link* is introduced. To alter the length of stroke, the radius at which the pin on the bull wheel rotates must be adjustable from outside the machine. This is achieved by mounting the pin on an inner block which fits in a radial slide in the bull wheel and is moved along the slide by a leadscrew. The leadscrew is rotated by a pair of bevel gears, as shown, and the spindle which operates them passes through the centre of the bull wheel spindle to the outside of the machine where it can be adjusted by a detachable handle.

191

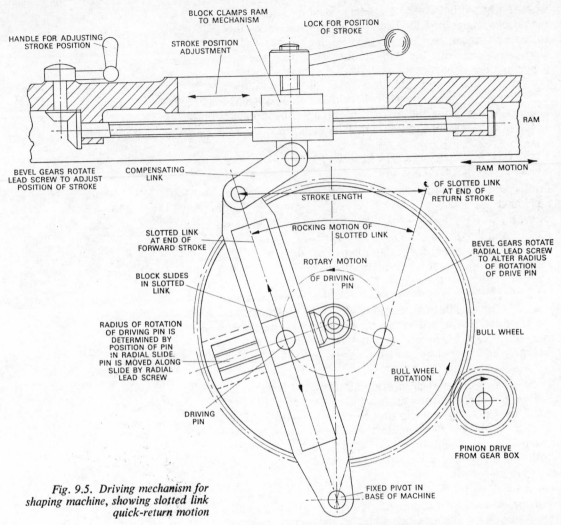

HANDLE FOR ADJUSTING
STROKE POSITION

BLOCK CLAMPS RAM
TO MECHANISM

STROKE POSITION
ADJUSTMENT

LOCK FOR POSITION
OF STROKE

RAM

RAM MOTION

BEVEL GEARS ROTATE
LEAD SCREW TO ADJUST
POSITION OF STROKE

COMPENSATING
LINK

STROKE LENGTH

℄ OF SLOTTED LINK
AT END OF
RETURN STROKE

ROCKING MOTION OF
SLOTTED LINK

SLOTTED LINK
AT END OF
FORWARD STROKE

BEVEL GEARS ROTATE
RADIAL LEAD SCREW
TO ALTER RADIUS
OF ROTATION
OF DRIVE PIN

ROTARY MOTION

BLOCK SLIDES
IN SLOTTED
LINK

OF DRIVING
PIN

RADIUS OF ROTATION
OF DRIVING PIN IS
DETERMINED BY
POSITION OF PIN
ÌN RADIAL SLIDE.
PIN IS MOVED ALONG
SLIDE BY RADIAL
LEAD SCREW

BULL WHEEL

BULL WHEEL
ROTATION

DRIVING
PIN

PINION DRIVE
FROM GEAR BOX

FIXED PIVOT IN
BASE OF MACHINE

*Fig. 9.5. Driving mechanism for
shaping machine, showing slotted link
quick-return motion*

SAFETY NOTE *Always ensure that this stroke-adjusting
handle is removed before starting the machine. It will rotate
at the same rate as the strokes of the ram and can do considerable damage if left on its spindle—and possibly more if it
flies off.*

(c) *Adjusting the position of the stroke*
The length of the stroke is adjusted to the length of cut required but it is also necessary to adjust the position of the
cut to suit the position of the workpiece, i.e., to adjust the
position of the stroke with respect to the table. The ram
carries a longitudinal slot through which a stud passes,
screwed into a block beneath and with a locking handle on
top, as in fig. 9.5. This block is connected through the com-

192

pensating link to the end of the slotted link of the main drive. When the locking handle is tightened, the ram is secured firmly to the block and thus moves with the end of the slotted link.

When the locking handle is freed and the block is released, the block can be moved to a new position in the ram slot by a leadscrew within the ram, which is operated through a pair of bevel gears driven by a rotating handle on top of the ram. This allows the ram position to be adjusted as required. After the adjustment, the block is re-locked.

(d) *The quick-return action*

In order to save time on the return stroke, when no work is being done, the drive mechanism provides a quick-return action, the geometry of which is shown in fig. 9.6(a). The driving pin on the bull wheel moves at a constant speed but, because the slotted link is pivoted at the bottom end, the pin travels through a larger angle A on the forward stroke than angle B on the return stroke. Since the pin is moving at constant speed it thus takes longer to traverse the forward stroke than the return stroke and, in fact, the ratio

$$\frac{\text{time for cutting stroke}}{\text{time for return stroke}} = \frac{\text{angle for cutting}}{\text{angle for return}} = \frac{A}{B}$$

Fig. 9.6. Geometry of quick-return motion

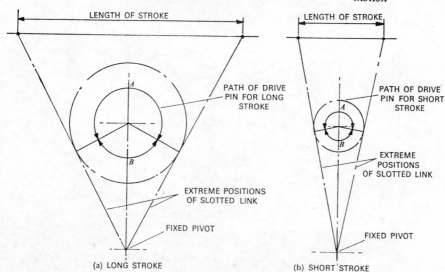

LENGTH OF STROKE

LENGTH OF STROKE

PATH OF DRIVE PIN FOR LONG STROKE

PATH OF DRIVE PIN FOR SHORT STROKE

A

B

A

B

EXTREME POSITIONS OF SLOTTED LINK

EXTREME POSITIONS OF SLOTTED LINK

FIXED PIVOT

FIXED PIVOT

(a) LONG STROKE

(b) SHORT STROKE

If we examine the conditions for a shorter stroke, shown in fig. 9.6(b), we see that these angles, A and B, are more nearly equal and therefore as the length of the stroke is reduced the quick-return action is much less marked.

It is of interest to note that the Butler Machine Tool Co., Ltd., will provide a perspex cover plate for the drive of a shaping machine, with interior illumination, which enables the details of the drive mechanism to be seen clearly.

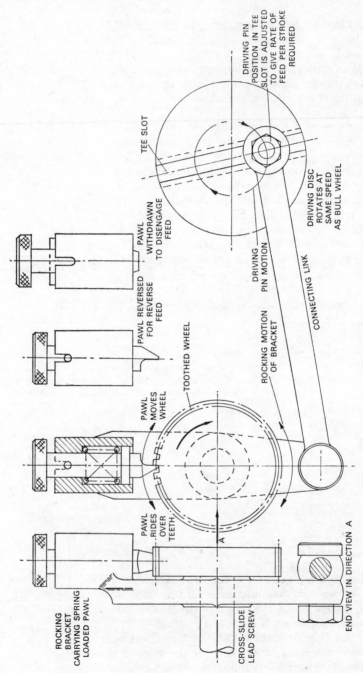

TEE SLOT

DRIVING PIN
POSITION IN TEE
SLOT IS ADJUSTED
TO GIVE RATE OF
FEED PER STROKE
REQUIRED

DRIVING DISC
ROTATES AT
SAME SPEED
AS BULL WHEEL

DRIVING
PIN MOTION

CONNECTING LINK

ROCKING MOTION
OF BRACKET

PAWL
WITHDRAWN
TO DISENGAGE
FEED

PAWL REVERSED
FOR REVERSE
FEED

TOOTHED WHEEL

PAWL
MOVES
WHEEL

PAWL
RIDES
OVER
TEETH

ROCKING
BRACKET
CARRYING SPRING
LOADED PAWL

A

CROSS-SLIDE
LEAD SCREW

END VIEW IN DIRECTION A

Fig. 9.7. Feed mechanism for shaping machine

THE FEED MECHANISM OF THE SHAPING MACHINE

Automatic feed is provided to the table cross-slide of a shaping machine, since this is usually the motion required to feed across the greatest width of work face. Unlike that of a lathe, where a continuous feed is used, the shaper feed must be intermittent, occurring during each return stroke of the tool, and it is therefore necessary to turn the cross-slide leadscrew a part of a turn on each return stroke. If we require a feed of 0·1 mm per stroke and the table cross-slide leadscrew has a pitch of 5·0 mm, the screw must rotate $\frac{0·1}{5·0} = \frac{1}{50}$ revolution per stroke. If a toothed wheel of 50 teeth is fitted to the end of the leadscrew, a rotation of the amount of one tooth will give the required feed of 0·1 mm per stroke, rotation to the extent of two teeth will give a feed of 0·2 mm per stroke and so on.

This feed of a few teeth at a time can be arranged by mounting a ratchet pawl on the toothed wheel in a bracket which rocks about the leadscrew axis, the rocking motion being provided by a connecting link attached to a crankpin on a disc which rotates at the same speed as the bull wheel. This arrangement is shown in fig. 9.7 and it will be noted that the crankpin radius can be adjusted to give a greater or lesser amount of rock to vary the feed as required.

The ratchet pawl is square on one side and bevelled on the other, so that it carries the toothed wheel as it rocks in one direction but rides over the teeth as it rocks in the other direction. Thus feed can be obtained in either direction by turning the pawl through 180°, or can be disengaged by withdrawing the pawl so that the cross-pin rests on top of the bracket and lifts the pawl clear from the toothed wheel.

TOOL MOUNTING IN THE SHAPING MACHINE

The shaping machine is one of the few machine tools in common use which is based on a reciprocating action, others being the slotting machine, the punch shaping machine, the gear shaping machine and the planing machine. In all these machines the tool would rub on the work during the return stroke and lose its edge if clamped rigidly. On the shaping machine, rubbing of the tool is avoided by use of the clapper box. On the front of the head slide is a *back block* which is mounted on a pivot screw near the bottom and fastened at the top by a screw which passes through a quadrant slot, as shown in fig. 9.8. This enables the back block to be swung at an angle on either side of the vertical. The *clapper block* is fitted in front of the back block between two side cheeks to which it is attached by a cross pin, or pivot pin, near the

195

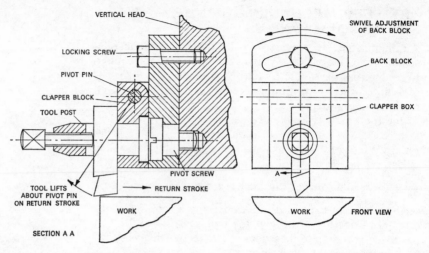

Fig. 9.8. General arrangement of clapper box

top, thus forming a *clapper box* in which the clapper block can swivel. The *toolpost*, which carries the cutting tool, is attached to the front of the clapper block.

On the cutting stroke, the clapper block sits firmly on the back block in its box, but on the return stroke, the tool, touching the workpiece, is lifted slightly, the clapper block being swung about its pivot pin. When the tool drops clear of the work the clapper block falls back into its box with a clapping sound, which gives the box its name. Some modern machines have a tool lifting device operated by a Bowden cable, which clears the tool on the return stroke.

As stated above, the clapper box can be swung about its pivot screw to either side of the line of the tool slide and it is this facility which enables vertical and inclined surfaces to

Fig. 9.9(a). Clapper box inclination and its geometry

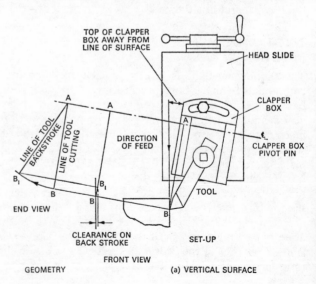

196

be machined. *The top of the clapper box is always swung away from the surface being machined*, as shown in the various diagrams of fig. 9.9. An examination of the geometry shows that this swings the tool clear of the surface on the return stroke instead of allowing it to dig in, as it would if the box was not correctly adjusted.

In fig. 9.9(a), which shows the clapper box set for cutting a vertical surface, line AB on the set-up is the radius from the centre line of the pivot about which the tool point swings. The action is shown at the left-hand side of the drawing as a geometric layout, and the end view of the geometry shows the line AB in the position AB_1 as the tool swings up on the back stroke. Projecting this position back to give the point B_1 in the front view reveals the clearance of the tool from the surface. Fig. 9.9(b) shows a corresponding set-up and geometry for the cutting of an inclined surface.

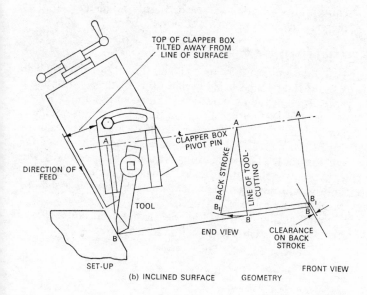

Fig. 9.9(b).

TOP OF CLAPPER BOX TILTED AWAY FROM LINE OF SURFACE

CLAPPER BOX PIVOT PIN

DIRECTION OF FEED

TOOL

BACK STROKE

LINE OF TOOL-CUTTING

CLEARANCE ON BACK STROKE

END VIEW

FRONT VIEW

SET-UP

(b) INCLINED SURFACE   GEOMETRY

THE SWAN-NECKED SHAPER TOOL The clapper box is a device to prevent the tool rubbing into the work on the back stroke. The swan-necked tool, shown in fig. 9.10, is sometimes used to prevent digging-in and chatter on the forward stroke. If the cutting load becomes excessive the tool bends slightly about point A and a straight tool bending about this point cuts deeper and increases the cutting load. This causes more bending, deeper cutting and increased load, and the process is progressive, making conditions worse until something gives or the depth of cut becomes too great and the work possibly undersize.

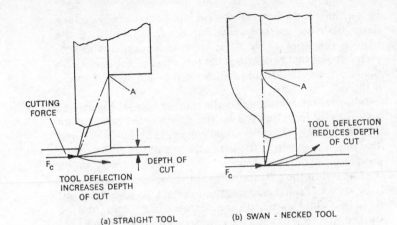

CUTTING
FORCE

A

TOOL DEFLECTION
REDUCES DEPTH
OF CUT

F_c

DEPTH OF
CUT

TOOL DEFLECTION
INCREASES DEPTH
OF CUT

F_c

(a) STRAIGHT TOOL

(b) SWAN - NECKED TOOL

Fig. 9.10. Effect of tool deflection in straight and swan-necked tools

The swan-necked tool bending about point A moves away from the work, and the cut and load are reduced until an equilibrium situation is reached with no danger and no increase in depth of cut.

METHODS OF HOLDING WORK

Large workpieces may be clamped directly to the machine table if their shape lends itself to this method, with clamp bolts fitted in the table tee-slots. The clamps should always be clear of the surface to be machined so that a complete cut can be taken over it: never clamp a workpiece so that the cut has to be stopped and the clamp removed to allow the cut to proceed. Incidentally it is surprising how many students suggest this during an examination, though they probably would never consider it if confronted with a shaping machine and the workpiece.

Suitably-shaped parts can be clamped or bolted to an angle plate which is itself bolted to the table.

Fig. 9.11. Shaping machine vice

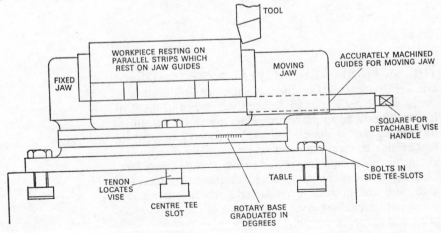

TOOL

WORKPIECE RESTING ON
PARALLEL STRIPS WHICH
REST ON JAW GUIDES

MOVING
JAW

ACCURATELY MACHINED
GUIDES FOR MOVING JAW

FIXED
JAW

SQUARE FOR
DETACHABLE VISE
HANDLE

BOLTS IN
SIDE TEE-SLOTS

TENON
LOCATES
VISE

CENTRE TEE
SLOT

TABLE

ROTARY BASE
GRADUATED IN
DEGREES

The Machine Vice

The commonest method of work-holding is probably by the machine vice, as shown in fig. 9.11. The machine vice is a piece of precision equipment which maintains the machine alignments and should be treated with care. It usually locates by a tenon in one of the table tee-slots and is mounted on a rotary base, graduated in degrees, so that it can be swung to any angular position, between jaws parallel to the stroke and jaws at right angles to the stroke. When the vice is in good condition, the fixed jaw is set accurately at right angles to the table and will remain so if the vice is used carefully. The moving jaw may lose its alignment through wear, so that when a surface is to be machined square to a previously-machined one, the machined surface should be held against the fixed jaw. If the opposite surface is rough or irregular it may tend to cant the work and a circular bar between it and the moving jaw will enable the fixed jaw to take control and maintain squareness, as shown in fig. 9.12.

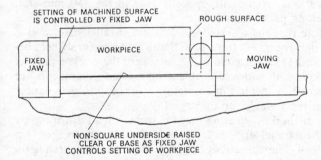

Fig. 9.12. Use of round bar to obtain a square setting in machine vice

The conditions usually required of a workpiece machined on a shaping machine, unless otherwise specified, are:
    (1) opposite faces must be parallel:
    (2) adjacent faces must be mutually perpendicular:
    (3) the finished part must be within specified limits of size.

In machining a rectangular block there are two possible procedures.

(1) Machine one surface, machine the opposite surface parallel to it and to the correct thickness, and repeat for all three pairs of opposite surfaces. This is not a good method; if a squareness error results there is no material left for its correction.

(2) Machine three sides mutually perpendicular to each other. The remaining three can then be machined parallel to their opposite sides and to the correct size. This method should be adopted, since it provides maximum material for obtaining initial squareness, after which machining the other sides parallel and to size is relatively easy.

199

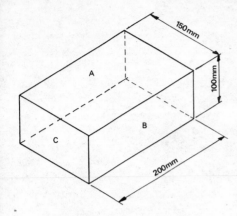

Fig. 9.13. Rectangular block to be machined all over to size and to be square and parallel

Thus, for a block to be finished 200 mm by 150 mm by 100 mm, shown in fig. 9.13, the procedure would be:

(1) Set block on parallel strips in vice and clean up face A.

(2) Turn block in vice with face A against fixed jaw and clean up face B.

Check faces A and B for squareness

(3) Turn vice so that jaws are at 90° to ram motion; grip block with face A downwards on parallel strips and B against fixed jaw, with C overhanging. Clean up face C and check for squareness with A and B. Any correction in the vertical plane can be made by adjusting the head slide on the ram. Note the need to swing over the clapper box.

(4) When face C is square in both directions turn the work end for end and machine the other end of the length of 200 mm.

(5) Without removing work from vice, turn vice through 90° and machine top face parallel to face A and to 100 mm size.

(6) Turn work so that face B is downwards on parallel strips and machine its opposite face to the 150 mm size, checking parallelism.

Note that the workpiece is held on parallel strips and if it is lightly tapped down until the strips are securely held between the vice base and the underside of the work, a parallel workpiece should result, unless the machine alignments are incorrect. A method of correcting error in the alignment for parallelism was given on page 189.

A method of ensuring that the work is held down tightly on the parallel strips is to use hold-down strips, as shown in fig. 9.14. These are wedge-shaped strips of metal, resting on parallel strips, between the vice jaws and the work. The angle A is greater than 90° so that the thrust of the jaw is directed obliquely downwards along the line between the points of contact at the work and the jaw. This force, being inclined,

Fig. 9.14(a). Use of hold-down strips

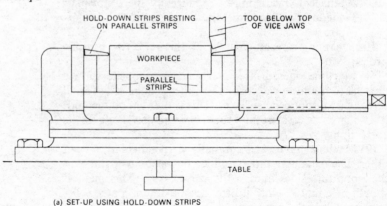

HOLD-DOWN STRIPS RESTING ON PARALLEL STRIPS
TOOL BELOW TOP OF VICE JAWS
WORKPIECE
PARALLEL STRIPS
TABLE

(a) SET-UP USING HOLD-DOWN STRIPS

200

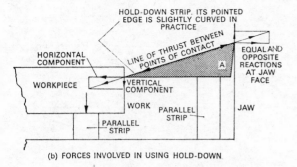

Fig. 9.14(b).

(b) FORCES INVOLVED IN USING HOLD-DOWN

has a vertical component which pushes the work down on to the parallel strips, and a horizontal component which grips the work. The actual clamping force is no less than that with a full vice jaw since the frictional force, which resists the tool cutting force, does not depend on the area of contact (see *Science for Mechanical Technicians*, Book 1, by M. G. Page).

Fig. 9.15. Adjustment of shaping machine vice to give parallel vertical faces

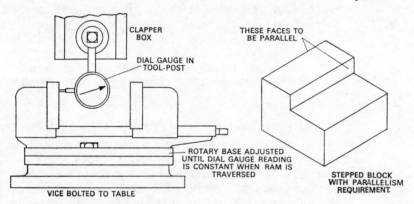

If the workpiece is to be stepped as shown in fig. 9.15, parallelism of the vertical faces can be achieved by attaching a dial gauge to the toolpost and running it along the fixed jaw of the vice, adjusting the setting of the vice until a constant dial gauge reading is obtained.

A component which has to have a face machined at a compound angle is shown in fig. 9.16. The compound angle can be produced by setting the vice at 15° from its square alignment and the head slide to 30°, with the clapper box tilted correctly away from the surface to be machined.

When practicable, the vice should be used with its jaws along the line of stroke. This generally allows a longer stroke to be used which is more economic than a greater number of

201

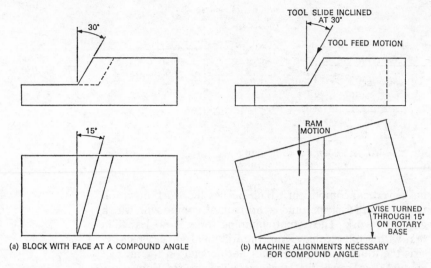

30°

TOOL SLIDE INCLINED AT 30°

TOOL FEED MOTION

15°

RAM MOTION

VISE TURNED THROUGH 15° ON ROTARY BASE

(a) BLOCK WITH FACE AT A COMPOUND ANGLE

(b) MACHINE ALIGNMENTS NECESSARY FOR COMPOUND ANGLE

Fig. 9.16. Shaping a face at a compound angle

short strokes because, as already shown, the quick-return action is more marked with a long stroke and, additionally, less time is spent 'cutting air'. Apart from this, the layout of the machine demands that when the jaws are across the line of stroke the cutting force is generally taken by the moving jaw and leadscrew of the vice. This should normally be avoided on any machine tool vice, if the jaw alignments are to be maintained. It must again be emphasised that a machine vice is a piece of precision equipment and should be treated with care for its accuracy to be maintained.

SHAPING MACHINE SPEEDS AND FEEDS

The cutting speed on a shaping machine should normally be less than the figures quoted in Chapter 6, for two reasons. Firstly, the cut is an interrupted one and the tool undergoes a shock load each time the cut is taken. Secondly, the ram does not move at a constant speed but reaches maximum speed at the mid-point of each stroke, the speed being zero at the beginning and end of the stroke. Thus the maximum speed reached by the tool is much greater than the average speed, on which calculations are based. Another factor to consider is the quick-return action which, as previously shown, is much more marked for a long stroke than a short one.

Bearing these factors in mind, consider a machine which is roughing a mild steel workpiece. Assume that the average cutting speed is 20 m/min and that the return stroke is twice as fast as the forward stroke.* If the workpiece is 340 mm long and allowing 30 mm overrun at each end:

* This quick return ratio is an assumption for this example only. It must not be assumed that the speed of the return stroke is generally twice that of the forward stroke.

202

Length of stroke $= 400$ mm

$\therefore$ Time for cutting $= \dfrac{400 \text{ mm}}{20 \text{ m/min} \times 1000} = \dfrac{1}{50}$ min

$\therefore$ Time for return $= \frac{1}{2}$ time for cutting $= \dfrac{1}{100}$ min

$\therefore$ Total time per stroke $= \dfrac{1}{50} + \dfrac{1}{100}$ min $\quad = \dfrac{3}{100}$ min

$\therefore$ Strokes per minute $= \dfrac{100}{3} = 33$ strokes/min approx.

A suitable feed for a roughing cut would be of the order of 0·25 mm per stroke, reduced to 0·10 mm per stroke for finishing unless a special broad-nosed tool is used, with a shallow cut and feed equal to the tool width.

Assume the workpiece described above is 100 mm wide and that a depth of cut of 5 mm is taken with a feed of 0·25 mm per stroke.

Over a 100 mm width, a feed of 0·25 mm per stroke would require 400 strokes, the approach and runout being neglected.

At 33 strokes/min the time required would be

$$\dfrac{400 \text{ strokes}}{33 \text{ strokes/min}} = 12 \cdot 1 \text{ min}$$

This should be compared with the same situation in milling on page 226.

GENERAL SAFETY NOTE *It is difficult to guard the cutting tool on a shaping machine because of its motion, and hands must be kept clear. The swarf produced can fly all over the place and be a hazard if it hits anybody, apart from being uncomfortable to walk on. It can be collected in a simple tray, made as shown in fig. 9.17, the tongues of which slide into the table tee-slots.*

Above all it should be remembered that the ram, on either the forward or return stroke, takes a lot of stopping, and will not stop for a delicate object like the human body. If it hits anybody who walks too near they usually get dented with painful results. The machine should be positioned so that nobody walks behind it in the path of the ram. Care should also be taken that clothing is not caught by the handle or other part of the feed mechanism.

It must again be emphasised that any machine tool is safe as long as it is respected and mastered, but stupidity and lack of respect will rapidly meet with painful retribution.

Fig. 9.17. Sheet-metal swarf tray and guard for shaping machine

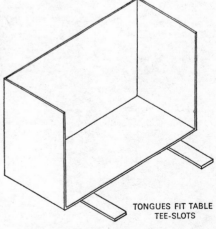

TONGUES FIT TABLE
TEE-SLOTS

10
The Milling Machine

CUTTING AND FEED MOTIONS

A milling machine may be defined as one whose main function is to produce flat surfaces with a rotary cutter, by either a copying or a generating process. This statement is true of both horizontal and vertical-spindle machines, and for each the basic table motions of the machine are the same, as shown in figure 10.1(a).

The motions are:

No. 1. *Rotation of Cutter*

As stated in Chapter 6, the largest force applied to a milling cutter is the tangential force F_t, which is therefore the motion through which the power is applied.

No. 2. *Longitudinal Table Motion*

This is the feed motion which, in conjunction with motion no. 1, produces the cutting action.

No. 3. *Vertical Table Motion*

This motion is used to set the depth of cut. On vertical-spindle machines it is also usually possible to feed the cutter axially downwards, an additional motion, no. 5.

No. 4. *Transverse Table Motion*

This crossward motion of the table is used to position the work under the cutter. It may occasionally be used as a cross-feed.

Fig. 10.1(a). Basic motions of tool and work on milling machine

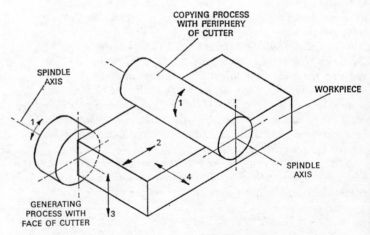

(a) MOTIONS REQUIRED FOR PLAIN HORIZONTAL MILLING MACHINE

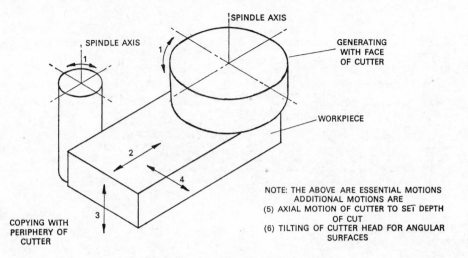

SPINDLE AXIS

SPINDLE AXIS

GENERATING
WITH FACE
OF CUTTER

WORKPIECE

NOTE: THE ABOVE ARE ESSENTIAL MOTIONS
ADDITIONAL MOTIONS ARE
(5) AXIAL MOTION OF CUTTER TO SET DEPTH
OF CUT
(6) TILTING OF CUTTER HEAD FOR ANGULAR
SURFACES

COPYING WITH
PERIPHERY OF
CUTTER

(b) MOTIONS REQUIRED FOR VERTICAL-SPINDLE
MILLING MACHINE

Fig. 10.1(b).

During cutting, only motions 1 and 2 are normally used, the other motions, i.e., adjustments, being locked.

It might appear at first sight that horizontal machines always utilise a copying process and vertical-spindle machines a generating process, but this is not so. With a face milling cutter mounted in the spindle, or a side-and-face cutter on the arbor, the horizontal machine can be employed for a generating process. Correspondingly, the periphery of an end mill copies a vertical surface when used in a vertical-spindle machine as shown in fig. 10.1(b).

MACHINE ALIGNMENTS

Certain relationships must exist and be maintained between these motions if the geometry of workpieces produced is to meet requirements. These relationships are the machine alignments and the important ones are given below. The diagrams in figs. 10.2 to 10.6 illustrate the errors induced if the alignments are incorrect.

Fig. 10.2. Taper produced by table motion being non-parallel to table surface

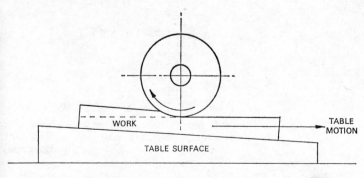

WORK

TABLE
MOTION

TABLE SURFACE

205

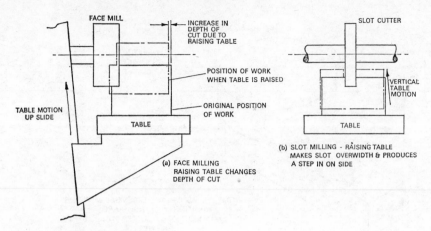

Fig. 10.3. *Effect of vertical table motion being out of square to table surface spindle axis*

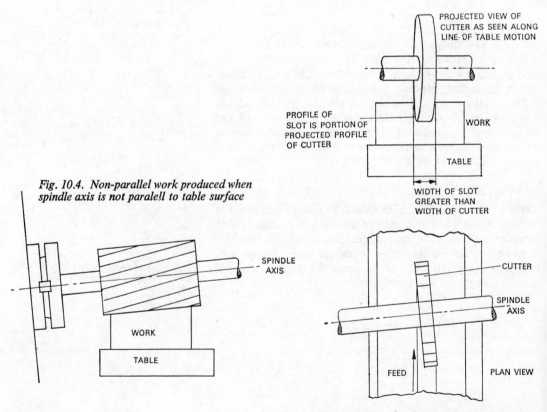

Fig. 10.4. *Non-parallel work produced when spindle axis is not paralell to table surface*

Fig. 10.5. *Shape of slot produced when spindle axis is not at right angles to table feed motion (much exaggerated)*

206

(1) TABLE SURFACE MUST BE PARALLEL TO ITS OWN MOTION This alignment applies to all machines in which the feed motion is produced by moving the table, e.g., surface grinders and shaping machines. Any error produces non-parallelism of the work as shown in fig. 10.2.

(2) CENTRE TEE-SLOT MUST BE PARALLEL TO TABLE MOTION The centre tee-slot is used to locate various milling fixtures such as the vice, rotary table and dividing head. If this alignment is not correct an incorrect datum is being used for the various operations.

With this in mind it is obviously necessary to ensure that the tee-slot and the fixture tenons which locate in it do not suffer damage, since a burr can destroy alignment locally even though the alignment is elsewhere correct.

(3) VERTICAL TABLE MOTION MUST BE AT RIGHT ANGLES TO TABLE SURFACE If all other alignments are correct, an error in this alignment will produce a side component of motion as the table is raised, and errors in depths of cut and widths of slots, as shown in fig. 10.3.

The above alignments are essential in all milling machines. Those peculiar to *horizontal machines* are:

(4) SPINDLE AXIS MUST BE PARALLEL TO TABLE SURFACE If this alignment is incorrect, non-parallel work across the surface will be produced and the machined surface will not be square to other faces, as shown in fig. 10.4.

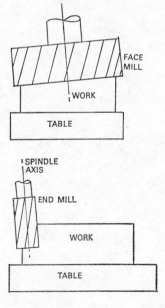

Fig. 10.6. *Effect of vertical spindle axis being out of square with table surface across table*

(5) SPINDLE AXIS MUST BE AT RIGHT ANGLES TO TABLE MOTION If this alignment is incorrect, slots produced by side-and-face cutters or by slotting cutters and saws will be too wide. The width of slot will be equal to the projected width of the cutter across the line of table movement, as shown in fig. 10.5. Note that the slot produced will not necessarily be out of alignment.

The most important alignment peculiar to *vertical-spindle machines* is:

(6) SPINDLE AXIS MUST BE AT 90° TO TABLE SURFACE IN BOTH DIRECTIONS This alignment is particularly important across the table; if it is in error, work produced will be non-parallel in that direction, or non-square if the cutter periphery is used to produce a vertical face, as in fig. 10.6.

In most vertical-spindle machines the cutter head can be swung in the other vertical plane and is often deliberately misaligned slightly in this plane to give clearance at the back of the cutter as it crosses the machined surface (see p. 134).

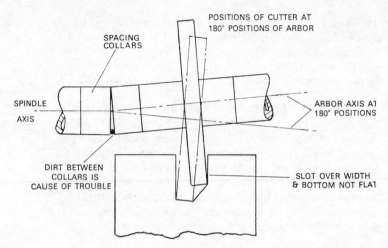

POSITIONS OF CUTTER AT
180° POSITIONS OF ARBOR

SPACING
COLLARS

SPINDLE

AXIS

ARBOR AXIS AT
180° POSITIONS

DIRT BETWEEN
COLLARS IS
CAUSE OF TROUBLE

SLOT OVER WIDTH
& BOTTOM NOT FLAT

Fig. 10.7. Effect of cutter running out of true because of bent arbor (much exaggerated)

Fig. 10.8(a). Block diagrams of column and knee-type plain milling machines. The motions and adjustment numbers refer to the motions in Fig. 10.1

Apart from these alignments the cutter spindle must 'run true', i.e., the spindle taper must not run out of truth and the arbor must be straight. If the cutter teeth are not concentric with the axis of rotation, all the cutting load has to be borne by the teeth running at the greater radius, with possible cutter damage or breakage or with a reduced cutter load to avoid such damage. In a horizontal machine a bent arbor will cause the cutter to oscillate from side to side and produce an overwidth slot, as shown in fig. 10.7, where the arbor is bent by dirt between the spacing collars.

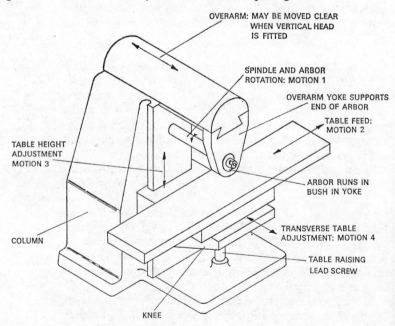

OVERARM: MAY BE MOVED CLEAR
WHEN VERTICAL HEAD
IS FITTED

SPINDLE AND ARBOR
ROTATION: MOTION 1

OVERARM YOKE SUPPORTS
END OF ARBOR

TABLE FEED:
MOTION 2

TABLE HEIGHT
ADJUSTMENT
MOTION 3

ARBOR RUNS IN
BUSH IN YOKE

TRANSVERSE TABLE
ADJUSTMENT: MOTION 4

COLUMN

TABLE RAISING
LEAD SCREW

KNEE

(a) PLAIN HORIZONTAL
MILLING MACHINE

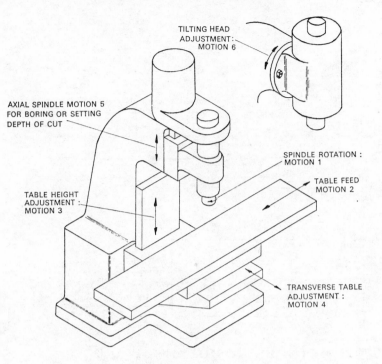

Fig. 10.8(b).

TILTING HEAD
ADJUSTMENT:
MOTION 6

AXIAL SPINDLE MOTION 5
FOR BORING OR SETTING
DEPTH OF CUT

SPINDLE ROTATION :
MOTION 1

TABLE FEED
MOTION 2

TABLE HEIGHT
ADJUSTMENT :
MOTION 3

TRANSVERSE TABLE
ADJUSTMENT :
MOTION 4

(b) FIXED-HEAD VERTICAL-SPINDLE
MACHINE.
THE SMALL DIAGRAM SHOWS AN ALTERNATIVE
SPINDLE HEAD WHICH SWIVELS AND ALLOWS THE SPINDLE
AXIS TO BE TILTED. THE AXIAL SPINDLE
FEED MOTION 5 IS STILL PROVIDED BY
A SIMILAR MECHANISM TO THAT USED ON
A DRILLING MACHINE, WITHIN THE HEAD ITSELF

Block diagrams of both horizontal and vertical-spindle
machines are given in fig. 10.8, which also shows how the
motions required are obtained and aligned.

The arbor of a horizontal machine is prone to misalignment through bending and its unsupported length should be
kept as short as possible. This is generally achieved by keep-
ing the cutters as near to the column as practicable, and
then moving an overarm support as close to the cutters as
possible, as shown in fig. 10.9. Further rigidity can be obtained by using braces to connect the overarm support to
the knee of the machine, thereby forming a rigid closed-box
structure. The braces have to be released, however, when the
cut is changed and removed to change the cutter, which is
often inconvenient, but for production work with long runs
and heavy cuts the increase in rigidity is well worthwhile.

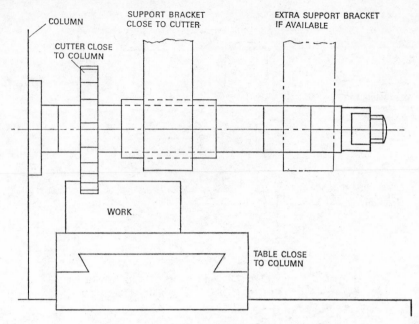

COLUMN

SUPPORT BRACKET
CLOSE TO CUTTER·

EXTRA SUPPORT BRACKET
IF AVAILABLE

CUTTER CLOSE
TO COLUMN

WORK

TABLE CLOSE
TO COLUMN

*Fig. 10.9. Support of cutter on
horizontal milling machine*

METHODS OF HOLDING WORK

The method used to hold the work depends on the type of workpiece, its size and shape, and on the operations to be carried out.

(1) CLAMPING DIRECTLY TO THE TABLE This method is generally used for large workpieces which cannot be conveniently held by other methods. It produces accurate work but sometimes presents a problem in aligning the work: two examples will be given.

(a) *Cleaning up the faces of 100 mm by 100 mm angle iron* This can easily be done on a horizontal machine by a shell end milling cutter. The work is clamped to the table, slightly overhanging the edge, as shown in fig. 10.10. To

*Fig. 10.10. Work clamped direct
to table. Facing angle iron*

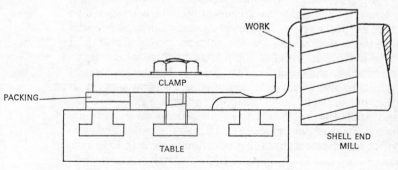

WORK

CLAMP

PACKING

TABLE

SHELL END
MILL

align the angle iron with the table motion, some form of in-dicator must be used, but a dial gauge should not be used on such a rough surface as this. A simple device known as a 'sticky pin' is used. This is simply a small scriber stuck to the cutter with a blob of plasticine. The table is adjusted to bring the top edge of the angle iron close to the pin, and then traversed by hand along the length of the iron to see if the gap between pin and work remains the same. The position of the angle iron is adjusted as necessary.

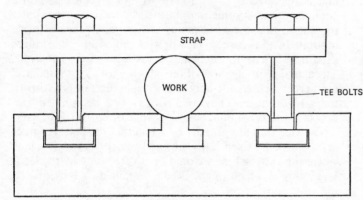

Fig. 10.11(a). Work clamped direct to table. Round bar located in centre tee-slot

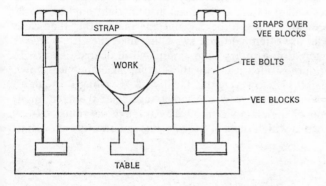

Fig. 10.11(b). Alternative method of locating and holding round bar

(b) *Cutting keyways in line at each end of a round bar*
The simplest way of doing this is to locate and clamp the bar along a tee-slot of the table, mill the keyway at one end and, at the same setting, traverse the table and mill the key-way at the other end of the bar. The set-up is shown in fig. 10.11(a). The bar could alternatively be clamped in vee blocks as shown in figure 10.11(b), and a dial gauge used to align it with the table motion, since the bar would either be machined or bright-drawn.

Note that the clamps and vee blocks would have to be clear of the cutting zones and, to reduce vibration and avoid deflection from the cutting load, it might be necessary to put supports under the ends of the bar.

If the keyways had to be at 90° to each other, one could be cut at one end with a slot cutter on the arbor, and the other with a slot drill or end mill, mounted in an adaptor in the spindle nose, without disturbing the setting of the workpiece.

(2) THE MACHINE VICE The plain (non-swivelling) machine vice consists of a base with a fixed jaw at one end and a moving jaw which slides along the base of the vice and is operated by a leadscrew. It is a piece of precision equipment and is sometimes located by tenons in the centre tee-slot so that the fixed jaw is at right angles to the table motion. In that case, a face or slot milled in a workpiece should be square to the face clamped against the fixed jaw. The actual gripping faces of the jaws are usually ground and are perpendicular not only to the table motion but also to the table surface. Thus, if a vice is well maintained and properly used it should produce work of correct geometry.

The vice should normally be set so that the cutting forces act against the fixed jaw and not against the moving jaw, where the cutting forces would be resisted only by the leadscrew thread which might become strained or loosened by the vibration.

The plain vice is normally limited to workpieces whose faces and slots are to be machined at right angles. Workpieces which have to be machined at angles other than right angles are often held in a swivelling machine vice, which is mounted on a rotary base, graduated in degrees, and is, in fact, almost identical with the shaping machine vice shown in fig. 9.11. However, this facility of swivelling through an angle is in some ways a disadvantage since the fixed alignments of the plain vice are lost. Although the rotary base is provided with a scale of degrees, it is not accurate enough to

Fig. 10.12. Swivel base vice set for angled slot in workpiece

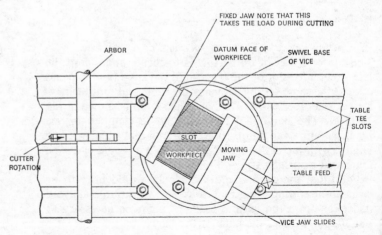

212

be relied upon for squareness or parallelism. For squareness, the fixed jaw should be checked with a dial gauge against the transverse table motion and, for parallelism, against the longitudinal table motion. This type of vice is shown in use for cutting a slot angled at 60° to the datum face of the work in fig. 10.12.

(3) THE ROTARY TABLE A vertical-spindle milling machine equipped with a rotary table can be used for an extremely wide variety of jobs. The rotary table is bolted on to the machine table and is usually located by tenons in the centre tee-slot. It has tee-slots cut in its own upper surface so that work can be cramped or bolted to it. A taper hole is accurately positioned at its centre so that, with the aid of a short mandrel, work can be accurately positioned over the centre of the table. If this is not possible the 'sticky pin' mentioned on page 211, the scriber of a surface gauge or a dial gauge can be used to set the work central, according to circumstances. The work is adjusted until its marked-out circle or circumference runs true when the table is rotated.

The table rotation is produced by a hand-operated worm drive. The angle of rotation is measured in degrees by a graduated scale around the table base and then to a further 3 minutes or 5 minutes of a degree, depending on the table, by graduations on the handwheel scale. Note that the base scale reads directly and does not take backlash into account. But the worm and wheel have a clearance which causes backlash and settings on the handwheel minute scale must always be made in the same direction to eliminate the effect of backlash. This precaution is unnecessary if the table scale is fitted with a vernier for fine readings and settings.

Apart from allowing accurate angular positioning on the table to be achieved, the worm drive also provides a hand

Fig. 10.13. Workpiece to be produced on a vertical spindle milling machine equipped with a rotary table

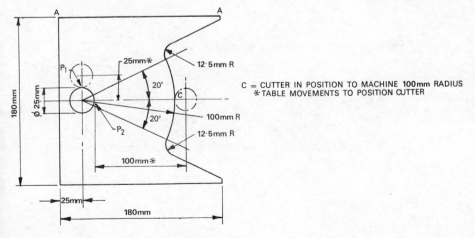

C = CUTTER IN POSITION TO MACHINE **100mm** RADIUS
✳ TABLE MOVEMENTS TO POSITION CUTTER

213

feed which can be used for milling arcs of circles, etc. A typical workpiece for production on a vertical-spindle machine equipped with a rotary table is shown in fig. 10.13 and the task may be resolved into two parts:

(1) setting-up the work on the rotary table:
(2) setting the cutter to the work.

Let us assume that the plate has been machined to a square of size 180 mm × 180 mm and the 25 mm diameter hole has been drilled and reamed. The procedure could then be as follows.

(1) Fit a suitable locating plug, of diameter to suit the hole in the workpiece, in the centre of the table and fit the workpiece on it, but resting on parallel strips to give clearance for the end of the cutter. Lightly clamp the workpiece.

(2) Set the rotary table to zero (0°) and mount a dial gauge on the vertical head so that it bears against side AA of the workpiece.

(3) Use the longitudinal table motion and adjust the work position on the rotary table until the dial gauge reading is constant. Tighten the clamp on the workpiece and recheck the setting.

The work is now positioned so that the centre of the 100 mm radius is over the centre of the rotary table, as shown in fig. 10.14, and the edges are parallel or square to the table motion.

(4) Fit a 25 mm diameter end mill in the spindle and adjust

Fig. 10.14. Workpiece of Fig. 10.13 set up on rotary table. Clamps and parallel strips not shown

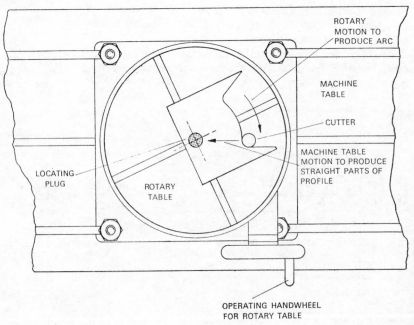

ROTARY MOTION TO PRODUCE ARC

MACHINE TABLE

CUTTER

MACHINE TABLE MOTION TO PRODUCE STRAIGHT PARTS OF PROFILE

LOCATING PLUG

ROTARY TABLE

OPERATING HANDWHEEL FOR ROTARY TABLE

214

the table movement until the cutter registers at point P1 on the locating plug. Set the cross-slide leadscrew dial to zero, traverse the cutter clear of the plug and move the table a distance of half the cutter diameter plus half the plug diameter to bring the cutter centre over the centre line of the plug.

$$\text{Table movement} = \frac{25 \text{ mm}}{2} + \frac{25 \text{ mm}}{2} = 25 \text{ mm}$$

Lock the cross slide. The cutter is now positioned over the centre line of the work.

(5) Traverse the table until the cutter registers at point P2 on the datum plug. Set the leadscrew dial to zero and move the table *more than* 100 mm to bring the cutter *beyond* point C in fig. 10.13. When it is moved back to point C for the finishing cut the backlash in the table leadscrew will have been eliminated, since the movements to point P2 and position C will have been in the same direction.

(6) Set the cutter position about 2 mm beyond the line of the finished radius, pierce the workpiece and rough out the arc and the two tapering sides. The arc is generated by traversing the rotary table 20° in either direction from the centre line, and the two tapering sides are generated by the longitudinal table motion, as shown in fig. 10.14. When the profile has been roughed out it can be finished by setting the table leadscrew dial to 100 mm from the datum position and taking suitable finishing cuts.

(4) THE DIVIDING HEAD The most important workholding device for indexing work on a milling machine is the dividing head. So much work is cylindrical in nature, requiring a number of equally-spaced slots, teeth or splines, or a number of flats positioned at stated angular relationships that the dividing head has become a standard piece of equipment on the general-purpose machine.

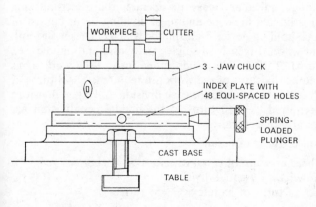

Fig. 10.15(a). Direct-indexing dividing head (vertical type). This type is often used in production work for milling flats on cylindrical heads, as shown

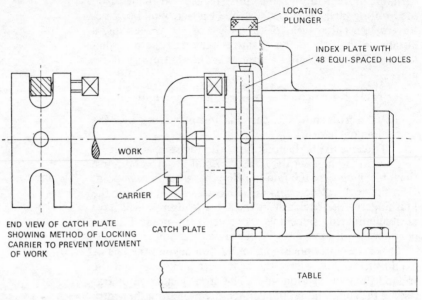

LOCATING PLUNGER

INDEX PLATE WITH 48 EQUI-SPACED HOLES

WORK

CARRIER

END VIEW OF CATCH PLATE
SHOWING METHOD OF LOCKING
CARRIER TO PREVENT MOVEMENT
OF WORK

CATCH PLATE

TABLE

Fig. 10.15(b). Direct-indexing dividing head (horizontal type)

Direct Indexing

The simplest form of dividing head consists of a work-holding attachment, usually a three-jaw self-centring chuck, attached to a spindle on which is mounted an index plate with a number of equally-spaced holes into which a taper plunger fits. The number of holes chosen is usually one with many factors, e.g., 48. This enables the chuck to be turned through 48, 24, 16, 12, 8, 6, 4, 3, and 2 equal divisions. A 24-hole plate is almost as useful, giving 24, 12, 8, 6, 4, 3, and 2 divisions. When the pin has been engaged in the correct hole the spindle is locked and the cut taken. Such a dividing head is shown in fig. 10.15(a) in its vertical form and in fig. 10.15(b) in its horizontal form, with a catch plate instead of a chuck.

Simple Indexing

Although quick and easy to operate, the direct-indexing head is limited in scope and most dividing heads consist of a work-holding device on a spindle which carries a 40-tooth worm wheel driven by a single-start worm and handle, i.e., 40 turns of the handle produce one turn of the work. Thus if 5 equal divisions of the work are required, $\frac{40}{5}=8$ turns of the handle are required for each division; if 4 equal divisions are required, $\frac{40}{4}=10$ turns of the handle per division are necessary, or generally:

No. of turns of handle $= \dfrac{40}{n}$

where n = no. of equal divisions of workpiece
Now let $n=7$ equal divisions
∴ No. of turns of handle $=\frac{40}{7}=5\frac{5}{7}$ turns.

216

In order to produce seven equal divisions of the workpiece it is therefore necessary to subdivide a complete turn of the handle. To achieve this the handle contains a spring-loaded plunger and can be adjusted for radius of rotation so that it can engage in any one of a number of rings of holes in an index plate, as shown in figs 10.16 and 10.17.

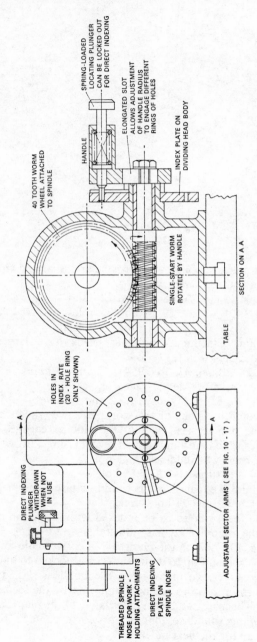

Fig. 10.16. Horizontal dividing head equipped for both direct and simple indexing. This is the simplest type. More complex types can be swung to any angle between vertical and horizontal

Note: When used for direct indexing the worm is normally disengaged from the worm-wheel

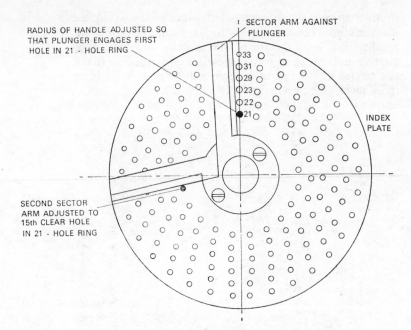

RADIUS OF HANDLE ADJUSTED SO
THAT PLUNGER ENGAGES FIRST
HOLE IN 21 - HOLE RING

SECTOR ARM AGAINST
PLUNGER

INDEX
PLATE

SECOND SECTOR
ARM ADJUSTED TO
15th CLEAR HOLE
IN 21 - HOLE RING

Fig. 10.17. No. 2 index plate set for indexing 7 equal divisions. The handle is turned 5 revolutions and a further 15 holes in the 21-hole ring

The index plates supplied with Browne and Sharpe dividing heads have three plates, viz.:

Plate No. 1: 15, 16, 17, 18, 19 and 20 holes
Plate No. 2: 21, 23, 27, 29, 31 and 33 holes
Plate No. 3: 37, 39, 41, 43, 47 and 49 holes

Parkinson and Cincinnatti dividing heads have larger, double-sided plates with (a) on one side:

24, 25, 28, 30, 34, 37, 38, 39, 41, 42 and 43 holes

and (b) on the reverse side:

46, 47, 49, 51, 53, 54, 57, 58, 59, 62 and 66 holes.

For seven equal divisions of the workpiece, we adjust the radius of the plunger arm so that the plunger engages a circle of holes which are a multiple of seven. Using a Browne and Sharpe head we could select 21 holes.

$$\frac{5}{7} \text{ turns} = \frac{5}{7} \times 21 = 15 \text{ holes.}$$

Thus to index 7 equal divisions would require 5 complete turns and 15 holes in a 21-hole circle.

To enable the 15 holes to be indexed without continual counting, the index plate has adjustable sector arms as shown in fig. 10.17. With the plunger in a correct hole, one sector arm is brought up to it and the second locked to indicate 15 *clear* holes. To index $\frac{1}{7}$ rev, the handle is turned 5 complete turns and on to the hole indicated by the second sector arm. The arms can be moved relative to the plate and are now swung round so that the first arm contacts the plunger ready for the next index.

218

Angular Indexing

It may be that a shaft is required with two keyways at an angle of 36° to each other. Since 40 turns of handle=360°

$\therefore$ 1 turn of handle=$\frac{360}{40}$=9° of work

or 36° of work=$\frac{36°}{9}$=4 turns of handle

Or generally:

$$\text{Turns of handle}=\frac{\text{angle required}}{9°}$$

Consider an angle of 43°:

Turns of handle=$\frac{43}{9}$=$4\frac{7}{9}$ turns

That is, 4 turns plus 14 holes in an 18-hole circle on a Browne and Sharpe No. 1 plate, or 42 holes in a 54-hole circle on a Parkinson plate.

If the angle required is quoted in minutes of a degree, one revolution of the handle=$9° \times 60$=540 minutes of the work or:

$$\text{Turns of handle}=\frac{\text{angle required in minutes}}{540'}$$

Thus for an index of 15° 40′ we have:

15° 40′=940′

Turns of handle=$\frac{940'}{540'}$=$\frac{94}{54}$=$\frac{47}{27}$=$1\frac{20}{27}$ turns

Thus the index is 1 turn plus 20 holes in a 27-hole circle.

Most dividing heads also carry a direct-indexing plate on the spindle nose so that for common numbers of divisions no calculations are required and the quicker direct-indexing can be used. This plate is shown in fig. 10.16.

Work-Holding in the Dividing Head

Work may be held in the dividing head in a three-jaw self-centring chuck, between centres or on a mandrel between centres. As usual, the accuracy of concentricity of self-centring chucks is not too reliable, particularly when wear has occurred. Thus work held between centres is to be preferred, but the chuck has the advantage that it can be used at any angle up to the vertical, whereas centres can only be used parallel to the table surface or nearly so (a height adjustment is provided on the tailstock).

When work which has to be machined parallel is held between centres or supported by the tailstock it should be checked with a dial gauge to ensure that it is parallel to the table motion, particularly if the tailstock alignment has been altered, e.g., to machine the flutes of a taper-pin reamer.

The same applies to chuck-held work when the chuck is returned to the horizontal after use in some other position.

CUTTER SETTING

Just as drilled holes are positioned relative to datum faces, so milled features are also positioned relative to some datum, either a datum face, reference line or reference point on a workpiece. To produce the required feature it is necessary to position the cutter relative to the datum. Furthermore, milled features often have prescribed widths, e.g., slots, and the width of slot produced may not be equal to that of the cutter, particularly if the cutter is running slightly out of truth. It is therefore often better deliberately to select a cutter thinner than the width desired and measure the slot produced after the first cut. The correct width can then be obtained with a finishing cut. Problems such as this will be dealt with in the following examples, all of which presume that the work is already set correctly, relative to the machine alignments.

Fig. 10.18. Profile of workpiece used to illustrate cutter-setting techniques

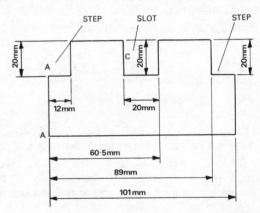

(1) *Setting a cutter to cut a step (fig. 10.18)*
Cutter: side-and-face, 20 mm wide × 100 mm diameter.

(a) With machine running, adjust cross-slide until side of cutter just contacts datum face AA. Set cross-slide dial to zero.

(b) Lower table until cutter clears and traverse across 12 mm on cross-slide. Lock cross-slide.

(c) Raise table until cutter just touches work and set vertical dial to zero.

(d) Back-off table and raise to take first cut. Continue to cut until vertical dial reads 20 mm.

(e) Lower table and move cross-slide until cutter is beyond other side of work. Bring table back and take a cut to mark a shoulder of greater width than 89 mm from datum face AA.

220

(f) Measure shoulder width and move cross-slide the remaining amount to reduce it to 89 mm. Check width and lock cross-slide.

(g) Take a cut at this setting and check width from datum face.

(h) Continue cutting at this setting until vertical dial reads 20 mm.

Note how backlash is eliminated by this procedure to obtain the 89 mm dimension.

On a vertical-spindle machine the procedure would have been similar but end mills would have been used.

(2) *Setting a cutter to machine a slot (fig.10.18)*
Cutter: side-and-face, 15 mm wide × 100 mm diameter.

In this case we assume the cutter to be unreliable for width, so an undersize cutter is used.

(a) Take a touch on face AA. Set cross-slide dial to zero.

(b) Lower table until cutter clears and traverse across 60·5 mm on cross-slide, using cross-slide dial.

(c) Cut slot to depth.

(d) Move table back to take a light cut on face C. This eliminates backlash.

(e) Measure width of slot using workshop-grade gauge blocks and subtract this measurement from 20 mm.

(f) Move table required remainder and finish slot. Again note elimination of backlash.

(3) *Setting a cutter to cut a keyway in a round bar (fig. 10.19)*
Cutter: slot cutter, 120 mm diameter × 12 mm wide.

In this case we assume the cutter to be reliable enough to produce the width of keyway to the required accuracy.

(a) Raise table and use cross-slide to touch side of cutter on diameter at A.

(b) Lower table and traverse cross-slide for half work diameter plus half cutter width.

$$\text{Table movement} = \frac{50 \text{ mm}}{2} + \frac{12 \text{ mm}}{2} = 31 \text{ mm}$$

Lock cross-slide.

(c) Raise table until cutter touches work. Traverse table until cutter clears work and raise table a further 6 mm. Lock vertical slide and proceed to cut slot.

(4) *Setting a cutter to cut a slot in a large-diameter disc (fig. 10.20)*
In this case the diameter of the work is too large to permit a touch by the cutter at the side (this would require a cutter about 8 in diameter).

Cutter: slot cutter, 100 mm diameter × 6 mm wide.

(a) Set a square on the machine table or on parallel strips if necessary to obtain the height. *Lightly* clamp the square in contact with the work as shown.

(b) Wring-up workshop-grade gauge blocks equal to half work diameter *minus* half width of cutter.

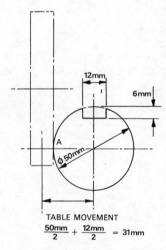

TABLE MOVEMENT
$$\frac{50mm}{2} + \frac{12mm}{2} = 31mm$$

Fig. 10.19. Setting slot cutter to a small diameter bar

221

$$\text{Gauge block width} = \frac{150 \text{ mm}}{2} - \frac{12 \text{ mm}}{2} = 69 \text{ mm}$$

(c) Adjust table until gauge blocks fit without shake when held between cutter face and try square.

(d) Check cutter setting from other side of disc and adjust as necessary.

(e) Machine slot to size.

Fig. 10.20. Setting a cutter to a large-diameter disc. Note: an alternative method is to set the cutter to the mandrel before mounting the disc on it

All the above operations have been based on the use of slot cutters or side-and-face cutters. They can also be performed by end mills and as a series of exercises the student can give corresponding descriptions of such operations.

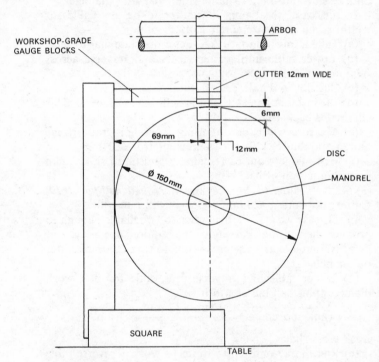

MORE SPECIALISED CUTTERS AND OPERATIONS

Form-relieved cutters

All the examples described have dealt with flat surfaces, except for the use of the rotary table to generate an arc. However, some shapes or forms need to be *copied* by specially-made cutters, such as that shown in fig. 10.21. These cutters are usually form-relieved, i.e., the form of each tooth is continued and preserved for the full depth of the tooth, clearance being obtained by making each tooth a small part of a spiral whose cross-section is the form of the tooth. Thus

222

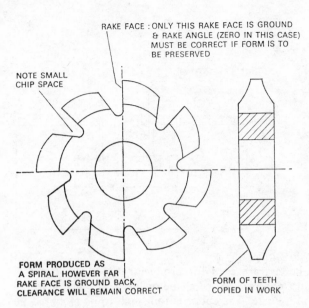

RAKE FACE : ONLY THIS RAKE FACE IS GROUND
& RAKE ANGLE (ZERO IN THIS CASE)
MUST BE CORRECT IF FORM IS TO
BE PRESERVED

NOTE SMALL
CHIP SPACE

FORM PRODUCED AS
A SPIRAL. HOWEVER FAR
RAKE FACE IS GROUND BACK,
CLEARANCE WILL REMAIN CORRECT

FORM OF TEETH
COPIED IN WORK

Fig. 10.21. Form-relieved cutter

however far the teeth are ground back on the rake face their form will remain correct. This is true only if the rake angle is correct and care must be exercised in sharpening such cutters to preserve the correct rake angle.

Dovetail cutters

A dovetail cannot be produced by a normal right-angled cutter and a special type of cutter is used, as shown in fig. 10.22. It machines the base surface with its end teeth and the angled surfaces with its inclined cutting face.

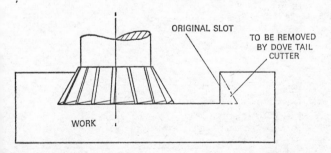

ORIGINAL SLOT

TO BE REMOVED
BY DOVE TAIL
CUTTER

WORK

Fig. 10.22. Action of dovetail cutter

Tee-slot cutters

Tee-slots are first machined by cutting the vertical slot to full depth with an end mill or slot drill. The tee of the slot is then cut by a special cutter as shown in fig. 10.23. It consists essentially of a small side-and-face cutter mounted on a shank, with a neck small enough to clear the vertical slot machined in the first operation. With the aid of a rotary table, a tee-slot can be machined to an arc of a circle.

223

Fig. 10.23. Action of tee-slot cutter

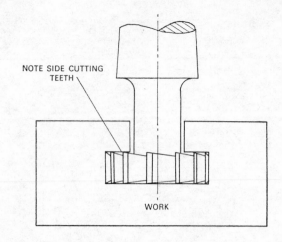

NOTE SIDE CUTTING TEETH

WORK

Woodruff cutters

These cutters are used for producing Woodruff key-seats and must conform to the shape of the key, which is a segment of a circle. The cutter is too small to be mounted on the machine arbor and it is made in the form of a slot cutter on a solid shank, side clearance being obtained by dishing. Unlike a tee-slot cutter it has no side-cutting teeth and can further sometimes be identified by the fact that its end is not flat but carries a centred spigot which allows a support centre to be used as shown in fig. 10.24. To produce the key-seat, the cutter is positioned over the work and sunk directly to the required depth. Different sizes of Woodruff keys, and therefore of Woodruff cutters, are used.

Fig. 10.24. Action of Woodruff key-seat cutter

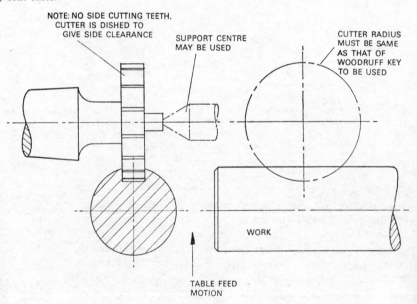

NOTE: NO SIDE CUTTING TEETH. CUTTER IS DISHED TO GIVE SIDE CLEARANCE

SUPPORT CENTRE MAY BE USED

CUTTER RADIUS MUST BE SAME AS THAT OF WOODRUFF KEY TO BE USED

WORK

TABLE FEED MOTION

224

STRADDLE MILLING Referring to milling example no. (1) on page 220 and its associated fig. 10.18, it would be possible by using a pair of matched cutters to cut the two steps simultaneously, provided the cutters were separated by a distance of 77 mm on the machine arbor, as shown in fig. 10.25. Such an operation is called straddle milling and although it takes longer to set the machine, production time is shorter because both steps are cut at one pass. This is important when a number of workpieces have to be machined.

Similarly, by using matched cutters with correct spacers on the arbor, features such as spanner flats, squares and hexagons can be cut two faces at a time, the work being held vertically in a direct indexing head of the type shown in fig. 10.15(a).

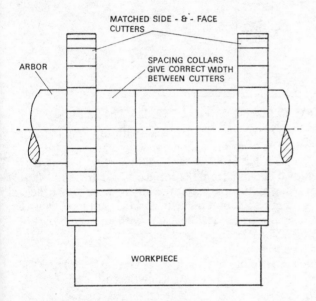

MATCHED SIDE - & - FACE CUTTERS

ARBOR

SPACING COLLARS GIVE CORRECT WIDTH BETWEEN CUTTERS

WORKPIECE

Fig. 10.25. Straddle milling

GANG MILLING Referring again to milling example no. (1) on page 220 and its associated fig. 10.18, by selecting suitable cutters it should be possible to machine the whole of the top surface in one pass, the cutters required being two side-and-face cutters, two slab mills, and one slot cutter. These cutters must be of correct appropriate diameters and thicknesses since the shape of the surface is a copy of the form produced by the cutters in combination, as shown in fig. 10.26. Such a process often calls for special cutters and is only economical where a considerable number of parts are to be machined.

Note that the slab milling cutters shown in fig. 10.26 are of opposite hand so that the end thrusts produced by the helix angles cancel each other out.

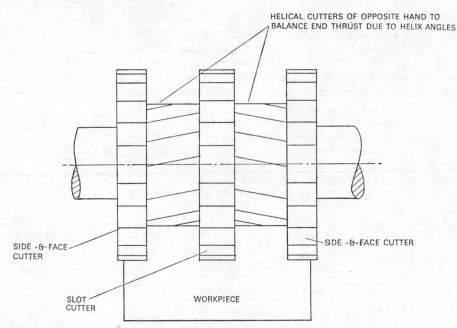

HELICAL CUTTERS OF OPPOSITE HAND TO
BALANCE END THRUST DUE TO HELIX ANGLES

SIDE -&-FACE
CUTTER

SIDE -&-FACE CUTTER

SLOT
CUTTER

WORKPIECE

Fig. 10.26. Gang milling. Matched
set of cutters machines complete and
correct profile on work

ESTIMATION OF CUTTING TIMES

In Chapter 9, on page 202, we dealt with the time required
for a roughing cut on a shaping machine and we will now
consider the same problem as a milling operation, that is,
the removal of 5 mm from the surface of a slab of mild steel,
340 mm long by 100 mm wide. We will assume that a helical-
tooth slab mill, 100 mm diameter by 125 mm long, is used
to remove the metal at one pass, with the same cutting
speed of 20 m/min and a feed per tooth of 0·25 mm, the
cutter having 4 teeth.

Circumference of cutter $= \pi \times 100$ mm $= 314\cdot2$ mm

$$\text{Rev/min} = \frac{\text{Cutting Speed (m/min)}}{\text{Circumference (m/rev)}}$$

$$= \frac{20}{0\cdot314} = \underline{64 \text{ rev/min}}$$

Feed/tooth $= 0\cdot25$ mm

Feed/rev $=$ Feed/tooth $\times$ no. of teeth

$\qquad\quad = 0\cdot25 \times 4$

$\qquad\quad = 1$ mm

Feed/min $=$ Feed/rev $\times$ rev/min

$\qquad\quad = 1 \times 64$

$\qquad\quad = 64$ mm/min

Time taken $= \dfrac{\text{Length (mm)}}{\text{Feed (mm/min)}}$

$\qquad\quad = \dfrac{340}{64}$ min

Time taken $= \underline{5\cdot32 \text{ min}}$

226

This is over twice as fast as with the shaping machine. In fact, the operation would take rather longer than 5·32 minutes since we have not allowed for the cutter to feed in to full depth of cut and to run out. However, with the shaping machine we used an average cutting speed of 20 m/min, knowing that the maximum speed at the midpoint of the stroke would be greater. With the milling machine we should in practice use a higher cutting speed, because the speed is constant during the whole cutting time.

Thus, under similar conditions, we have a higher metal removal rate with the milling machine than with the shaping machine, for the following reasons:

(a) For each revolution of the mechanism of the shaping machine there is only one cutting edge in operation. For each revolution of the milling machine spindle, four teeth engage the work.

(b) On the shaping machine nearly half the operating time is wasted on the return stroke. This is not so on the milling machine, which has an almost continuous cutting action.

The question then arises, 'Why use shaping machines?' The answer is given if a similar comparison is made for a surface 375×200 mm. The milling machine would require two passes and the total time would be more than doubled because of the time needed to feed back, cross-traverse the table and restart the cut. The shaping machine would still be cutting and thus as surface areas increase the shaping machine becomes more economic. Furthermore, the shaping machine uses relatively simple hand-ground tools, while the cutters of a milling machine are expensive to buy and maintain. The milling machine is, however, capable of much more sophisticated work, while the shaping machine is mainly suited to the machining of large flat surfaces. Each has its own special functions for which it is purchased and used.

SAFETY NOTES *The following safety notes, which have again been left until the end of the Chapter, not only deal with the safety of the operator but also with safety of the equipment.*

(1) Always use the guard supplied for the machine. The time taken in fitting and adjusting the guard may save a lifetime as a one-handed operator.

(2) Milling attachments are heavy. Never try to lift a vice, dividing head, rotary table or other attachment unless you know it is well within your capabilities, and be modest rather than conceited about these. Get assistance or use a portable hoist, or you may do yourself an injury.

(3) Some operations are difficult to guard. Keep your hands away from cutters and never brush swarf away when the cutter is running. Use a coolant feed, not a brush.

The following safety notes are concerned more with the machine than with the operator:

(4) The machine attachments should be regarded as instruments rather than just work-holding attachments. Treat them with care to maintain the built-in alignments. Ensure that the bases and tenons do not get damaged, by always resting the attachments on wood blocks, not on a concrete floor.

(5) The tee-slots of the machine are important, since they provide locations for the attachments. Maintain the tee-slots in good condition and, if a burr is raised scrape or file it off carefully.

(6) Ensure that the table and the underside of any attachment are clean before setting-up and bolting down the attachment.

(7) Ensure that the spindle-nose taper and the arbor tapers are clean before fitting an arbor and pulling it home with the drawbolt.

(8) Ensure that collars and cutter faces are clean when mounting or changing a cutter.

DATA SHEET – LIMITS AND FITS

EXTRACTED FROM B.S. 4500.

THE FOLLOWING SELECTION OF LIMITS AND FITS WILL MEET THE NEEDS OF A LARGE PROPORTION OF THE REQUIREMENTS OF GENERAL ENGINEERING. DETAILS FOR OTHER FITS CAN BE FOUND IN B.S. 4500

UNITS 0.001 mm.	TYPE OF FIT					
	LOOSE CLEARANCE	AVERAGE RUNNING	PRECISION LOCATION	AVERAGE LOCATION	PUSH	PRESS (FERROUS PARTS)

HOLES

```
+0.060
+0.040    H8        H8                      H8
+0.020              H7                              H7            p6
                                                            k6   H7
   0  ────────────────────────────────────────────────────────────
-0.020                        g6              h7
-0.040                   f8
-0.060
-0.080   e8
-0.100
```

SHAFTS

TO SCALE FOR DIAMETER RANGE 30mm – 50mm

NOMINAL SIZES		H8	e8	H8	f8	H7	g6	H8	h7	H7	k6	H7	p6
OVER	To												
—	3	+14 / +0	−14 / −28	+14 / +0	−6 / −20	+10 / +0	−2 / −8	+14 / +0	−0 / −10	+10 / +0	+6 / +0	+10 / +0	+12 / +6
3	6	+18 / +0	−20 / −38	+18 / +0	−10 / −28	+12 / +0	−4 / −12	+18 / +0	−0 / −12	+12 / +0	+9 / +1	+12 / +0	+20 / +12
6	10	+22 / +0	−25 / −47	+22 / +0	−13 / −35	+15 / +0	−5 / −14	+22 / +0	−0 / −15	+15 / +0	+10 / +1	+15 / +0	+24 / +15
10	18	+27 / +0	−32 / −59	+27 / +0	−16 / −43	+18 / +0	−6 / −17	+27 / +0	−0 / −18	+18 / +0	+12 / +1	+18 / +0	+29 / +18
18	30	+33 / +0	−40 / −73	+33 / +0	−20 / −53	+21 / +0	−7 / −20	+33 / +0	−0 / −21	+21 / +0	+15 / +2	+21 / +0	+35 / +22
30	50	+39 / +0	−50 / −89	+39 / +0	−25 / −64	+25 / +0	−9 / −25	+39 / +0	−0 / −25	+25 / +0	+18 / +2	+25 / +0	+42 / +26
50	80	+46 / +0	−60 / −106	+46 / +0	−30 / −76	+30 / +0	−10 / −29	+46 / +0	−0 / −30	+30 / +0	+21 / +2	+30 / +0	+51 / +32
80	120	+54 / +0	−72 / −126	+54 / +0	−36 / −90	+35 / +0	−12 / −34	+54 / +0	−0 / −35	+35 / +0	+25 / +3	+25 / +0	+59 / +37
120	180	+63 / +0	−85 / −148	+63 / +0	−43 / −106	+40 / +0	−14 / −39	+63 / +0	−0 / −40	+40 / +0	+28 / +3	+40 / +0	+68 / +43
180	250	+72 / +0	−100 / −172	+72 / +0	−50 / −122	+46 / +0	−15 / −44	+72 / +0	−0 / −46	+46 / +0	+33 / +4	+46 / +0	+79 / +50
250	315	+81 / +0	−110 / −191	+81 / +0	−56 / −137	+52 / +0	−17 / −49	+81 / +0	−0 / −62	+52 / +0	+36 / +4	+52 / +0	+88 / +56
315	400	+89 / +0	−125 / −214	+89 / +0	−62 / −151	+57 / +0	−18 / −54	+89 / +0	−0 / −57	+57 / +0	+40 / +4	+57 / +0	+98 / +62
400	500	+97 / +0	−135 / −232	+97 / +0	−68 / −165	+63 / +0	−20 / −60	+97 / +0	−0 / −63	+63 / +0	+45 / +5	+63 / +0	+108 / +63

Appendix 2

From the City and Guilds of London Institute's Examinations for the Mechanical Engineering Technicians' Courses, no. 293, Part I—Workshop Processes and Practice.

These have been converted to SI units by the author.

MAY 1966

This paper contains nine questions: answer any FIVE.

All questions carry equal marks.

Where possible illustrate your answers with pencil sketches in the answer book.

You should have the following for this examination:

An answer book, which includes squared paper (inches and tenths).

Drawing instruments.

1. (a) Explain briefly what is meant by plate moulding, using sketches to show:
   (i) the plate in relation to the mould,
   (ii) the way in which several castings can be made at one pouring.
   (b) Give two important advantages and two disadvantages of this method of moulding.

2. (a) Using simple sketches or diagrams, show the following features of a twist drill:
   (i) the web,
   (ii) the land,
   (iii) the cutting edges,
   (iv) the cutting edge top rake,
   (v) the cutting clearance.
   Which of these features can vary and must be controlled during re-grinding?
   (b) The top rake of any cutting tool should be adjusted to suit the metal being cut. Explain how this can be accomplished in the case of the twist drill.

3. Explain clearly and concisely the method of performing any workshop experiment carried out during your course concerned with turning operations on the centre-lathe, giving details of:
   (i) the set-up,
   (ii) the procedure,
   (iii) the observations made,
   (iv) the results obtained.

4. (a) What is the object of tempering plain high carbon steel?
   (b) State the temperature range within which the simple tempering of plain high carbon steel is usually carried out.
   (c) Explain why it is necessary to have a range of temperature rather than a single temperature for the tempering process.
   (d) State a type of furnace and method of temperature control suitable for use in tempering small batches of punches.

5. Sketch any small assembly suitable for joining together by brazing, and give the following information about it:
   (i) of what material is each part of the assembly made?
   (ii) what is the approximate composition and melting point of the spelter or filler metal?
   (iii) how are the parts located or held to ensure correct position after brazing?
   (iv) how is a suitable temperature attained?
   (v) how does one know whether the joint is sound?

6. (a) The 'swan-neck' or equivalent type of tool for a shaping machine is designed so as to bring the cutting edge approximately into line with the support face of the tool. Using sketches, explain the reason for this, and give a typical application for such a tool.
   (b) Many shaping machines are fitted with a knee or table support bracket. Using simple line diagrams show:
   (i) that this bracket is provided to absorb and counteract the forces produced by cutting,
   (ii) what provision is made with the bracket to permit the table cross-feed to be used.

7. (a) Explain, with the aid of sketches, the procedure for 'boxing a hole' in the process of marking out.
   (b) Explain the advantages of the above procedure compared with scribing a circle on the hole centre.

8. Second-operation turning is often done by mounting the work on a temporary mandrel made by turning a peg or spigot.
   (i) Give an example of a typical component which could be machined in this way, and show a sequence of operations.
   (ii) A high degree of concentricity can be achieved by this method. Explain the reason for this.

231

(iii) State the main disadvantages of the method and suggest an alternative way of holding the work.

9. (a) Outline the machining conditions which generally give rise:
    (i) to a continuous chip,
    (ii) to a discontinuous chip.
  (b) Give *two* examples of accidents which can be caused by each type of swarf, and the precautions which should be taken to avoid them.

MAY 1967
This paper contains nine questions: answer any FIVE.
All questions carry equal marks.
Where possible illustrate your answers with pencil sketches in the answer book.
You should have the following for this examination:
  An answer book, which includes squared paper (inches and tenths).
  Drawing instruments.
  B.S. 4500 — Data Sheet

1. Describe the main features of any workshop investigation or experiment on *either*
  (a) a single point lathe tool, *or*
  (b) a twist drill.
        The description should cover the following headings:
      (i) the object of the investigation,
      (ii) the set up used, indicating the main items of equipment,
      (iii) the readings or observations taken,
      (iv) the information obtained from the observations.

2. (a) With the aid of simple sketches, explain why the Brinell and Vickers Diamond Pyramid hardness tests are called indentation tests and show clearly which feature of the indentation is measured in each case.
  (b) Give an example of a typical mistake in heat-treating plain high-carbon steel, the fault it would produce and the way in which this fault could be revealed by a hardness test.
  (c) Why is a normal indentation test unreliable if carried out on the surface of case-hardened parts?

232

3. (a) Make a neat sketch to show the approximate proportions of a British Standard slip or block gauge and indicate the gauging faces.
   (b) State, approximately, the accuracy requirements for a 25 mm grade 01 gauge block.
   (c) Explain briefly how wear in the screw of a 25 mm external micrometer could be detected by using gauge blocks.

4. (a) The workpiece in *Fig. 1* has to have a 40 degree taper produced upon it by turning in the lathe. Using simple diagrams of tool shapes and tool movements, explain clearly the difference between forming and generating as basic methods of machining this taper.
   (b) With reference to one of the above methods, outline the practical machining process, including the tool shape and feed, the work-holding arrangement and the means of controlling the dimensions of the taper.

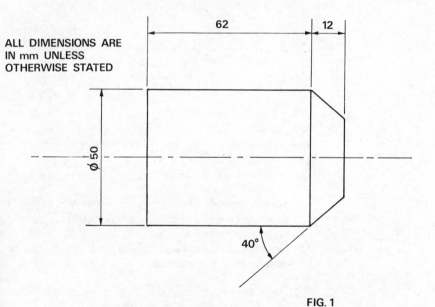

ALL DIMENSIONS ARE
IN mm UNLESS
OTHERWISE STATED

62   12

Ø 50

40°

FIG. 1

5. A standard 20 mm. diameter hexagon-head steel bolt could be headed by any of the following methods:
   (a) machining from the side,
   (b) permanently fixing a nut to the end of a bar,
   (c) forging.

233

For *each* method,

(i) state the form in which the material should be supplied,

(ii) state the kind of bolt or application which would justify the method,

(iii) describe briefly the heading procedure.

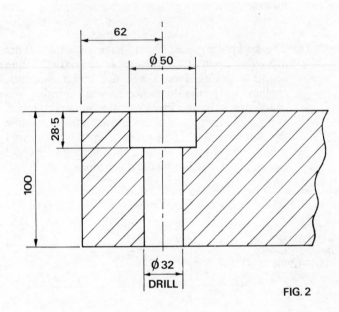

FIG. 2

6. A rectangular cast iron base-plate, size 1·25 m × 1 m, is received planed on both sides, and has a hole at each corner as shown in *Fig. 2*.

(*a*) Specify the most suitable type of drilling machine for producing the holes.

(*b*) Make a neat sketch of the counterbore tool required showing clearly the cutting edges and their cutting angles.

(*c*) Describe how the depth of the counterbore can be controlled and measured.

7. (*a*) Give *two* main reasons why castings are often marked out before they are machined.

(*b*) Make a neat sketch showing the approximate shape of the casting for a typical lathe tail stock indicating where the casting would be machined.

(*c*) Describe how this casting could be marked out stating the equipment required.

8. (*a*) Explain briefly the difference between interchangeable manufacture and selective assembly.

(*b*) The barrel of a lathe tail stock does not rotate. It must slide freely for adjustment, but is clamped up tight when in use.

Using the data provided, state
   (i) what type of fit should be used, giving reasons,
   (ii) the limits of size and tolerance to which machining must be carried out, assuming a nominal size of 65 mm diameter,
   (iii) the machining processes suitable for finishing the barrel and for finishing the bore in view of the tolerances involved.

9. Explain, with the aid of diagrams, a typical application of the dial indicator for setting-up purposes on:
(*a*) the milling machine,
(*b*) the drilling machine.
   In *each* case show and/or state clearly:
   (i) the attachments required,
   (ii) the method of mounting the indicator,
   (iii) the motions to be used,
   (iv) the object of the test.

MAY 1963

This paper contains nine questions: answer any FIVE.
Where possible illustrate your answers with pencil sketches in the answer book.
Logarithmic tables are supplied. At the end of the examination, they should be handed to the Invigilator.
A sheet of graph paper is supplied; drawing instruments may be used if desired.
The attached sheet shows the Figures referred to in the questions.
All questions carry equal marks.

1. (*a*) What sort of grinding equipment should be used when grinding (*i.e.* re-sharpening)
   either (i) single point lathe tools,
      or (ii) twist drills,
   in order to ensure the necessary finish and accuracy? It is not necessary to draw the equipment, but line diagrams may be used if desired.
   (*b*) Outline the steps which should be taken to prevent accidents in the use of the above equipment, indicating some of the main causes of injury.

2. Two of the main reasons for the efficiency of the standard straight-edged lathe tool is that the cutting edge is at the same height and the cutting angles are constant over the whole depth of cut.

235

Use sketches to show the meaning of this statement and so explain the disadvantages of badly shaped cutting tools, such as round-nosed 'hooked' tools.

3. (a) Describe a practical thermo-couple pyrometer outfit, as supplied with muffle furnaces operating up to 1 000°C. Show how the equipment is arranged relative to the furnace.

   (b) What precautions are necessary for the protection of the pyrometer equipment?

   (c) State briefly what is meant by re-calibration and why it is necessary.

4. (a) To what accuracy and degree of finish can the following products usually be made:
   (i) sand castings; (ii) die castings; (iii) drop forgings?
   Give reasons for the differences in the values for these products.

   (b) Explain briefly which of the above products would be best for
   (i) the steering drop arm of a motor car,
   (ii) a vee-belt pulley for the drive of a power hacksaw.

5. (a) Describe the main difficulties encountered when parting-off in a centre-lathe and state how they can be minimised or overcome.

   (b) Discuss the relative advantages of using material in the form of sawn-off billets or in the form of bar stock when producing quantities of similar components on the centre lathe, taking into account size of work, size of machine and any other relevant factors.

6. The disc shown in *Fig. 1* is the indexing plate for a milling fixture.
   Assuming that other machining is completed, explain how you would machine the slots, giving details of the settings required, the cutting tool or tools to be used and the method of holding the work. Note that the slots must be accurately spaced to within $\pm$ 10 min.

7. When the indexing plate shown in *Fig. 1* is in use, a tapered plunger engages in the slots which tend to wear and should be hardened.

   (a) Give the approximate composition of the material which you consider most suitable for the plate.

   (b) State what heat-treatment would be given to the plate and give details of the equipment and temperatures needed.

236

DIMENSIONS GIVEN ARE IN mm UNLESS OTHERWISE
STATED.   FIRST ANGLE PROJECTION

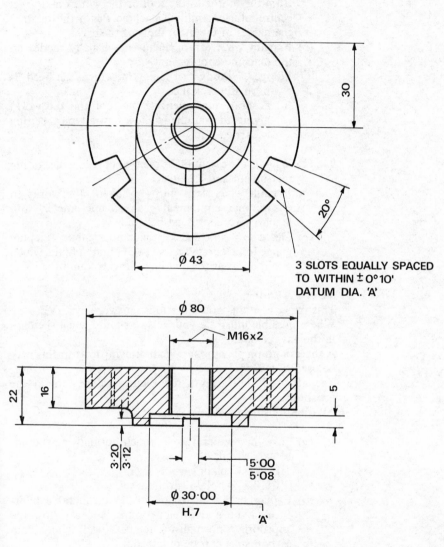

Ø 43

3 SLOTS EQUALLY SPACED
TO WITHIN ± 0°10'
DATUM DIA. 'A'

30

20°

Ø 80

M16x2

22

16

5

3·20 / 3·12

5·00 / 5·08

Ø 30·00

H.7

'A'

FIG. 1

(c) In view of possible distortion during heat-treatment, what steps should be taken to ensure the accuracy of the finished work?

8. (a) Describe, with the aid of a simple line diagram, the line of drive through which power is transmitted from the motor to the tool or the work on *either* a centre-lathe *or* a milling machine. Put on the diagram the names of the main units of the drive.
   (b) Explain what arrangements are usually made, on the machine chosen, for
      (i) feed, stating the units in which the feed is normally reckoned,
      (ii) accurate movement of the tool and the work, giving an example to show how a typical setting is carried out.

9. (a) What is the essential difference between a measuring instrument and a gauge?
   (b) Explain what steps must be taken in a works to ensure that equipment such as micrometers and gauges give continued accuracy.
   (c) Describe how to check either a micrometer or a plug gauge for accuracy; name two common faults which might account for any inaccuracies found.

JUNE 1964
This paper contains nine questions: answer any FIVE.
Where possible illustrate your answers with pencil sketches in the answer book.
A sheet of graph paper is supplied; drawing instruments may be used if desired.
The attached sheet shows the Figures referred to in the questions.
All questions carry equal marks.

1. (a) Give the temperature at which normalising should be carried out on:
      (i) a 1%C plain carbon steel,
      (ii) a 0·3%C plain carbon steel.
   (b) Explain briefly the reason for the considerable difference in the above temperatures and say how the appropriate normalising temperature for any plain carbon steel can be obtained.
   (c) State two reasons for carrying out a normalising process.

2. (a) The accuracy of a *certain* cast-iron surface plate is required by B.S. 817 to be 'within 0·005 mm'. Explain the meaning of this statement.

238

(b) Describe the characteristic texture of the surface of a standard cast-iron surface plate. Using any practical example, explain how the quality of the surface limits the use of the plate for precision measuring purposes.

3. (a) Using simple outline diagrams, explain the difference between radial arm and compound table drilling machines. Put arrows on the diagrams to show the main motions of each machine.

(b) For ONE of the above machines explain a typical set-up and work piece for which it is specially suitable.

4. (a) Make a simple cross-sectional diagram showing a single-point cutting tool in action on a ductile material. Using this diagram show by arrows:
   (i) the direction of the cutting motion and of chip flow,
   (ii) the forces acting on the tool.

(b) Explain, briefly, how the shape and life of the tool are affected by the strength and ductility of the metal being cut.

(c) What is meant by a 'built-up edge'?

5. An existing shaft S projects from the side of a machine as shown in *Fig. 1*. The shaft is 30 mm in diameter and is known to be to B.S. 4500 e8 limit viz. $\frac{-0 \cdot 040}{-0 \cdot 073}$ mm

It is necessary to provide the shaft with an out-board bearing in the form of a bushed cast-iron bracket. This may be bolted to the surface XX which already is satisfactorily machined.

(a) Outline the steps necessary to machine the bracket so that it will fit without adjustment.

(b) Suggest an alternative arrangement or method which would avoid the accurate machining involved in part (a).

6. In *Fig. 2*, M represents a machine frame which stands on a large cast-iron bed-plate B. The frame M has a machined top face size 1 m × 0·33 m which must be flat and level. It is therefore set up on the bed-plate by means of a dial gauge, but a circular bar placed on the top face rolls, showing that the operation is not successful.

(a) explain the most likely reasons for the error and say how to investigate and correct it.

(b) how could you ensure that the top face was set at a uniform height of 450 mm above the surface of the bed-plate to an accuracy of ± 0·12 mm?

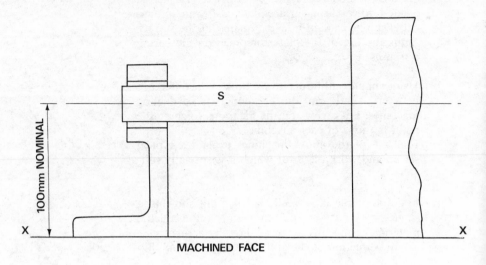

MACHINED FACE

FIG. 1

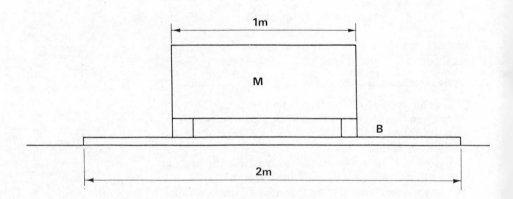

FIG. 2

7. A left-hand thread of 30 mm diameter 0·9 mm pitch is to be cut on a centre lathe which has a lead screw of 5 mm pitch.

   (a) What gear ratio is required between the work spindle and the lead screw?

   (b) Explain any arrangement normally available on a standard centre lathe for setting up the gear ratio, including provision for the left-hand thread.

   (c) What must be done to ensure that the cutting tool engages the thread correctly on successive cuts?

8. The effects of stress and strain on materials are sometimes unwisely ignored in the workshop. Give an example in each of the following to show typical practical cases of overloading or incorrect loading, explaining the nature of the loading and the stresses produced:

(a) in which damage to machines or equipment may result,

(b) in which there is no visible effect, but inaccurate work may result,

(c) in which personal danger may result.

9. (a) Give an example of a typical form-milling operation and explain how a form-relieved milling cutter differs from those with orthodox cutting-clearance.

(b) Explain the main advantages and disadvantages of form-milling.

(c) State one alternative machining method for the type of work performed by form-milling.

DECEMBER 1964

This paper contains nine questions: answer any FIVE.
Illustrate your answers with pencil sketches in the answer book where appropriate.
A sheet of squared paper, quarter inches, is supplied; drawing instruments may be used if desired.
All questions carry equal marks.

1. B.S. 3643—1963 (ISO Metric Screw Threads) includes recommendations for special threads, and a thread of 1·5 mm pitch is recommended for a screw of 36 mm diameter.

   Fig. 1 is an extract from the Standard, showing the basic form for unified threads.

   (a) State the advantages and disadvantages of drilling and tapping compared with boring and screw cutting, for producing a batch of nuts with the above thread.

   (b) Using the information given, state the maximum drill size that should be used in each case.

BASIC FORM FOR UNIFIED THREADS

The basic form of the ISO Metric Screw Thread is shown opposite. It is derived from an equilateral triangle disposed with one side parallel to the axis of the screw thread. This triangle is truncated by an amount equal to one-eighth of its height at the major diameter and by an amount equal to one-quarter of its height at the minor diameter.

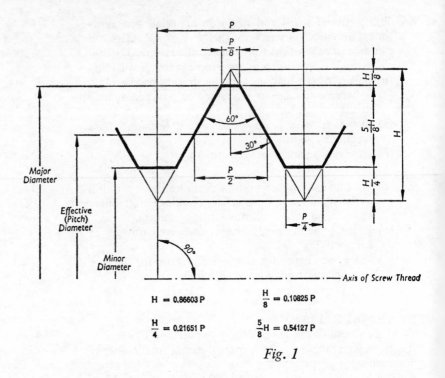

$H = 0.86603\ P$ $\dfrac{H}{8} = 0.10825\ P$

$\dfrac{H}{4} = 0.21651\ P$ $\dfrac{5}{8}H = 0.54127\ P$

Fig. 1

2. When a cutting tool is in use on a centre-lathe, the chip produced sometimes turns blue with heat.
   (a) With the aid of a simple cross-sectional diagram of the cutting tool in action, explain how the heat in the chip is generated.
   (b) Why must the temperature at the tool point be kept to a minimum?
   (c) State *two* ways in which the heating effect on the tool can be minimised.

3. Plain carbon steel is hardened by heating uniformly to a given temperature and cooling rapidly in a quenching medium.
   (a) Explain briefly how the simplified iron/carbon diagram can be used to decide the temperature to which the steel must be heated.
   (b) Why must the heating be uniform, and how is this usually achieved?
   (c) Name *two* common quenching media. Explain the differences each would produce in the properties of the same type of steel as a result of quenching in them.

4. Give an account of an experiment which you have done during which you investigated some aspect of:
   either (*a*) the use of a drilling machine,
   or (*b*) the use of a shaping machine.
   Arrange your answer so as to give the following information:
   (i) the object of the experiment,
   (ii) details of the test piece (if any) and the set-up,
   (iii) details of the procedure,
   (iv) the results obtained.

5. (*a*) Use simple sketches to show the differences between an end-milling cutter and a slot drill.
   (*b*) Explain why the slot drill can be used with an axial feed and the end mill cannot.
   (*c*) B.S. 49 (Keys and Keyways) gives the information shown in *Fig. 2* for a 50 mm diameter shaft. Explain carefully what settings would have to be made on the milling machine, using the index dials, in order to cut the keyway correctly.

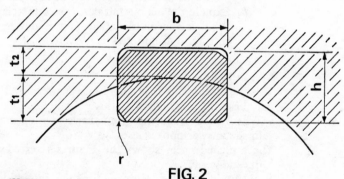

FIG. 2

b = 14 mm
h = 9 mm
t₁ = 5·5 mm
t₂ = 3·8 mm

6. (*a*) Using simple diagrams, explain how large angles of taper can be turned using the settings available on the compound slide and toolpost.
   (*b*) Accurate circular scale settings are not normally available on the compound slide. Explain any way in which an accurate male taper (i.e. one that will fit the other member accurately) of say 60° included angle can be turned. Give details of any measurements or tests required.

7. Metals expand and contract in response to changes in temperature, and this has important consequences when machining or measuring metal articles.

   (*a*) Using simple diagrams of typical machining operations explain how expansion may:

      (i) produce inaccuracy in the work,

     (ii) cause damage to the machine.

   (*b*) What particular problems of measurement arise with temperature changes when working with non-ferrous metals?

8. Choose any simple, typical component and, using sketches,

      (i) explain the purpose of using a core in the moulding process,

     (ii) describe the method of making the core, and

    (iii) name the materials used for making the core.

9. (*a*) By means of a simple diagram explain the main motions and adjustments available on a standard shaping machine. What factors determine the maximum size of work which can be accommodated?

   (*b*) Explain the action and purpose of the clapper box. What is the disadvantage of this device for large cutting tools and how is it overcome?

MAY 1965

This paper contains nine questions: answer any FIVE.
All questions carry equal marks.

Where possible illustrate your answers with pencil sketches in the answer book.

The attached sheet shows the Figures referred to in the questions.

You should have the following for this examination:

One answer book, which includes squared paper (inches and tenths).

Drawing instruments.

1. The first stage in the manufacture of the collar shown in *Fig. 1* is to turn a plain ring. A centre lathe fitted with a four-way tool-post is to be used. A quantity of 50 is required.

      (i) If the material to be used is mild steel, state the form in which the material should be supplied. Give reasons for your choice.

     (ii) Using clear sketches show the shape of the cutting tools and their setting relative to the work. Describe a simple operation cycle which will require a minimum of resetting for each plain ring produced.

244

2. After the turning of the ring shown in *Fig. 1* a hole is to be drilled and counter-bored as shown to take a pinching screw.

   (i) Explain why it is difficult to drill this hole directly, taking into account the shape and construction of a twist drill and its behaviour under load.

  (ii) To ease the problem of drilling the hole, it is proposed to mill a flat right across the collar, as shown in *Fig.1a*, at the same time as the slot is cut. Explain how the milling cutter could be arranged for such an operation, and point out the advantages and disadvantages of this idea.

 (iii) Suggest any other way in which the drilling difficulty can be overcome.

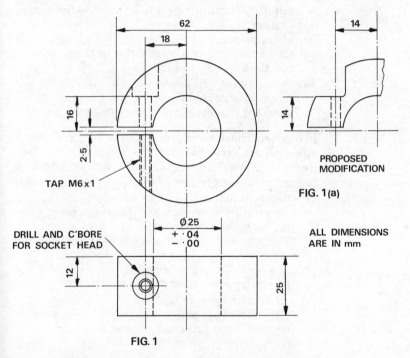

PROPOSED
MODIFICATION

FIG. 1(a)

TAP M6 x 1

DRILL AND C'BORE
FOR SOCKET HEAD

Ø 25
+ ·04
– ·00

ALL DIMENSIONS
ARE IN mm

FIG. 1

3. (*a*) Make a simple diagram showing the main constructional features of a salt bath suitable for the surface hardening of steel. Explain how the temperature of the bath is measured and controlled.

   (*b*) What type of salt is commonly used for case-carburising? State the approximate carbon content of the case obtained, and explain briefly the factors governing the depth of case.

   (*c*) All pieces of steel should be pre-heated before being placed into the salt-bath. Explain why this is necessary.

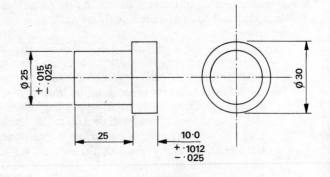

FIG. 2

4. A batch of 500 headed pins is to be made to the dimensions shown in *Fig. 2*.
   (i) Using sketches, explain how a dial gauge can be set up and used as a comparator to measure the 30 mm thickness of the head.
   (ii) What type of dial gauge would be suitable for this purpose, what graduations should it have, and what would be the accuracy of measurement obtainable?

5. In a certain rough turning operation a 50 mm diameter mild steel bar has to be reduced to 30 mm diameter for a length of 75 mm. This roughing could be done by taking one cut at a suitable rate of feed or by taking several lighter cuts at higher feed rate.
   (*a*) Compare the advantages and disadvantages of these two methods of procedure.
   (*b*) State which of the methods you consider best, and why.
   (*c*) Give the following information:
      (i) cutting speed to be used in m/min,
      (ii) spindle speed in rev/min,
      (iii) depth of cut and rate of feed,
      (iv) tool shape and cutting angles,
      (v) material of which the tool is made.

6. (*a*) What are the main objections to grinding on the flat side of a standard off-hand grinding wheel?
   (*b*) Give details of the form and method of use of a grinding wheel and rest that is suitable for single-point tool grinding. Explain its advantages compared with the use of the curved periphery of a disc grinding wheel.

7. (*a*) Explain briefly a suitable method of milling the surfaces *A* and *B* of the cast iron bracket shown in *Fig. 3*. The faces must be square with each other.

Give clear details of the cutters used and the equipment and method used for setting up.

(b) How could the squareness of the surfaces be checked accurately after milling?

8. (a) Explain briefly how a mould would be made for the cast iron bracket shown in *Fig. 3*.

(b) What work must be carried out on the casting after it leaves the mould before it is ready for machining?

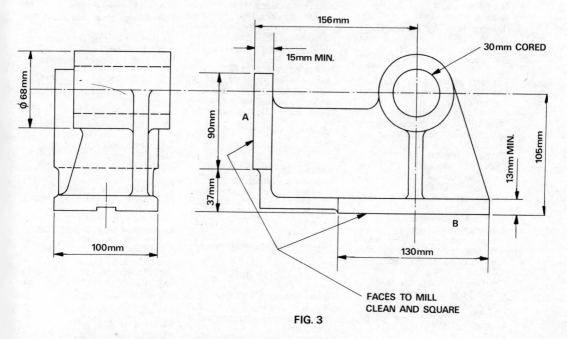

FIG. 3

9. (a) Using sketches, describe the correct technique for measuring the diameter of a 200 mm hole in a 18 mm thick plate using
   (i) a stick type internal micrometer,
   (ii) a vernier caliper.

(b) What is meant by measuring pressure? How can excessive measuring pressure be produced in the two cases mentioned above, and what are its effects?

247

Index